ALFRED'S COLLEGE

The Concept of
Utopia

The Concept of Utopia

Ruth Levitas

PHILIP ALLAN

New York   London   Toronto   Sydney   Tokyo   Singapore

First published 1990 by
Philip Allan
66 Wood Lane End, Hemel Hempstead
Hertfordshire HP2 4RG
A division of
Simon & Schuster International Group

Typeset by Keyboard Services, Luton, Beds
Printed in Great Britain by
BPCC Wheatons Ltd, Exeter

British Library Cataloguing in Publication Data

Levitas, Ruth
The concept of Utopia.
1. Utopias   2. Marxism
I. Title
321.07

ISBN 0–86003–400–3
ISBN 0–86003–700–2 pbk

---

1 2 3 4 5   94 93 92 91 90

For my mother
Liz Levitas
who first introduced me to
News from Nowhere

Contents

Acknowledgements

Many people have contributed directly or indirectly to the writing of this book. I inherited my sense that the world does not have to be like this from my parents, Liz and Maurice Levitas. Together with the rest of a large and complex extended family, and friends of various red and green persuasions, they have sustained my commitment to the quest for utopia, and have constantly reminded me that there are many ways of venturing beyond the present or participating in the Great Refusal.

The academic study of utopia is not well established in Britain. Over the years, my conviction that it is a proper area of investigation has been supported by several people, including Krishan Kumar and Lyman Tower Sargent. Keith Taylor, who convened a study group on utopian thought in the early 1980s, played a large part in encouraging me to ignore general scepticism. My immediate colleagues made possible a term's study leave to begin work on the book. They have also been sufficiently tolerant to encourage me to teach a course on Ideology and Utopia. I am grateful both to them and to the students who have chosen to take the course, who have forced me to clarify my ideas and have shared their own.

Rebecca Amiel and Andrew Chester loaned their *Collected Works of Marx and Engels*. Vincent Geoghegan, Robert Hunter and Keith Taylor made invaluable comments on an earlier draft of the manuscript; without these I would undoubtedly end up with even more egg on my face than I now will. Participants in the conference on Utopian Thought and Communal Experience at New Lanark in July 1988 and in the Third International Congress on the Study of Utopia in Italy in May 1989 made useful and challenging comments on material included here. Parts of Chapter 5 originally appeared in 'Marxism, Romanticism and Utopia: Ernst Bloch and William Morris', in *Radical Philosophy* **51**. I am grateful to Basil Blackwell for permission to quote extensively from Ernst Bloch's *The Principle of Hope*. Philip Cross and Clare Grist of Philip Allan and Simon and Schuster have shown remarkable forbearance over the prolonged non-completion of the manuscript.

Writing can be both anti-social and dispiriting at times. Graham Hunter has had much less of my attention that he is entitled to expect, and has cheered me up on many occasions. Robert Hunter has made the entire project possible, both by his active political and intellectual interest in it, and by his unfailing emotional and practical support. I promise to do my share of the chores in 1990.

Introduction

Ah love, could thou and I with Fate conspire
To grasp this sorry Scheme of Things entire,
Would we not shatter it to bits – and then
Remould it, nearer to the Heart's Desire![1]

Utopia is about how we would live and what kind of a world we would live in if we could do just that. The construction of imaginary worlds, free from the difficulties that beset us in reality, takes place in one form or another in many cultures. Such images are embedded in origin and destination myths, where the good life is not available to us in this world but is confined to a lost golden age or a world beyond death. They may also be religious or secular, literary or political. Although various in form, content and location, they are sufficiently common for some commentators to speculate about the existence of a fundamental utopian propensity in human beings. Sometimes utopia embodies more than an image of what the good life would be and becomes a claim about what it could and should be: the wish that things might be otherwise becomes a conviction that it does not have to be like this. Utopia is then not just a dream to be enjoyed, but a vision to be pursued. Yet the very term utopia suggests to most people that this dream of the good life is an impossible dream – an escapist fantasy, at best a pleasant but pointless entertainment. Those utopians who seek to make their dreams come true are deemed to be hopelessly unrealistic, or worse, actively dangerous.

The view that utopia is not escapist nonsense but a significant part of human culture is a fundamental assumption of the expanding field

1

of utopian studies. The variation in the forms of utopian expression means that it can be looked at from the perspective of a range of disciplines: history, literature, theology, cultural anthropology, sociology, political theory, psychology may all concern themselves with representations of the worlds we would like to inhabit. Yet although utopia attracts increasing attention there is much confusion about exactly what makes something utopian, and disagreement about what utopia is for and why it is important. Are all images of the good life utopian, or only those set in the future and intended to be implemented? Should the pursuit of spiritual perfection be included, or paradises beyond death, or does utopia refer only to transformed versions of the social world in which we live our lives before death? Are there lines to be drawn between utopia and religion, or utopia and 'real' politics? And what is utopia for? Does it help to change the world or to stabilise existing societies? Although we may initially think we know what utopia is, when we try to define it, its boundaries blur and it dissolves before our eyes.

This book sets out to clarify the meaning of the term utopia and provide a new definition. Such a project could be undertaken from many points of view: definitions are tools, not ends in themselves. The aim here is to address some of the problems that arise in the field of utopian studies from the absence of a clear and agreed definition. The purpose is firstly one of clarification, to show the basis of the current variation in usage of the concept of utopia. Since this variety arises only in part from a lack of conceptual rigour on the part of commentators and more fundamentally from the range of questions and approaches that are involved, it is important that any common definition which is proposed takes account of this variety. The object is not to impose an orthodoxy, but to encourage communication about issues which are already being addressed and to suggest new ones. Above all, it is to encourage a greater degree of conceptual clarity in discussions of utopia.

Many of the problems which beset utopian scholars arise from the absence of a clear definition of utopia which separates its specialist academic use from the meanings current in everyday language. It is helpful, therefore, to begin with a consideration of how the term is generally used. Utopia as colloquially understood contains two meanings: a good, but non-existent and therefore impossible, society. The elision stems from Thomas More's book, *Utopia*, first published in Latin in 1516. The title, like many of the names in the book, is a joke. It contains deliberate ambiguity: is this eutopia, the good place, or outopia, no place – and are these necessarily the same thing? The pun has left a lasting confusion around the term utopia, and one which constantly recurs like a familiar but nonetheless rather troublesome ghost. More is frequently represented as a benevolent founding father of the utopian genre and consequently of the field of utopian studies; conceptually, however, his legacy has not been an unmitigated blessing.

The ambiguity persists in contemporary dictionary definitions. *Chambers Twentieth Century Dictionary* gives both a non-evaluative and an evaluative meaning. Utopia is 'an imaginary state described in Sir Thomas More's Latin political romance or satire *Utopia*' or 'any imaginary state of ideal perfection'.[2] Utopian, however, may mean (besides an inhabitant of Utopia) 'one who imagines or believes in a Utopia' or 'one who advocates impracticable reforms or who expects an impossible state of perfection in society'. The *Shorter Oxford English Dictionary* reflects the same issues. We have both the initial reference back to More, and 'a place, state, or condition ideally perfect in respect of laws, customs and conditions' or 'an impossibly ideal scheme, especially for social improvement'.[3] The adjective utopian is again more unequivocally derogatory than the noun. Apart from the direct connection with More's island of Utopia, we have 'impracticably ideal; of impossible and visionary perfection . . .' and 'indulging in impracticably ideal projects for social welfare, etc.' – and then, as an afterthought, the less evaluative 'believing in or aiming at the perfecting of polity or social conditions'.

Colloquial usage thus tends to dismiss speculation about the good society as intrinsically impractical. This dismissal may be tolerantly good-humoured, seeing utopia as an interesting if esoteric byway of culture and the utopian as a well-meaning dreamer. It may, on the other hand, be extremely hostile, seeing attempts at instituting utopia as highly dangerous and leading to totalitarianism. This anti-utopian position is typified by Karl Popper and Friedrich Hayek.[4] The enemies of utopia are dealt with by George Kateb,[5] and are only fleetingly referred to in this book – not because they are unimportant, but because they are tangential to the present purpose, which is to explore the usage by the increasing number of scholars who wish to take utopia seriously. For this book is primarily about the way in which the concept of utopia has been used in the growing secondary literature which examines the history and variety of utopian thought, or in arguments for the value or necessity of utopia.

Both the colloquial definitions and the anti-utopian position illustrate the fact that the concept itself is an ideological battleground. The elision between perfection and impossibility can serve to invalidate all attempts at change, reinforcing the claim that there is no alternative, and sustaining the status quo. Perhaps, as Khayyam suggests, we would do better to forget the future and drown our sorrows. But even among different groups committed to change, the derogatory meaning attaching to utopia is what dominates. People rarely claim that their own aspirations are utopian but even dreamers may hurl the epithet at others. The rejection of other people's projects as utopian and unrealistic is part of the process of promoting the merits of one's own plans, and is thus an intrinsic part of the political process.

The variety of definitions within utopian studies operates in the opposite way. Rather than utopia being a term of abuse directed at what other people study, there is a temptation to try to limit the field to one's own area of interest and to set up boundaries which exclude large areas of material as not properly utopian. And indeed, without a definition, it is difficult to establish exactly what we are looking at. If utopia is merely the good/impossible society, this may include literary fictions, satire, fantasy, science fiction, religious or secular paradises, political theories, political programmes and manifestos, small-scale attempts to create ideal communities and nationwide attempts to create the good society, to name but a few areas. If all of these diverse areas are to be included, we need to be clear about what it is that they have in common. In practice, however, most commentators limit what they consider to be properly utopia; but without agreement as to what the proper limits, if any, are, there is a danger of researchers in the area making arbitrary and subjective selections of material; or, even if they are clear and methodical in their own use of the term, using it in an idiosyncratic way and talking past each other; or, indeed, wasting too much time arguing over what is or is not utopian.

In exploring existing definitions of utopia we can consider three different aspects: content, form and function. Firstly, there is content. There is a common assumption that utopia should be a portrayal of the good society. It is however obvious that this will vary, being a matter not just of personal taste, but of the issues which appear to be important to different social groups, either in the same society or in different historical circumstances. Content is for many people the most interesting aspect of utopia, inviting them to consider whether, in fact, this would be a good society, if it existed. The variation in content, however, makes it particularly difficult to use this as part of the definition of utopia. Definitions in terms of content tend to be evaluative and normative, specifying what the good society would be, rather than reflecting on how it may be differently perceived.

The issue of possibility also relates directly to the content of a utopia, and again judgements differ. Some wish to reverse the colloquial meaning and assert that utopias – or at least important utopias – are not impossible at all, but derive their significance from the fact that they are realistic. Such an assertion involves recognising that our notions of what is realistic are socially structured, and thus our judgements must be tempered with caution. But it retains the suggestion that unrealistic images of the good society are less worthy of our attention and consideration than realistic ones. I shall argue that while this may be true for the purposes of particular questions, it is not generally so. And the fact that it is untrue releases us from agonising overmuch about our judgements of possibility or impossibility in most instances. Some utopias may be possible worlds, others not; and while it may be fruitful to reflect on these issues, they are not definitive ones.

Secondly, one can attempt to define utopia descriptively, in terms of form. The common sense equation of utopia with a description of a good society (leaving aside the question of possibility) is one version of such a definition. Another is the equation of utopia with an ideal commonwealth. Some commentators take the form of More's *Utopia* as a model and argue that utopia is a literary genre, involving the fictional depiction of an alternative society in some detail. However, as we have already suggested, depictions of the good society do not necessarily take the form of literary fictions – and indeed this form is only available under certain very specific historical conditions; is it then to be assumed that when these conditions do not exist, there are no utopias? Broader historical comparisons require more inclusive definitions, to accommodate changes in the way in which aspirations for a better life may be expressed.

Thirdly, one may define utopia in terms of its function. This is less obvious; to focus on the function of utopia is already to move away from colloquial usage, which says nothing about what utopia is for, but implies that it is useless. Even those who define utopia in terms of form and content, however, see it as having some function. Many commentators quote Oscar Wilde:

> A map of the world that does not include Utopia is not even
> worth glancing at, for it leaves out the one country at which
> Humanity is always landing. And when Humanity lands there,
> it looks out, and seeing a better country, sets sail. Progress is the
> realisation of Utopias.[6]

Thus utopia is seen as presenting some kind of goal, even if commentators, as opposed to the authors of utopias, do not see them as necessarily realisable in all their details. At the very least, utopias raise questions about what the goal should be. Many commentators, however, go further and use the function of utopia as a defining characteristic – although that function is differently represented by different authors.

The bulk of the book explores the consequences of definitions in terms of form and function. Broadly, one may divide approaches to utopian studies into two streams. The liberal–humanist tradition tends to focus on definitions in terms of form. In contrast a largely, but not exclusively, Marxist tradition has defined utopia in terms of its function – either a negative function of preventing social change or a positive function of facilitating it, either directly or through the process of the 'education of desire'. Contemporary utopian studies draws on both these traditions, and definitions of both kinds may be found, although those in terms of form tend to predominate. Here one may also find attempts to bring together issues of form and function, with an additional function of 'constructive criticism' becoming a defining characteristic.

The first part of the book explores the implicit definitions in early commentaries on utopia – implicit, because the problem of definition is not always directly addressed. On the whole, these can be situated in a liberal–humanist tradition. Most of their definitions rely upon form, but they equally draw on an emerging tradition of the works which are to be considered utopian. To some extent this tradition is little more than a collective habit; yet at the same time, many authors actively create through their selection a version of the utopian tradition in order to argue a particular case about utopia.

The second, and longest, part of the book addresses attempts to define utopia in terms of function. It begins with a discussion of Karl Marx and Friedrich Engels and their rejection of utopia. Although this rejection can be shown to be a local political judgement upon particular movements described as utopian socialism, it has had continuing implications for the development of Marxism – albeit based upon a misunderstanding of the original objections. Whereas Marx and Engels define utopia negatively in terms of its function, Karl Mannheim reverses this judgement and defines utopia as that which transforms the status quo, irrespective of its form. The effect of Mannheim's position is very similar to that of Georges Sorel, although the use of terms is diametrically opposed; Sorel uses utopia in a derogatory sense, and uses the term myth for Mannheim's utopia. Attempts to reintegrate Marxism and utopia have focused upon function, again defining it positively rather than negatively, as a catalyst of radical change. This is true of both Ernst Bloch and Herbert Marcuse (although Marcuse's use of the term is both ambiguous and inconsistent) and, indirectly, of the approach to the problem expressed through recent commentaries upon the work of William Morris. Here the function is that of the 'education of desire' – a function which, on reflection, also forms an intrinsic part of the arguments put forward by Marcuse and Bloch.

Three points need to be made here. First, the fact that these approaches are more analytical means that on the whole concepts are used with much greater precision than elsewhere. It also follows that it is impossible to make sense of the use of a particular term such as utopia without reference to the general problematic within which it is situated. It has thus been necessary to show how the concept and its use fits into an overall argument. Secondly, when we do this, we find that the Marxist utopia differs in content as well as in definition. Its goal lies not in a defined set of institutional arrangements but in the pursuit of another way of being; what is sought is disalienation. It throws up more profound questions about human nature and its potential than do many ideal commonwealths, but it also means that the form of describing the institutions of an ideal society is less appropriate – quite apart from the fact that the legacy of orthodox Marxism makes the stipulation of institutional arrangements unpopular. Thirdly, since the functions of utopia are the education of desire and the transformation of the world, issues of the merit and possibility of what is sought (i.e. issues of content) necessarily leak back in, leading both Bloch and, eventually, Marcuse to make a distinction between 'abstract' and 'concrete' utopia.

The third part of the book examines the way in which concepts of utopia are currently deployed in contemporary utopian studies. There is some indication of a rapprochement between traditions, but not much sign of an emerging consensus. Working definitions range from the refusal of any definition at all, through definitions in terms of form, form and content, function, function and form. An awareness of the questions surrounding the relationship between form and function is also emerging. The changing nature of contemporary utopian fiction has also had an impact here; the emphasis has changed from the presentation of finished perfection to a more open exploration in which the construction of the individual, and thus the question of another way of being, has become the central issue. Nevertheless, while there is a flourishing variety of approach, it is characterised by a conceptual plurality which is anarchic to the point of confusion.

The last chapter of the book therefore seeks to establish a concept of utopia which will contain these various approaches. It is argued that all definitions in terms of form, function or content are problematic. Not only do they place limits upon what may properly be regarded as utopian and thus upon the field of enquiry itself; they also obscure variations in the utopian genre. In order to make such a claim, one must of course be able to locate something which remains constant while content, form and function vary. This element, I would argue, is that of desire – desire for a better way of being and living. To say this is not to make a claim that there is an essential ingredient in human nature with its source deep in the human psyche, reaching towards utopia (as suggested by Marcuse and Bloch). We may claim that all utopias have something in common without making claims about the universality of utopia or the existence of a fundamental utopian propensity. Rather, where such desire is expressed – and the scope for this will itself be historically variable – it will not only vary markedly in content but may be expressed in a variety of forms, and may perform a variety of functions including compensation, criticism and the cata-lysing of change. The most useful kind of concept of utopia would be one which allowed us to explore these differences and which ulti-mately might allow us to relate the variations in form, function and content to the conditions of the generating society. At the same time, it would not exclude from the field of utopian studies any of the wide variety of related work that currently is defined by practitioners as part of the field.

In conclusion then, a new definition of utopia is offered, which recognises the common factor of the expression of desire. Utopia is the expression of the desire for a better way of being. This includes both the objective, institutional approach to utopia, and the subjective, experiential concern of disalienation. It allows for this desire to be realistic or unrealistic. It allows for the form, function and content to change over time. And it reminds us that, whatever we think of particular utopias, we learn a lot about the experience of living under any set of conditions by reflecting upon the desires which those conditions generate and yet leave unfulfilled. For that is the space which utopia occupies.

1

Ideal commonwealths:
the emerging tradition

The study of utopia as a field of academic enquiry did not emerge on any scale until the 1960s. Nevertheless, the perennial fascination of utopia is reflected in the fact that there were in the preceding decades a number of commentaries on various novels, works of political philosophy and social and political movements deemed to be utopian. These early works are interesting and important for a number of reasons. Not only do they provide an insight into what was seen as utopian at the time, and into the role utopia was thought to play in the processes of social change, but they did much to construct a series of assumptions about which phenomena are properly to be labelled utopian. Sometimes the criteria are spelt out with clarity, sometimes not; but in all these compendia and commentaries, the material selected for inclusion provides an implicit definition of the utopian object and the proper field of utopian studies. The effect of these selections can still be felt in contemporary work, and the issues about the boundaries of utopia which are raised continue to be pertinent.

There are a very large number of works which could be considered in trying to characterise the approach to utopia in the period in question. In a discussion of the historiography of utopia, J. C. Davis divides works on utopia into three sections. First, various catalogues and bibliographies which, he says, wrestle with inadequate definitions. Secondly, commentaries and compendia which use what the Manuels call the 'daisy-chain' approach – that is, they consist of a discussion of a chronologically arranged list of utopias, sometimes including substantial excerpts from the texts. Some such commentaries are arguing a case in relation to utopia – for its danger or its utility – and others purport to be neutral; some focus on particular issues or institutions in utopia, such as education or welfare economics. Thirdly, Davis puts in a separate category works which are 'extended studies of, exhortation to or admonition against' utopia.[1]

Only a selection of material can be considered here, and I have chosen to focus on Davis's second category. Several of these commentaries in fact contain bibliographies, but because these can be relatively extensive we learn more about what is regarded as the core of the field of study by considering the works chosen for discussion in the text. Six of the eight books which form the basis of this chapter are probably the best-known and most frequently cited commentaries of the period, through which many contemporary scholars must have been introduced to the field. They are Moritz Kaufmann's *Utopias* (1879), Lewis Mumford's *The Story of Utopia* (1922), Joyce Hertzler's *History of Utopian Thought* (1923), Marie Berneri's *Journey Through Utopia* (1950), A. L. Morton's *The English Utopia* (1952) and Glenn Negley and J. Max Patrick's *The Quest for Utopia* (1952). The other two books included (for different reasons) are Henry Morley's *Ideal Commonwealths* (1885) and Harry Ross's *Utopias Old and New* (1938).

In this chapter we will discuss four themes in relation to these works. First, the material selected as utopian by the various authors, and thus the identification of the utopian object. This varies enormously, with some writers including the whole of nineteenth century socialism, others excluding all of this apart from the occasional novel; and some crossing what others would see as a boundary between utopia and religion. This leads to the second theme, the different attempts to delineate the utopian form and the difficulties encountered therein. Thirdly, there is the issue of the existence of a utopian propensity in human beings, posited by several of these commentators, as well as by authors discussed in subsequent chapters. The final consideration is the treatment of the function of utopia and particularly its relationship to progress. Since the treatments of these themes by individual authors are interwoven and dependent on the overall argument being advanced about utopia, the books will be considered first in chronological order. We can then return to a summary of the treatment of each theme in turn.

The tradition which emerges from these surveys can be characterised as essentially liberal and humanist, despite the fact that Berneri was an anarchist, Morton a Marxist and Kaufmann (apparently) some kind of Christian Socialist. With the partial exception of Morton, they share assumptions of evolution and progress and a preoccupation with reason and freedom. They are anti-statist, wary of utopia's tendency to authoritarianism and wary of prescriptions for radical and precipitous social change. The virtue of utopia is that it holds up an ideal, an ideal

10

which encourages social progress – but that progress is seen as properly a gradual process, which the literal attempt to institute utopia would interrupt. There is an ambivalence here: utopia fascinates as an expression of the felt problems and solutions of particular historical situations; it inspires as a response to the recurrent problems across history; yet it provokes fear that the revolutionary may make the mistake of taking it literally. There is an implied model of the process of social change, as well as its direction: ideas are the motive force in social progress, so that utopia must be taken seriously as a contribution to this – but not too seriously, or evolution and progress may turn to revolution and disaster.

For most of these writers, the ultimate importance of utopia lies in its connection with progress and thus in its social role. However, the dominant character of the commentaries is descriptive. What they contain are accounts (and sometimes texts, excerpts or translations) of the content of various literary or political utopias. A central theme is the variation of the content of these utopias over time. Nevertheless all of them, whether implicitly or explicitly, define utopia primarily in terms of form – for example, the depiction of an ideal commonwealth. The definitions vary, some commentators maintaining that utopia is primarily a literary fiction, others that it is a political vision. And even where the definitions are essentially similar they may be differently applied, or temporarily laid aside, when it comes to selecting material for inclusion. There is also disagreement about the boundaries of utopia, not just as regards the line between the literary and the political but on the inclusion or exclusion of satires and dystopias. Some works are almost universally regarded as utopias; but this 'core' is minute and does not relate to the consistent application of any identifiable criteria, being rather the outcome of habitual assumptions. There are also some works which are apparently recognised as 'traditionally' utopian, in that their exclusion calls for justification. We would be hard put to it to identify an emerging consensus as to definition or the boundaries of the field, but a tradition does emerge as to what are the 'key' utopias. If we were to identify a handful of texts as the agreed core of utopias, it would be Plato's *Republic*, Thomas More's *Utopia*, Francis Bacon's *New Atlantis*, Tomasso Campanella's *City of the Sun* and Etienne Cabet's *Voyage en Icarie*. These are the works least often excluded from discussion (though rarely from mention); More's *Utopia* is the only work which is universally discussed.

Moritz Kaufmann: *Utopias*

Kaufmann's book was published in 1879, just a few years after Friedrich Engels's *Socialism: Utopian and Scientific* (discussed below, Chapter 2). It is subtitled *schemes of social improvement from Sir Thomas More to Karl Marx*. Kaufmann describes his own book as a consideration of the 'principal socialistic schemes' since the Reformation, and as a 'History of Socialism'.[2] It focuses on those who are now conventionally regarded as utopian socialists; indeed, Kaufmann shows the influence of Engels's argument both in his choice of subjects and in his claim to trace the evolutionary process of socialism through its imaginative, critical and ultimately scientific stages – hence the inclusion of Marx. For Kaufmann, utopia is virtually synonymous with socialism. Nevertheless, the book opens with a consideration of three of our five key authors, More, Bacon and Campanella, before moving on to a survey of socialism. The roll-call holds few surprises: Morelly, François Babeuf, Claude Henri de Saint-Simon, Charles Fourier, Robert Owen, Etienne Cabet, Louis Blanc, Pierre-Joseph Proudhon, Ferdinand Lassalle, Karl Marx – and one totally obscure and pseudonymous German cooperative socialist, Karl Marlo, included despite the 'utter absence of . . . fantastic pictures of impossible societies'.[3] Despite this choice of subject-matter and his dependence upon Engels, Kaufmann was far from being a Marxist. He was a clergyman and seems, like the Christian Socialists in the mid-nineteenth century, to have been removed to favour social reform largely through a fear that revolution might otherwise ensue.

Kaufmann does provide us with a definition of utopia:

> What is a Utopia? Strictly speaking, it means a 'nowhere Land', some happy island far away, where perfect social relations prevail, and human beings, living under an immaculate constitution and a faultless government, enjoy a simple and happy existence, free from the turmoil, the harassing cares, and endless worries of actual life.[4]

There is an implication here that utopia is impossible, confirmed by his observation (in relation to Cabet) that utopians are apt to present us with images of people minus all the faults of human nature. Elsewhere, he remarks that all utopian schemes aim 'to remove . . . the extremes of wealth and poverty' (which follows less from his definition than from his equation of utopia with socialism).[5] Kaufmann's definition rests substantially on form and content. The suggestion is made, however, that the form may vary with the social context, all such utopian expressions being the product of a general human propensity:

12

the social ideal, in one form or another, is to be found in the human mind itself; . . . the various modes of giving it shape and form, according to different circumstances, are the manifestations of the same tendency in all men to realise a social ideal.[6]

Mercifully, in Kaufmann's view, there is yet another general human propensity which accounts for the failure of utopian schemes:

The cause of this – the general failure of Utopian systems, as a whole, and the partial acceptance of some truths they contain – is to be found in that wholesome tendency of average men to be guided by practical rather than ideal considerations, to prefer tentative measures to thoroughgoing schemes of social improvement.[7]

His general orientation to utopia is revealed in explorations of its social role. Utopia is an expression of discontent which has both positive and negative aspects. Even where it is unrealistic, as in Cabet's ignoring of the weakness of human nature, it provides a useful corrective to those who see only the prevalence of selfishness. By holding up a higher, if unattainable, ideal, utopia points us in the right direction and contributes to progress:

here we see the value of utopias, in that they hold up a higher ideal of society and prevent a stationary, or rather a stagnant, condition of humanity, satisfied with the base facts of life. They point to a goal of higher moral and material improvement, and so direct man onwards on the way of progress and social reform.[8]

Utopias can do this despite being intrinsically unrealistic, since essentially fantastic and fictional alternatives can function as critiques of the present. Kaufmann even suggests that the intention of utopian schemes is to promote social reform rather than secure their implementation, which is not always true:

Still, it must be remembered that their object was more frequently to satirise existing social inconsistencies than to recommend the literal application of the social schemes which they contained. They aimed at social improvements and reforms by describing fictitious states of society. . . .[9]

The 'wholesome tendency of average men' is not, however, sufficient bulwark against the dangers of utopia. In explanation of the rise and decline in the popularity of Owenism in England, Kaufmann argues that the appeal of utopia is directly proportional to the level of social discontent; and being the expression of popular discontent, utopias are the product of social disharmony, indeed social pathology. Thus 'at all times Socialism is rampant where society is disorganised'.[10] And such germs of truth as exist in socialist utopias generally refer to processes which Kaufmann sees as already being brought to fruition through social progress. As long as socialist utopias do no more than contribute to this inexorable progress they are acceptable, but if utopia is taken seriously and acted on – if it becomes the catalyst of social change rather than merely a critique of existing conditions – it is deeply dangerous. In conclusion, he argues that 'the proper attitude towards Socialism is to regard it as a movement of mankind towards progress which requires to be checked and to be conducted into safe channels'.[11] The acceptable function of utopia is, then, the embodiment of an impossible ideal in the form of a description of a fictitious state of society, as inspiration to the continued march of progress.

Henry Morley: *Ideal Commonwealths*

Morley's contribution does not use the term utopia in its title. Moreover, it is a collection of texts rather than a commentary, and is therefore not amenable to discussion in terms of our four themes. Nevertheless it is worthy of brief comment for two reasons. Both the title and the selection of texts appear to have influenced later commentators, many of whom refer back to this collection and many of whom define utopia as synonymous with an ideal commonwealth.

The selection consists of five texts. The first of these is Plutarch's *Life of Lycurgus*. This is followed by three of the texts which make up our core five, those by More, Bacon and Campanella, and a fragment of Joseph Hall's *Mundus Alter et Idem* (a satire whose status as a utopia or as an ideal commonwealth is therefore contested by some writers). There is little doubt that this volume contributed to the availability of these works and thereby to their routine consideration by students of utopia. This is not to say that Morley was responsible for inventing the tradition of their inclusion, since the central three writers were discussed by Kaufmann six years earlier; but he does appear to have played a role in reproducing this tradition.

Lewis Mumford: *The Story of Utopia*

Mumford's book echoes Morley's title in its subtitle, *ideal common-wealths and social myths*. His roll-call of utopias contains some curious judgements. Plato and More are included, but both Bacon and Campanella receive a passing and dismissive mention by comparison with Johann Valentin Andreae's *Christianapolis*, although he does feel called upon to justify this exclusion; Bacon is described as 'incredibly childish and incoherent'.[12] In the nineteenth century, the principle of selection involves the association of utopias with 'movements like state socialism, the single tax and syndicalism'.[13] Space is given to Fourier and Cabet and to James Buckingham, Thomas Spence, Theodor Hertzka and Edward Bellamy. Owen is marginalised in terms which recall William Cobbet's epithet 'parallellograms of paupers': 'his work belongs more to the "real" world than to the idola of utopia', and his 'projects . . . have more of the flavour of a poor colony than that of a productive human society'.[14] This dismissal, taken with his grounds for the exclusion of John Ruskin and the Guild of St George, constitute an exclusion of the communitarian tradition from the field of utopia – such experiments do not 'embrace the whole of society', are 'utopian only in the sense that the Oneida Community . . . was utopian', and are as fragmentary as Bacon's *New Atlantis*.[15] These nineteenth-century utopias are designated utopias of reconstruction; yet because Mumford regards them as having very limited vision, and being concerned with machinery and inventions rather than with the ends to which these are put, he includes, under the designation utopias of escape, novels by William Morris, W. H. Hudson and H. G. Wells.

Mumford does not consistently identify utopia with an ideal commonwealth because of the distinction he draws between utopias of escape and utopias of reconstruction. The former category refers to the projection of desire without the consideration of limiting conditions, which Mumford regards as primitive and potentially dangerous if indulged in to excess. Indeed, such utopias are not necessarily social fictions at all, but include egocentric fantasies of private, personal fulfilment. Mumford uses the following (sexist and heterosexist) example: 'What man has not had this utopia from the dawn of adolescence onwards – the desire to possess and be possessed by a beautiful woman?'[16] The dangers are illustrated in an interesting (and equally sexist) reversal of this utopia. If we stay in utopia too long we lose our capacity to deal with things as they are. Thus 'the girl who has felt Prince Charming's caresses too long will be repulsed by the clumsy embraces of the young man who . . . wonders how . . . he is going to pay the rent if they spend more than a week on their honeymoon'.[17]

The only suggestion that utopia represents some fundamental human propensity is in relation to utopias of escape.

Utopias of reconstruction are another matter; these, it seems, are roughly synonymous with ideal communities. Utopia becomes 'a vision of a reconstituted environment which is better adapted to the nature and aims of the human beings who dwell within it . . . [and] better fitted to their possible developments'.[18] What is entailed is 'a new set of habits, a fresh scale of values, a different set of relationships and institutions, and possibly . . . an alteration of the physical and mental characteristics of the people chosen, through education, biological selection and so forth'.[19] Where historical utopias are concerned, therefore, Mumford includes 'such plans for the improvement of the human community as had been embodied in complete pictures of an ideal commonwealth' – thereby excluding, for example, James Harrington's *Oceana*, as well as 'any treatment of abstract idealisms which . . . did not exemplify the essential utopian method'.[20] The completeness of the description is important to Mumford. It is, he says, only in the writings of utopians that the transformation of the material and mental world is addressed as a single unified problem. Utopia 'pictures a whole world, but it faces every part of it at the same time'.[21]

Although for most of the book the equation between utopia and the ideal commonwealth operates (and hence so does an implicit definition of utopia in terms of form), this equation is severely qualified. Not only do utopias of escape not correspond to descriptions of an alternative society, but Mumford also discusses 'social myths'. Mumford takes this term from Georges Sorel (see below, Chapter 3), but uses it differently. Whereas utopias as pieces of literature are the product of an individual, there are also collective utopias or social myths which are nowhere set out in detail, but have a more nebulous existence. Mumford's myths are not, like Sorel's, catalysts of action; rather the reverse:

> we are rather interested in those myths which are, as it were,
> the ideal content of the existing order of things, myths which,
> by being consciously formulated and worked out in thought,
> tend to perpetuate and perfect that order. This type of social
> myth approaches very closely to the classic utopia, and we could
> divide it, similarly, into myths of escape and myths of
> reconstruction.[22]

The dominant myths discussed by Mumford are the Country House, Coketown and Megalopolis – labels which evoke their content. These myths are also referred to as 'fake utopias', which need to be

16

replaced by genuine eutopias. The switch in spelling here is significant. Since all the classic utopias, according to Mumford, whether of escape or reconstruction, 'placed desire above reality' and found their fulfilment only 'in the realm of fantasy', they are both good place and no-place, eutopia and outopia, and thus properly utopia.[23] Mumford's goal is a replacement which is sufficiently grounded in reality, but addresses itself adequately to the fundamental questions of human existence – an ideological construct which is eutopia, not outopia.

Although the definition is largely in terms of form, as Mumford's argument develops the emphasis is more upon the function of utopia. The 'separate reality of Utopia' is that of 'a world by itself, divided into ideal commonwealths, with all its communities clustered into proud cities, aiming bravely at the good life'.[24] Yet the equation of utopia with the unreal and the impossible is rejected, since the 'idolum' or 'subjective world' (containing 'all the philosophies, fantasies, rationalizations, projections, images and opinions in terms of which people pattern their behaviour') is real because real in its effects.[25] As Emile Durkheim (whom Mumford cites as an influence) would say, utopias are social facts and one must treat social facts as things; as Mumford puts it, 'Nowhere may be an imaginary country, but News from Nowhere is real news'.[26]

At this point Mumford turns to the functions of the idolum, and of utopia in particular. It is on the one hand a means of escape, a compensation, an aimless substitute for the external world. On the other hand it is an attempt to change the situation, to transform the external world. These compensatory and transformative functions of utopia are not, for Mumford, paradoxical attributes of a single entity; rather, as we have seen, the distinction forms the basis of a division between bad and good utopias (even if existing utopias of reconstruction are not, in fact, seen as very good at all). And as ever, the function is social progress. Mumford quotes Anatole France:

> Without the Utopians of other times, men would still live in caves, miserable and naked. It was Utopians who traced the lines of the first city. . . . Out of generous dreams come beneficial realities. Utopia is the principle of all progress, and the essay into a better future.[27]

Joyce Hertzler: *The History of Utopian Thought*

The next of our commentaries, published in 1923, just one year after Mumford's, is similarly preoccupied with progress. Utopias are seen as unattainable goals but goals which, despite 'constantly receding', nevertheless lead us 'onward and upward'.[28] Utopia is identified with an impossible perfection, contrasted with the virtue of evolutionary progress assumed to be taking place, yet able to play a part in it. Again we find Plato, More, Bacon and Campanella, this time with the inclusion of Harrington in the ranks of the seventeenth-century utopians – although Harrington is suggested to be not quite a proper utopian, being primarily concerned with the setting up of political ideals. There is a substantial section on utopian socialism, including again Morelly, Babeuf, Saint-Simon, Fourier, Cabet, Blanc and Owen, though omitting Proudhon, Lassalle, Marx and the obscure Marlo. A final section includes Bellamy, Hertzka and Wells under the heading 'Pseudo-utopians', a designation which we shall explore further. The first third of the book, however, consists of a discussion of biblical treatments of utopia, contrasting the Hebrew prophets with the later apocalyptists, considering the idea of the Kingdom of God, and the importance of the figure of Jesus. Both Augustine's *City of God* and Savonarola's Florentine theocracy at the end of the fifteenth century receive attention in this context.

In some ways, this remains the most interesting section of the book. The material may be well-worked by theologians, but it is rarely discussed in any detail in the context of utopianism. Hertzler locates a historical shift which has echoes in what has happened in contemporary utopian thought. Whereas the prophets believed the Kingdom of God to refer to a this-worldly Messianic state which was essentially the outcome of ordinary political processes, later writers were no longer able (for reasons of historical circumstance) to believe this. Instead, they hypothesised deliverance through miracle, and ultimately the hope of an eternal kingdom on earth was abandoned in favour of a spiritual heaven. The pushing of the Kingdom of God into an after-life took place because there seemed to be no way of bridging the gap between is and ought; the transition was only possible through the agency of divine intervention.

Hertzler regards the apocalyptists as 'markedly inferior to the prophets', being less realistic and less of a stimulus to social reform:

> While they breathe religious fervour and pious learning, they are childish, fanciful, ornate, unreal and highly emotional, almost useless from the social point of view. . . . They are not stern social reformers such as the prophets, struggling with their feet firmly planted on the ground, and laying down elements of idealism and principles of life which will hold for all time, nor

do they seem to be aware of the laws of life. As a moral stimulus they are practically *nil*.[29]

The effect of the absence of a belief in progress or a mundane agency of transformation in pushing utopia back into the realm of fantasy is something which can be observed in contemporary utopianism too, where it is sometimes seen as the collapse of the genre or, in terms similar to those set out here, its possibly fatal weakening (see Chapter 8 below). Hertzler's observation suggests that the content, form and social role of utopia vary markedly across time, but in ways which are explicable in terms of the generating society.

Hertzler does, however, define utopia largely with reference to form and, despite the discussion of biblical and classical utopias, with reference to More, although it is added that utopia should not be conceived too narrowly as a literary field. Utopia is 'the general term for imaginary ideal societies', the distinctive feature of More's work being the depiction of 'a perfect, and perhaps unrealizable, society, located in some nowhere, purged of the shortcomings, the wastes, and the confusion of our own time and living in perfect adjustment, full of happiness and contentment'.[30] There is reference too to a utopian spirit, but it is not clear that this refers to a universal propensity, being 'the feeling that society is capable of improvement and can be made over to realize a rational ideal'.[31] Both here and in the reference to More there is a suggestion that there is an intrinsic connection between utopia and reason, and that to some extent at least utopia is defined by its rational content. The designation of the utopian spirit as utopianism, and the ensuing definitions at the beginning and end of the book, tend to stir rather than settle the confusion. Utopianism is defined as:

> *a conception of social improvement either by ideas or ideals themselves or embodied in definite agencies of social change [original italics].*[32]

It is also defined as:

> the role of the conscious human will in suggesting a trend of development for society, or the unconscious alignment of society in conformity with some definite ideal.[33]

Both of these refer to function although the meaning is obscure, largely because it assumes a model of social change so idealist as to be almost beyond credibility.

Comments in the text upon particular examples of utopia do little to clarify what is intended here. What makes something utopian seems to be its unattainability. Thus the utopian socialists are held to be so se their future was separated from the present by an unfathomable abyss. One must presume this to be the author's judgement, in spite of the recognition that utopias are often declared unrealistic as a result of vested interests, since the utopian socialists did not themselves hold this to be the case. Further, it seems to be the unattainability of a mode of behaviour, rather than of a set of institutions, that primarily interests Hertzler. Of Saint-Simonism we are told 'it . . . was truly religious in character . . . and as such was the most sublime utopianism',[34] and of More's *Utopia*, 'as an ideal it offered the purest utopianism'.[35] Jesus's teaching is described thus:

> like every ideal, [it] is beyond our perfect practice; but like every true ideal, it is the point toward which our endeavors may growingly converge and approximate. . . . It is a doctrine of optimism and hope, for it looks to the future and not to the past, to human possibilities and not miraculous occurrences, to the perfection of all and not to the glory of a remnant. As utopianism it stands without parallel.[36]

The equation of utopia with impossibility is emphasised by the argument that utopia is coming to an end. It is because utopia is a static state representing perfection as opposed to progress that Bellamy, Hertzka and Wells are described as pseudo-utopians: their utopias 'were not so much high flights of the imagination as the calculated product of beneficent forces now at work'.[37] Because these utopias 'are based in most cases upon proved potentialities, and depend upon normal evolutionary advance for attainment', they are not proper utopias at all.[38] Hertzler plainly believed in the possibility of evolutionary advance in the direction described by Bellamy, and the book ends with a long section extolling the virtues of progress over the pursuit of perfection, while asserting that the merit of utopia is that it holds up a unattainable ideal towards which one may strive, thus acting as a stimulus to progress.

Harry Ross: *Utopias Old and New*

This book, published in 1938, is much less well-known. It (rightly) does not appear on the list in Negley and Patrick as being 'generally reliable and correct',[39] a list which includes Kaufmann, Hertzler and Berneri. Nevertheless, it raises directly a number of problematic issues about the boundaries of utopia, as regards both form and content. The book was written for use in adult education classes and explicitly reflects the author's interests. However, it purports to include the most familiar utopias as well as a few less well known. It includes our old friends Plato, More, Bacon, Campanella and Cabet. The last is the only one of the utopian socialists to receive much attention, the ideas of Babeuf, Owen, Saint-Simon and Fourier being described, astonishingly, as 'dilutions of the existing system with the tonic of co-operation and profit-sharing'.[40] The other less obscure utopias included are those of Andreae and Harrington in the seventeenth century and a selection of novels by William Mallock, Hudson, Edward Bulwer Lytton, Gabriel Tarde, Bellamy, Wells, Huxley and, finally, Morris. Some of the judgements in the book are bizarre, and some contradictory. Hertzka's *Freeland* is presented as the model for the Israeli kibbutz and described as 'the first Zion', with the assertion that 'in Palestine . . . Utopia is coming true'.[41] Plato, More and Harrington are all accused of at least approaching fascism, largely because their education systems are seen as systems of indoctrination, and even Bellamy, about whom Ross is in many ways very positive, is seen to reflect 'the germ of an American Fascism';[42] at the end of the book, however, we are told that to describe More, Andreae or Plato as fascist is absurd.[43]

Ross observes that there is a difficulty in deciding what is a utopia. Two areas where he sees the boundary as problematic are satire and political plans. Although the dividing line is ultimately arbitrary, there is a difference:

> There is such a fine gradation between satire and criticism, between Utopias and projected political programmes, between textbooks of theoretical economics and plans for the future, that we must be content with a very arbitrary division.[44]

Several satirical works are excluded. One of these is Hall's *Mundus Alter et Idem* (included in Morley's collection); others are Samuel Butler's *Erewhon* and *Erewhon Revisited*, and Jonathan Swift's *Gulliver's Travels*. Daniel Defoe's *Robinson Crusoe* is 'not a Utopia though the shipwrecked hero found it a pleasant enough place' because 'you cannot have a Utopia of one' – Friday having mysteriously disappeared.[45] The reason for excluding these works is that their authors plainly did not intend them to be taken as descriptions of ideal societies; they serve purely as vehicles for criticism of the present.

The criterion of authorial intention leads Ross to include material which most commentators do not even consider. Although there is general agreement that utopias are not necessarily places that the reader would find appealing, that one person's utopia may be another person's hell, and that many utopias are alarmingly authoritarian,

Ross is the only writer to take this to its logical conclusion and include a discussion of the fascist utopia (and its differences from communism); he also included Adolf Hitler's *Mein Kampf* in his bibliography. Plainly, utopia cannot be defined by its content. The question of an author's intentions is not, however, an unproblematic criterion. Ross describes Huxley's *Brave New World* (along with some other dystopias of anti-communist intent) as a false utopia; it is 'not so much a Utopia as a nightmare and warning to all who would plan a Utopia'.[46] However, readers may differ not only in their evaluation of the merits of a portrayed society, but also (sometimes as a result) in their interpretation of the intended meaning of particular works. Both *Brave New World* and, later, B. F. Skinner's *Walden Two*, were received by some as utopias and by others as anti-utopias.

Ross defines utopia in terms of form as 'the picture of an ideal society in action, whether that society is historical or not'.[47] It is a definition which could include much of utopian socialism (as shown by Kaufmann and Hertzler), but the selection here focuses on literary utopias, plus the small group whose inclusion is becoming an almost unchallenged convention. The fictional element appears to be crucial: Laurence Gronlund's *The Cooperative Commonwealth* is excluded on the grounds that it is a purely theoretical treatise. Ross also requires that the description be reasonably complete. Thus Ebenezer Howard's *Tomorrow* is excluded on two grounds:

> not only are [Howard's] books intended as a direct guide to
> action, but they confine themselves to only a small part of what
> a Utopia must be. A Utopia must comprehend the whole of the
> social structure.[48]

On this basis, as Berneri is to point out, one might also exclude Bacon; nor does Plato describe the whole social structure. Indeed, most utopias would fail this test given that almost without exception they ignore the issue of child-care (as distinct from education).

For Ross it is form and intent rather than content, or indeed function, which define utopia. It is not necessarily holding up an ideal to which we would aspire, nor even encouraging us to reflect critically upon the present, let alone do anything to change it. There is a suggestion that utopia has something to do with the future, since Ross attributes the absence of 'genuinely Utopian thought' in the Middle Ages to the fact that it was difficult to envisage a future organised differently.[49] Escape, on which Mumford frowns, seems to be regarded as a legitimate function – and one which, far from challenging the status quo, reconciles us to it. Both Mallock's *The New Republic* and Hudson's *A Crystal Age* are described as 'a way of escape'.[50] Lytton's

The Coming Race and Tarde's *Underground Men* are also escapist, the latter enabling us to 'laugh . . . and return to this sad grim world refreshed'.[51] Ross observes that the effect of these books is to return the reader to reality 'more ready to accept the real world and to agree that perhaps this is not such a bad old world after all'.[52]

Marie Berneri: *Journey Through Utopia*

Berneri's book was published posthumously in 1950 and is the first of the post-war commentaries. An untroubled assumption of progress had been severely shaken. Fascism, the Holocaust and the militarily unnecessary bombings of Hiroshima and Nagasaki left a legacy of anxiety and pessimism. The US action, taken to limit the potential Soviet sphere of influence in Asia,[53] precipitated the cold war between the super-powers; the new enemy was communism, despite the role of the Soviet Union in defeating Nazism. These preoccupations were reflected not only in the prevalence of dystopian fiction but in the tenor of commentaries on utopia. Berneri's book begins with a foreword by George Woodcock, commenting on the intolerant and authoritarian nature of most utopias with the exception of a few such as those by Morris, Denis Diderot and Gabriel de Foigny. The dangers of utopia are argued to be increasingly recognised, with people increasingly writing and reading anti-utopias. The function of Berneri's book, as of these anti-utopias, is to constitute a warning 'of the doom that awaits those who are foolish enough to put their trust in an ordered and regimented world'.[54]

Journey Through Utopia is both anthology and commentary, and the intention to make particular texts more widely available affects the selection and the attention given to particular topics. The classical utopias discussed are those of Plato, Plutarch and Aristophanes (these last being satires). Berneri raises the question of authorial intention, remarking that in this period it is difficult to determine which works are to be considered utopian, since it is hard to distinguish between what is intended as fact and as fiction: 'the difference between imaginary and historical accounts is sometimes a very tenuous one'.[55] Renaissance utopias include More, Campanella (in a new translation), Bacon and Andreae, as well as François Rabelais's *Abbey of Theleme*, despite the fact that 'it cannot be honestly described as an ideal commonwealth'.[56] In general, with the Renaissance period Berneri includes only 'works which can be defined as ideal, imaginary commonwealths or communities' rather than 'treatises on government or politics'.[57] Harrington's *Oceana* is thus excluded and the section on utopias of the English Revolution is dominated by discussion of Gerrard Winstanley (although only of *The Law of Freedom in a Platform*, not the earlier, more mystical and apocalyptic, texts). Berneri argued Winstanley to be overlooked and neglected, despite his reflecting popular currents of the revolutionary period. Discussion of French utopias of the Enlightenment, particularly those of de Foigny and Diderot, follows.

For the nineteenth and twentieth centuries, Berneri decides against utopian socialism and concentrates upon literature. The authors chosen are Cabet, Lytton, Bellamy, Morris and Eugene Richter, followed by Hertzka, Wells, Yevgeny Zamyatin and Aldous Huxley. Both *Erewhon* and *Gulliver's Travels* are excluded because they are satires 'in which an imaginary civilisation is used as a device for criticising our own', rather than ideal commonwealths.[58] The same might be said of Richter's *Pictures of a Socialistic Future*, but ideological imperatives override consistency: Richter is included because he 'illustrates many objections which the utopias of state-socialism arouse in one's mind'.[59] The book concludes with the words of the tramp's utopia, the American folksong 'The Big Rock Candy Mountain'.

The decision to focus on literary texts is taken after some consideration. Berneri comments on the difficulty of establishing the boundary between utopia and socialism in the nineteenth century:

> The history of utopias in the nineteenth century is closely linked with the creation of the socialist movement, and it is sometimes difficult to distinguish between schemes which belong to the province of utopian thought and those which come within the province of social reform. There is hardly a single work dealing with social problems, published during this period, which has not, at some time or other, been described as utopian.[60]

This situation, however, results from a trick of definition, of which Berneri deeply disapproves. The responsibility is laid at the door of those 'self-styled scientific socialists' who have subverted the original meaning of the term 'utopian' and contrasted it with 'scientific', turning it into a term of abuse to be hurled at opponents. 'It is thanks to these Marxist judges that the list of nineteenth century utopias has assumed such enormous proportions.'[61]

The influence of Engels's *Socialism: Utopian and Scientific* was considerable and the distinction impressed not only Marxists but other commentators upon utopia and socialism, as is demonstrated by Kaufmann's commentary. Berneri is surely wrong, however, to attribute the connection between socialism and utopia in the nineteenth century purely to a trick of definition. The boundaries were already obscure, and in reality the conjunction occurs because of a coincidence in the dominant content of utopia with that of socialism. Further, the alternative meaning given to utopianism by Marx and Engels built on the existing assumption of impossibility; but it did not override the existing definition.

Until Engels, argues Berneri, 'utopia was considered as an imaginary ideal commonwealth whose realisation was impossible or difficult'. His much wider meaning 'included all social schemes which did not recognise the division of society into classes, the inevitability of the class struggle and of social revolution'.[62] The definition in terms of form is replaced by one in terms of content (although the point of Engels's distinction actually relates to function, as we shall see). Berneri contends that there is no reason to suppose 'utopian' socialism to be in reality any more unrealistic than 'scientific' (meaning, of course, that there is no reason to consider scientific socialism, i.e. Marxism, to be any more realistic than utopian socialism), and thus chooses to adhere to the 'original' definition in terms of form:

> It might be wiser, therefore, to leave aside what seems to-day an arbitrary division between utopian and scientific socialists, and to consider only the most representative of those works which remain in the utopian tradition by describing ideal commonwealths in some imaginary country or in an imaginary future.[63]

Berneri's definition, then, is unequivocally in terms of form, although she does not always apply it rigorously. She is more ambivalent about the function of utopia, which receives little direct attention in the text. On one hand, the association between utopia and progress is not entirely abandoned. The book opens with a series of quotations, including those by Anatole France and Oscar Wilde (cited above) which would give utopia a key role in the unrolling of human progress. On the other hand – and this is the more central argument – the realisation of utopia has become a major danger. This is behind her lack of sympathy with the literary utopias of the nineteenth century (apart, that is, from *News from Nowhere*): they provoke an 'utter boredom', with their authors' 'conceit . . . in thinking themselves the saviours of mankind . . . who would kill their sons with attention and kindness rather than let them enjoy one moment of freedom'.[64] The last section, on modern utopias (Hertzka, Wells, Zamyatin, Huxley), reiterates the same concerns. Berneri argues that the fashion for utopian schemes is dying out, with the trend of modern literature being increasingly anti-utopian. As utopia becomes realisable, it is no longer something to hope for, but something to fear. As Nicholas Berdiaev put it:

> Utopias appear to be much more capable of realisation than they did in the past. And we find ourselves faced by a much more distressing problem: How can we prevent their final realisation? . . . Utopias can be realised. Life advances towards utopia. And perhaps a new century is beginning, a century in which the intellectuals and the cultivated classes will dream of the means by which the utopias can be avoided and how we can return to a non-utopian society, less 'perfect' and more free.[65]

Berneri argues that this entirely appropriate suspicion of utopias can be attributed to a number of factors, including new totalitarian regimes, a turning away from a belief in progress, an increasing distrust rather than confidence in the beneficence of machinery and a new understanding of the problem of the relationship between the individual and the state. The traditional utopia assumed a coincidence between these interests which is now seen to be problematic, and it is the consequent authoritarianism of the nineteenth-century utopia which Berneri holds chiefly responsible for the rise of anti-utopianism. Having said that, a few utopias (and Morris's *News from Nowhere* is included among these) remain 'the living dreams of poets'.[66]

Negley and Patrick: *The Quest for Utopia*

The *Quest for Utopia*, published in 1952, is relatively untouched by the concerns which beset Berneri and retains the sense of connection between utopia and progress. It, too, is an anthology of selections largely from literary utopias, with some commentary, and contains a more extended consideration of the definition of utopia. It is the only collection not arranged in chronological order, since utopias written between 1850 and 1950 constitute the first half of the book, followed by earlier examples from classical sources onwards. As with Berneri the object of the collection is said to be in part to make available or more widely known some of the more obscure utopias, besides providing 'a representative sample of utopian thought in Western civilization';[67] thus one cannot necessarily infer that these are seen as the most central and important constituents of the field. Criteria for inclusion include relative unavailability. Nevertheless, More is included, since it 'seemed improper to present an anthology of utopian literature' which excluded him;[68] so too are Bacon, Harrington, Cabet and Campanella (again in a new translation), as well as Hall. Bellamy also figures in the section on modern utopias: 'as in the case of More, Bellamy's name has become almost synonymous with utopia'.[69] Here, though, we are not offered excerpts from *Looking Backward*, it being widely available.

The other main criterion for inclusion, apart from the requirement that the authors concerned be allowed to speak in their own words, rests on the definition of utopian literature, a matter which Negley and Patrick describe as difficult and arbitrary. Utopia is defined clearly in terms of form:

> The utopist . . . is not merely a reformer or satirist, not just a dreamer, nor yet only a theorist. Utopia is a distinct vehicle of expression. . . . Utopia is distinguishable from the other forms in which men have expressed their ideals, as philosophy is from poetry, or legal codes from political tracts. . . . [It] is impossible to understand utopian literature if all manner of speculations, idealizations, vagaries, plans, political platforms and programs are to be considered utopias.[70]

The characteristics which distinguish utopia from these other forms of expression which presumably border upon it are three-fold. Utopia is fictional, it 'describes a particular state or community' and its 'theme is the political structure of that fictional state or community'. In particular, the use of a fictional state 'eliminates from utopian literature all speculation the form of which indicates that it should properly be designated political philosophy or political theory';[71] hence, presumably, the exclusion of the whole of 'utopian socialism', with the exception of Cabet's *Voyage en Icarie*. On the periphery of the field of utopian literature, or perhaps outside it, lie 'those works which should be designated predictions, fantasies, and planning administration'.[72] In an entirely separate category is the discussion of utopian communities. Within the category of utopian literature there are two main classifications based upon literary form: the speculative or constructive utopia and the satire. Thus Negley and Patrick include in the genre that problematic group which uses the device of a social fiction, but one which takes the form of a critical commentary on the present rather than an ideal commonwealth. Fantasy, too, may occasionally be included.

The function of utopia is only hinted at, but Negley and Patrick seem to share Hertzler's view. Utopia, far from being the nonsense as which it is usually regarded, 'represents . . . one of the noblest aspirations of man':

> What could be of more significance in the history of civilization than that man, since he first began to think and write, has

27

continued ever to dream of a better world, to speculate as to its possible nature, and to communicate his longings to other men in the hope that the ideal might, at least in part, become reality?[73]

Progress too depends upon utopia: 'the vision of one century is often the reality of the next', and utopia moves on, prodding humanity to 'reshape reality closer to the ideal'.[74] The utopian propensity is a feature of the human condition: 'the tendency to utopianize is common to primitive and sophisticated men'. Interestingly, the justification for this claim draws on material which their definition would exclude from the category of utopia – 'Paradise, Arcadia, the Golden Age, the Island of the Blest, Gardens of Eden and the Land of Cockaigne',[75] as well as 'incipient utopianism' in the Hebrew prophets.[76] Proper utopias, however, are argued to begin with the Greeks, written either as 'escapes from harsh reality' or as a means of philosophical speculation or propaganda.[77]

The role of utopia in encouraging progress does however place some constraints upon its content. The imagination cannot be given complete licence, and sheer fantasy ceases to be utopian. Indeed, 'it is well that the fictional state of utopia should be an idealized vision of the existing state, for only thus could men gain from the utopian vision a hint of the direction of progress beyond their own present society'.[78] On the other hand the whole point of utopia is its difference from the present, and the absence of the restraint either of existing institutions or existing human character. Thus 'the utopist may populate his fictional state with a race of men wiser, healthier and more generous than any society has ever seen', as well as 'construct a configuration of institutions the like of which the world has never known'.[79] What Negley and Patrick are grappling with here, but cannot articulate because they do not directly address the question of function, is the relationship between the function of utopia and the possibility or plausibility of its content. This is an issue to which we will return in Chapter 8.

Again, then, we have utopia defined in terms of form, and largely confined to a literary genre, with certain specific exclusions of material other commentators would wish to include as utopian. And, again, we have the liberal–humanist idea that social progress continues and that utopia plays a part in this which is not very clearly defined, but has to do with the projection of ideals or of goals which carry progress onwards.

A. L. Morton: *The English Utopia*

The English Utopia is written from a Marxist viewpoint and therefore has a rather different perspective from the other works considered in this chapter. Given the antagonism of most Marxists at the time to utopian speculation, it is perhaps surprising that the book was written at all. But Morton sees utopia as an aspect of social history, in the understanding of which his *A People's History of England* was a pioneering work; and he treats utopia primarily as a vehicle of aspiration. The second surprise is that, given his Marxist perspective, he in fact shares both the definition of utopia and the underlying assumption of progress with several other authors discussed here, although his view of the direction and content of that progress is very different.

The fact that Morton is writing about English utopias accounts for the exclusion of Plato, Campanella and Cabet, among others. There is, of course, a long discussion of More, besides consideration of Bacon, Harrington and two more minor figures, Samuel Hartlib and Samuel Gott, as well as (albeit briefly) Winstanley. Defoe and Swift receive extended attention. He draws too on a wider field of literature, including William Godwin, William Blake and Percy Bysshe Shelley, as well as addressing utopian socialism as represented by Owen and a more obscure disciple, John Goodwin Barmby. Samuel Butler is included, as well as Lytton, Bellamy, Hertzka, Richter and of course Morris. Wells, Huxley and Orwell are accompanied by E. M. Forster and G. K. Chesterton. While utopia is seen primarily as a literary text, both satire and anti-utopia are included and the boundaries are widely drawn.

Although most of the book treats utopia primarily as a literary phenomenon, Morton notes that there is a popular theme which runs alongside this. His first chapter is called 'Poor Man's Heaven'. Here Morton discusses the poem *The Land of Cokaygne* and the recurrence of elements of this in the folk utopias of the poor from antecedent myths to the much later 'The Big Rock Candy Mountain'. Thus the serf's dream of Cokaygne persists 'as an almost secret tradition under the surface' of the literary tradition, until the two strands are brought together in *News from Nowhere*.[80] This for Morton is the epitome of the English utopia, as Morris unites the dream of the oppressed for a land of abundance, leisure and social justice with the active movement of the working class, and expresses both through the vehicle of the literary utopia.

Morton defines utopia in terms of both form and function. Utopia is 'an imaginary country described in a work of fiction with the object of criticising existing society'.[81] He is, however, anxious not to be too strictly bound by this definition, and indeed includes some works which are not fictional, as well as some in which the critical element is slight. The inclusion of anti-utopias does not quite fit the definition either. It means that he takes from More only the 'no-place' element of utopia (and indeed he says that 'Utopia . . . comes from two Greek words meaning "No place" '), while simultaneously binding utopia to a future location: 'Utopia is really the island which people thought or hoped or sometimes feared that the Britain of their day might presently become'.[82] On the other hand, utopia has at its heart the aspiration for a *better* future – an aspiration whose form and content change over time. 'In the beginning Utopia is an image of desire', and while it later 'grows more complex and various', developing into an elaborate means of satire and social criticism, it is still 'always . . . based on something that somebody actually wants'.[83]

The definition of utopia in terms of form and function is reiterated in the discussion of the 'end of utopia' in the final chapter. This phrase has a double meaning for Morton. On the one hand, utopia is no longer necessary as the working classes see the emergence of utopia itself as reality:

> We can see today in the building of socialism a transformation of
> man and of nature on a scale never before attempted. The
> fantasies of Cokaygne, the projects of Bacon, the anticipations of
> Ernest Jones are in effect being translated into facts in the plans
> which are now beginning to change the face and the climate of
> the U.S.S.R. and other socialist countries. . . . This realisation of
> Utopia through the power of the working class, which the
> Huxleys and Orwells find so terrifying, is the vindication of the
> belief that has lain at the roots of all the great utopian writings
> of the past, the belief in the capacity and the splendid future of
> mankind.[84]

This realisation of utopia means that the speculative utopia is no longer necessary: 'the working class and their allies who are actually fighting to win or to build socialism are seldom inclined to construct imaginary pictures of a future shaping itself under their hands'.[85] But on the other hand, the utopian *form* is now so established that it continues even when its original function has disappeared. In attacking the anti-utopias of Huxley and Orwell, Morton cites (but critically) the quotation from Berdiaev which was used by Berneri, and which appears in the preface to *Brave New World*. Morton sees these anti-utopias as degenerate, the product of a bourgeoisie who 'see in their own future the future of civilisation [and] cannot now contemplate that future with anything but despair'.[86]

Morton's judgements are more overtly coloured by his political standpoint here than elsewhere in the book. For our purposes, what is important is that the books in question are deemed to be utopian in form but not function: the essential utopian function is, at this point, to be the catalyst of social change:

> the essence of the classical utopias of the past was a belief that by satire, by criticism or by holding up an example to be followed, they could help to change the world. In this they have had a positive part to play, they have stimulated thought, led men to criticise and fight against abuses, taught them that poverty and oppression were not a part of a natural order of things which must be endured.[87]

Both his pessimistic assessment of the anti-utopias and his optimism about the realisation of utopia stand in stark contrast to Berneri's conclusion, and perhaps both judgements should be qualified by recalling the words of William Morris himself:

> men fight and lose the battle, and the thing that they fought for comes about in spite of their defeat, and when it comes turns out not to be what they meant, and other men have to fight for what they meant under another name.[88]

Themes and issues

Both the range of material and the approach to utopia vary a great deal among the commentators discussed here and it is time to draw together their treatment of the four themes identified at the beginning of this chapter. These are the identification of the utopian object, the definition of utopia, the question of a utopian propensity and the function of utopia.

There is a core of writers almost universally recognised as utopian: Plato, More, Bacon, Campanella, Cabet – although even here some cavil at the inclusion of Bacon on the grounds of the incompleteness of his description, if utopia is supposed to be an ideal commonwealth. Once we move away from this core, disagreements multiply. The difficulties have to do with the boundaries between literature and politics, between utopia and religion, and with differences of content and intent within the literary genre, and thus the possible distinctions between utopia, dystopia, anti-utopia and satire. But they also have to do with habit, which affects what is neglected, as opposed to explicitly excluded, as well as what is chosen for discussion. It is notable that not one of these commentators discusses Charlotte Perkins Gilman's *Herland*, despite the insights that can be gained by comparing this with *Looking Backward* and *News from Nowhere*. Women's utopias are conspicuously absent from the tradition as it emerges in the first half of the twentieth century, although more recent scholarship proves conclusively that this is not because they did not exist.

The question of the distinction between politics (especially socialism) and utopia is resolved in opposite directions by Kaufmann and Berneri. Whereas Kaufmann regards utopia as primarily a political phenomenon, Berneri insists upon the identification of utopia with a fictional description of an ideal commonwealth; the result of her argument is to exclude from the field of utopianism most of the material discussed by Kaufmann. Similar problems surround the question of the inclusion or exclusion of Harrington's *Oceana*. Morton discusses Harrington (as do Hertzler, Ross and Negley and Patrick), for precisely the reasons which lead Berneri (and Mumford) to reject him:

> the fact that in both the American and French Revolutions Harrington's Utopia was the one to which the acutest political theorists turned, is proof of its close relation to the actual problems of a revolutionary age.[89]

Whichever way the difficulty is resolved, it presents itself as a problematic distinction between literary and political texts. Social and political movements, as well as the communitarian tradition, are largely ignored. This is most curious in the case of Morton, although he does attend to a wider range of textual material than most and is less bound by issues of literary form. The reason for this general bias may lie in the nature of liberal academic enquiry: the text is an identifiable object, its contents verifiable and easily shared, if amenable to alternative interpretations. Even differences of view about the meaning or importance of a text carry little threat to the status or identity of contestants. Utopian images which exist as the kind of social myths to which Mumford refers (whether supportive of or oppositional to the status quo), precisely because they are nebulous and nowhere written down, are much more difficult to study and claims of objectivity much more difficult to substantiate. Moreover, the political arena is one where partisan loyalties have far deeper significance; the stakes are higher.

The relatively messy and difficult nature of non-textual utopias may explain why few commentators cross our second boundary, between utopia and religion. Of the commentators discussed here only Hertzler explores the area at any length, although Morton makes some interesting points about the continuities and contrasts between *The Land of Cokaygne* and biblical accounts of Eden and the New Jerusalem. (Paul Bloomfied's *Imaginary Worlds*, published in 1932, discusses, albeit most superficially, Christian, Jewish and Islamic paradises.) The only other reference to this sort of material comes in Negley and Patrick, where it is mentioned in passing but is not, according to their definition, part of utopia proper.

Even within the field of literature there are problems about what constitutes a utopian text. Cabet, Bellamy, Hertzka and Wells are almost universally discussed; Hudson, Lytton and Morris frequently so, and never specifically excluded. Morton alone offers Milton, Blake and Shelley. One dispute centres on the status of satire. Thus Ross excludes Butler and Swift, as does Berneri, while Morton discusses *Gulliver's Travels* at length; Morley includes Hall, as do Negley and Patrick (who include satire as a distinct genre from 'constructive utopias'), while Ross excludes him. The significance of writers such as Richter, Orwell and Huxley and the inclusion of their works among utopias is also in dispute. Here the problem is not one of form, but of the content of the text, the author's intentions and the social role of such novels; utopia, it seems, is not just a matter of form but also of content and function.

Nevertheless, most of the definitions of utopia that we are offered are expressed in terms of form. The dominant description of utopia is an ideal commonwealth, an imaginary ideal society; and one which is more or less complete and couched in fictional terms. The problem over satire and negative images of the future is that utopia is also presumed to be better than existing conditions – in the case of Hertzler and Berneri at least, impossibly so. Both Berneri and Morton are explicit about utopia's location in the future, a point which is assumed by most commentators.

Despite this concentration on the form of utopia, there is a recognition that not only the content but the form of utopia may vary across time. Hertzler's discussion of the prophets and apocalyptists is the most direct version of this point to be found in these commentaries, while Morton's presentation of utopia as an aspect of social history takes it for granted. Morton locates a popular tradition, including Cokaygne, as a second current running underneath or alongside the literary tradition, the vehicle of the aspirations of oppressed classes. Negley and Patrick indirectly make a similar point. While defining utopia in terms of a fictional form available only to the literate classes of literate society, they posit a universal human propensity to imagine utopias. The popular forms which they list suggest that the study of utopia might profitably include cultural anthropology, although this might be deemed to be a source merely of the 'incipiently' utopian. Yet if we are to take seriously the idea that there is a fundamental human 'tendency to utopianise', the question of this variation in form will need to be more rigorously addressed and, with the other issues raised in this chapter, will be returned to at a later stage.

Definitions in terms of form do not preclude a concern with function. The dominant concern is with utopia's role in relation to progress – a progress assumed by almost all these writers. The main function identified for utopia is as an ideal which, while strictly speaking impossible to realise, nevertheless (in some unspecified way) helps history to unfold in a positive direction. Other functions are also identified, however. Both Mumford and Ross identify some utopias as escapist and compensatory, Mumford finding this role less acceptable, although suggesting that it permits freer reign to the imagination than the utopia of reconstruction. The acceptance that the proper role of utopia is to criticise the present is universal. The view of its relationship to change varies. Morton suggests that once change is underway utopia becomes redundant; it is how desire is expressed when the good society cannot be built. Kaufmann and Berneri both fear that utopia might be implemented, that it can catalyse change, and not necessarily in a direction they would welcome. Three different functions, not necessarily mutually exclusive, are thus identified: compensation, critique, catalyst.

Questions of function are not, however, pursued with much rigour and indeed cannot be because of the overwhelming insistence on a definition in terms of form. Although the issue of social change is clearly present in these works, it is not (except in Morton's case) the dominant concern. In the following chapters we shall see how a more analytical and largely Marxist tradition has addressed the relationship between utopia and social change, and in the process defined utopia primarily in terms of function rather than form. The reason for this is that a different question becomes central: how can the good society be implemented? If hitherto utopists have largely sought to understand the world, the point, for Marxists, is to change it.

2

Castles in the air:
Marx, Engels, and utopian socialism

The Marxist tradition has for the most part been strongly antipathetic to utopianism, which it has understood as the construction of blueprints of a future society that are incapable of realisation; the charge of utopianism has also been levelled at Marxism by its opponents, using a similar definition. Throughout the twentieth century there have been notable exceptions to the dominant unpopularity of utopianism (including the views of Ernst Bloch, Herbert Marcuse and Edward Thompson, discussed in subsequent chapters) but the idea that utopia can be valuable for Marxists has always been a minority view. The roots of Marxist objections to utopia can be found in the writings of Marx and Engels; however, their criticisms of utopian socialism have been used illegitimately as justification of a general rejection of descriptions of the future socialist society. The concept of utopia deployed in this rejection, besides being a political weapon in a process of 'annihilation by labels',[1] confounds two issues: speculation about the future, and the possibility and means of transition to socialism. The real dispute between Marx and Engels and the utopian socialists is not about the merit of goals or of images of the future but about the process of transformation, and particularly about the belief that propaganda alone would result in the realisation of socialism. The general orientation to utopia that has developed not only mis-represents the views of both Marx and Engels, but has had thoroughly deleterious effects on the socialist project in the past hundred years. In this chapter we shall try to unravel the real grounds of the distinction between utopian and scientific socialism and its implications for speculation about the future and for the concept of utopia.

The term utopia is in fact hardly every used by Marx or Engels other than as the adjective 'utopian', generally in the terms 'utopian socialism' and 'utopian communism'. Indeed the term 'utopia' does not appear as an entry in the recent comprehensive *Dictionary of Marxist Thought* (perhaps surprisingly, given the inclusion of an entry on Ernst Bloch).[2] 'Utopian socialism' is a term with a particular historical meaning and refers initially to the ideas of and movements inspired by Saint-Simon and Fourier in France and Robert Owen in England, although the field is subsequently widened. By 'utopian communism' Marx and Engels chiefly referred to the followers of Cabet in France and of Wilhelm Weitling in Germany. In one sense the whole of the collaborative project of Marx and Engels can be seen as a critique of utopian socialism, but in order to understand the significance of their specific criticisms we need to look briefly at the ideas of the utopian socialists themselves.[3]

The utopian socialists

Saint-Simon, Fourier and Owen all drew up schemes for the institution of a society which would overcome the manifest evils of poverty and degradation that characterised early industrial society. All were critical of the extremes of wealth and poverty they saw around them, of the unbridled power of private property and of conventional sexual morality and family relationships. Both the nature of their criticisms and their solutions differed considerably, but all emphasised the importance of cooperation, association and harmony – and all justified their schemes in terms of their basis in a scientific understanding of human nature. Like Marx, they claimed to be accurate analysts of the status quo and to derive their proposed solutions – which they also claimed to be inevitable – from these empirical analyses; they too rejected the designation 'utopian' because of its dominant meaning of impossibility.

Like Marx, Saint-Simon believed that industrial development laid the basis for the development of the good society because it provided the conditions for abundance and thus for the elimination of poverty, idleness and ignorance. The ills currently besetting society were the effect of an inevitable historical process and would just as inevitably be overcome. The society of the future would not be perfectly egalitarian, but would provide the greatest possible scope for the development of human capacities (and hence for the expansion of production). These capacities were not, however, equally distributed throughout the population and Saint-Simon's ideal society consisted of three classes, each appropriate to the talents of three human types, scientists, artists and producers; this triadic view of human nature was claimed to be scientific. Social harmony would prevail largely because of the congruence between people's activities and their inclinations, so that the need for government would decline to be replaced by administration. Towards the end of his life, however, Saint-Simon also argued for the need for a more effective social cement to ensure harmony, to be provided by a new religion whose moral code prescribed love and proscribed violence.

Saint-Simon, like Fourier and Owen, wished to see the new society instituted by persuasion, and not by force. Unlike them, his aim was a transformation of the whole society, not a gradual process of change through the institution of small experimental communities. No opposition was seen between the interests of owners and workers; bourgeoisie and proletariat were both seen as part of a class of producers to be contrasted with parasites, the latter being made up mainly of the nobility and clergy:

> The producers have no wish to be plundered by any one class of
> parasites rather than by any other. . . . It is clear that the
> struggle must end by being played out between the whole mass
> of parasites on the one hand and the mass of producers on the
> other. . .[4]

The Saint-Simonist movement founded on Saint-Simon's death in 1825 therefore sought to persuade both bourgeoisie and proletariat of the merits of his plans, and because of the central opposition to violence and conflict was essentially socially quiescent. However, by the early thirties its emphasis had shifted from stressing the 'scientific' nature of the doctrines and Saint-Simonism declared itself a religion. The doctrine of love which it preached, however, included a liberation of sexual passion and opposition to the bourgeois family. In 1832 the leaders of the movement were brought to trial and jailed and the movement was declared illegal. This did not in itself lead to the movement's demise and it continued to exist until after 1848, but at no stage had great appeal to the working class and continued to be engaged primarily with moral and religious questions.

Fourier also deduced his scheme for the perfect society from a speculative anthropology claimed as empirical fact. In his view, human nature consisted of twelve passions, present in different degrees in each individual and whose precise mix determined each person's uniqueness. From these passions and the resultant human types, Fourier went on to derive 810 different temperaments, and thus argued that the minimum number of people for a harmonious community is 1620, the optimum number being between 1700 and 1800. His ideal society would be made up of these small self-supporting communities, with individuals integrated into a variety of groups within them. Choice of occupation, congenial company and variety in the work itself would mean that labour would cease to be an imposition: 'attractive work does not cause physical pain or mental distress; for the worker it is an amusement, a free exercise of his faculties'.[5]

To a much greater extent than Saint-Simon, Fourier railed against the repressive morality of his own society and placed sexual pleasure at the centre of life in his ideal communities; his analysis of the ills of society also involved an elaborate cosmology and the fear that the discord in human society might presage a disruption of the order of the universe. Fourier not only claimed that his analysis of human nature was scientific, but explicitly rejected the view that his plans were utopian and unrealistic:

> What is Utopia? It is the dream of well-being without the means
> of execution, without an effective method. Thus all
> philosophical sciences are Utopias, for they have always led
> people to the very opposite of the state of well-being they
> promised them.[6]

The Fourierist movement stressed the setting up of small communities which would be self-supporting and primarily agricultural. It had links with the wider cooperative movement in France, just as Owenism influenced the cooperative movement in England, but did not have substantial support among the emergent working class, nor was it ever perceived as sufficiently threatening to be suppressed.

Owen, like Fourier, saw the path to the salvation of society as the setting up of small self-supporting communities. But although he identified the three main evils of society as religion, private property and marriage, his communities were not designed to be enclaves of sensual or sexual indulgence. They involved community of property, but the elimination of poverty depended upon the elimination of waste and of excessive consumption; there is a puritanical element in Owen's utopia which is conspicuously lacking in those of his French counterparts. His view of human nature is also different: whereas both Saint-Simon and Fourier made specific claims about the content of human nature, Owen stressed its malleability. People were the products of circumstances and not responsible for the defects in their characters; education thus had a central role to play in producing human beings capable of cooperation in the new society. Indeed, the 'doctrine of circumstances' is the central element of Owen's philosophy:

Any general character from the best to the worst, from the most ignorant to the most enlightened, may be given to any community, even to the world at large, by the application of proper means; which means are to a great extent at the command and under the control of those who have influence in the affairs of men.[7]

Owenism as a movement had much deeper roots in the emergent working classes in England than did either Saint-Simonism or Fourierism in France, but it was a movement which underwent several changes in character. Owen's attempts to reconstruct society began with the development of a model factory at New Lanark, and attempts to have communities set up to solve the problem of unemployment – hence Cobbet's description of his plans as parallelograms of paupers. Failure to gain support for his ideas in the corridors of power led to his initial interest in the working classes as a vehicle for social change, and during the 1830s his major preoccupation was the establishment of a single, all-embracing trade union, which did gain some popularity. When this venture collapsed and the goal of the movement became focused on community-building there was an extensive structure of branches, particularly in northern England, which provided social and educational facilities for members as well as supporting the community experiments. Owenite emphasis on the oppressive and damaging effects of the patriarchal family meant it also had considerable support among women; socialism and feminism were integrated in Owenism. However, towards the end of the 1840s, as the experimental communities were repeatedly unsuccessful, the Owenite movement, like Saint-Simonism, increasingly took on the characteristics of an esoteric and millennialist sect.

Saint-Simon, Fourier and Owen all rejected existing society as unjust, immoral and generally insupportable. All sought its replacement by a society which would be radically different, characterised by cooperation rather than antagonism, and in which human nature would find its true expression. All saw this transformation as at least necessary and sometimes as inevitable. And all saw their own schemes for the new society as so indisputably and self-evidently beneficial to all that they could be instituted through adequate propaganda and the triumph of reason. In spite of these claims to realism, Marx and Engels came to reject all as utopian.

Communist society

The liberal–humanist definition of utopia that emerges from the previous chapter is one which sees utopia as a description of a (probably impossible) ideal society. One of the reasons why Marxism itself can be said to be utopian in exactly the same way as the so-called utopian socialists is that an outline of the principal features of communist society can be pieced together from the writings of Marx and Engels, even though it was never presented by them in a single description. The similarity of this vision, in many respects, with those of the utopian socialists has also been widely observed. Several attempts have been made to bring together the various scattered references to communist society which can be found in the works of Marx and Engels, including Bertell Ollman's 'Marx's vision of communism',[8] and Paul Meier's attempt to demonstrate the identity between both the transitional and final stages of communism and the content of Morris's *News from Nowhere*.[9] To agree that Marxism contains a utopia in this sense, however, has no bearing on whether the goal is achievable; as Ollman says, that remains an open question. Before moving on to questions of the process of transformation it is worth looking at the nature of the goal itself.

Marx's suggestions as to the nature of communist society range from very abstract principles put forward in the *Economic and Philosophical Manuscripts* to the more specific statements in the *Grundrisse*. In Marx's early writings the goal of communism is the transcendence of alienation, the overcoming of the estrangement of human beings from themselves which results from the institution of private property:

> *Communism* as the *positive* transcendence of *private property as human self-estrangement*, and therefore as the real *appropriation* of the *human* essence by and for man; communism therefore as the complete return of man to himself as a *social* (i.e. human) being – a return accomplished consciously and embracing the entire wealth of previous development. This communism, as fully developed naturalism, equals humanism, and as fully developed humanism equal naturalism; it is the *genuine* resolution of the conflict between man and nature, and between man and man – the true resolution of the strife between existence and essence, between objectification and self-confirmation, between freedom and necessity, between the individual and the species. Communism is the riddle of history solved, and it knows itself to be this solution.[10]

The abolition of private property through social ownership transforms the nature of work. It is alienated labour which is the root of alienation; hence it is only through the transformation of the work process and its place in communist society that human estrangement can be overcome. A key issue here is the division of labour, which turns people into extensions of the productive process and prevents the full development of each individual's broad potential. Hence the familiar statement in *The German Ideology* that

> in communist society, where nobody has one exclusive sphere of activity but each can become accomplished in any branch he wishes, society regulates the general production and thus makes it possible for me to do one thing today and another tomorrow, to hunt in the morning, fish in the afternoon, rear cattle in the evening, criticise after dinner, just as I have a mind, without ever becoming hunter, fisherman, shepherd or critic.

Similarly, 'in a communist society there are no painters but only people who engage in painting among other activities'.[11] The division between mental and manual labour is abolished, and the division between town and country. On this point, the utopian socialists were commended by Engels in *Anti-Dühring*:

> The utopians were already perfectly clear as to the effects of the division of labour, the stunting on the one hand of the labourer, and on the other of the labour function, which is restricted to the life-long uniform mechanical repetition of one and the same operation. The abolition of the antithesis between town and country was demanded by Fourier, as by Owen, as the first prerequisite for the abolition of the old division of labour altogether . . . abolition of the antithesis between town and country . . . has become a direct necessity of industrial production itself. . . . The abolition of the separation between town and country is therefore not utopian.[12]

Whether the sexual division of labour is also to be entirely abolished is less clear. There is certainly support for communal living arrangements as a new productive force, involving the development of new machinery and the abolition of the family, in *The German Ideology*, which is entirely congruent with Engels's praise for the saving in labour power implied in Owen's planned communities.[13] Ollman argues that the communal raising of children is implied by the need that parents be prevented from exercising a destructive influence over their children without forcibly separating them from each other. He does concede, however, that this is never made explicit in Marx's writing, and that Marx never deals with the limitations child-rearing imposes upon the self-development of adults, in practice usually their mothers, although Ollman asserts that 'he was surely aware of it'.[14] Although it is clearly intended that the all-round development of the individual in communist society should apply to women as well as to men, the means by which this is to be made possible have to be inferred or invented.

In the *Grundrisse* it is made clear that the new human being who develops with communist society does so through the expansion of 'free time – which is both leisure and time for higher activity', which transforms 'its possessor into another subject'. Work remains a realm of necessity in contrast with the realm of freedom outside work, where human development is an end in itself. This does not mean, however, as one commentator has suggested, that the problem of freedom is in the *Grundrisse* reduced to the problem of free time, nor does it mean that the realm of work consists of alienated labour. Work does not become 'pure fun, pure amusement, as in Fourier's . . . childishly naive conception', since 'really free work . . . is also the most damnably difficult, demanding the most intensive effort'. But if 'labour cannot become a game, as desired by Fourier', it remains to his great credit that he 'stated that the ULTIMATE OBJECT is the raising of the mode of production itself, not [that] of distribution, to a higher form'. And the nature and conditions of work are to be transformed to that work, while necessary, is nevertheless free:

> Work involved in material production can achieve this character only if (1) its social character is posited; (2) if it is of a scientific character and simultaneously general [in its application], and not the exertion of the worker as a natural force drilled in a particular way, as a subject, which appears in the production process not in a merely natural, spontaneous form, but as an activity controlling all natural forces.[15]

Work in communist society is both greatly reduced and trans-formed in character. These features depend upon the expansion of productive powers, made possible in the first instance by capitalism but then exponentially so by its demise. Abundance is a necessary condition for communism. These four key features – the abolition of the division of labour, the development of individual potential, the transformation of work and the increase in material prosperity (made possible by the social ownership of the means of production) – are summed up in the *Critique of the Gotha Programme*:

> In a higher phase of a communist society, after the enslaving subordination of the individual to the division of labour, and

therewith also the antithesis between mental and physical labour, has vanished; after labour has become not only a means of life but life's prime want; after the productive forces have also increased with the all-round development of the individual, and all the springs of common wealth flow more abundantly – only then can the narrow horizon of bourgeois right be crossed in its entirety and society inscribe on its banners: From each according to his ability, to each according to his needs![16]

Finally this new society entails the production of a different kind of person, not just in the sense of increasing their powers as atomised individuals but (and in fact this is how the increase of individual powers is possible) as the production of fully social human beings. Alienation affects not just the relationship of people to themselves and to their work, but to one another. The recognition of interdependence and of the social nature of production and of human existence in general leads not only to a transformation of work, but also means that the relationships between individuals both within and outside the work process cease to have the instrumental and competitive nature they assume in capitalist society.

If, however, the goal outlined here in some ways reflects the desire for harmony characteristic of utopian socialism, there are of course fundamental differences. In the first place it does not imply a fixity of either institutional patterns or of human capacities, as the schemes of the utopian socialists do. Secondly, although it is in one sense a goal, it is not very specific about the precise institutional arrangements which will prevail. There are two reasons for this. The more fundamental objection to describing communist society is that the needs, wants and capacities that will develop within it are neither static nor predictable from within the constraints of capitalism. In addition there is a strategic reason for silence: the criticism of utopian socialism in terms of its supposition that its schemes would be self-realising would be undermined by appearing to offer a competing plan of the good society. Hence Marx's reluctance to identify communism as a state rather than a process:

> Communism is for us not a *state of affairs* which is to be established, an *ideal* to which reality [will] have to adjust itself. We call communism the *real* movement which abolishes the present state of things.[17]

The issue of the process of transition is crucial:

> Between capitalist and communist society lies the period of the revolutionary transformation of the one into the other.

43

Corresponding to this is also a political transition period in which the state can be nothing but *the revolutionary dictatorship of the proletariat*.[18]

Marx did not refrain from describing in a much more specific way the institutional parameters of the first stage of the communist future, through which full communism would eventually be achieved. In the *Manifesto of the Communist Party*, a list is given of ten measures which the proletariat is expected to implement once it has seized power, its objective being 'to wrest . . . all capital from the bourgeoisie, to centralise all instruments of production in the hands of the State, *i.e.*, of the proletariat organised as the ruling class; and to increase the total productive forces as rapidly as possible'. The list includes the abolition of all property in land and all right of inheritance; the centralisation of the means of communication and transport in the hands of the state, and of all credit by means of a national bank with an exclusive monopoly; confiscation of the property of all emigrants and rebels and a heavy progressive income tax; the equal liability of all to labour and the establishment of industrial armies, especially for agriculture; the abolition of the distinction between town and country, with the redistribution of the population across the country, the extension of factories and the improvement of agricultural production; and free education for all children and the abolition of child labour – although this is only to be abolished 'in its present form', and education is to be combined with industrial production.[19] Elsewhere Marx outlines the best form of education with reference to Owen:

As Robert Owen has shown us in detail, the germ of the education of the future is present in the factory system; this education will, in the case of every child over a given age, combine productive labour with instruction and gymnastics, not only as one of the methods of adding to the efficiency of production, but as the only method of producing fully developed human beings.[20]

Further comment on the nature of the first phase of communism can be found in *Capital*, in the *Critique of the Gotha Programme* and in *The Civil War in France*. The forms of political organisation supported in the last work suggest that local and central governing bodies should consist of people elected by universal suffrage, mandated by and accountable to their constituents. In the *Critique of the Gotha Programme* there is further emphasis upon the expansion of production and upon the simultaneous reduction in the length of the working day – possible because of the large number of people who in capitalist society do not work but who, with the equal liability of all to labour, would do so. Marx is contemptuous of demands for the equal distribution of the whole product of labour. First, not all that is produced may be consumed because investment is necessary, and not all that may be consumed may be distributed since there are costs of administration and of collective consumption such as schools, health care and provision for those unable to work. Secondly, distribution cannot be treated as an independent issue since 'any distribution whatever of the means of consumption is only a consequence of the distribution of the conditions of production themselves' which depends on the mode of production. Initially, therefore, distribution must be on the basis of the labour-time contributed by the worker, not, at this stage, according to need. This is ultimately inequitable because it takes account neither of people's different capacities to contribute to the social product nor of their different needs; it regards them purely as workers, and not as the full individuals which communism will eventually produce.

> But these defects are inevitable in the first phase of communist society as it is when it has just emerged after prolonged birth pangs from capitalist society. Right can never be higher than the economic structure of society and its cultural development which this determines.[21]

Full communism will take a little longer.

It is plain that the suggestions drawn together here do not add up to the kind of detailed blueprint supplied by Owen and Fourier, who were prepared to supply specifications of the numbers of people to be accommodated in individual settlements, and architectural plans of the settlements themselves as well as, in Owen's case, prescriptions of the social life and educational arrangements within the communities. However, it can hardly be claimed that the nature of socialist and subsequent communist society is left entirely for the future to reveal. If it is utopian to have an image of the good society, then indeed Marx and Engels may rightly be included in the ranks of utopian socialists; but this was certainly not the basis of their distinction between their own revolutionary and scientific socialism and that of Owen, Fourier and Saint-Simon.

Paths to utopia

The difference between Marxism and utopian socialism does not, then, rest on the existence or otherwise of an image of the socialist society to be attained, nor even on the content of that image. It rests upon disagreements about the process of transition. Even here the question of who is most utopian in the sense of unrealistic is a matter of dispute. Martin Buber, in *Paths in Utopia*, defends the orientation of utopian socialism (including not just Saint-Simon, Fourier and Owen, but Proudhon, Kropotkin and Landauer) to this problem. Buber's argument is that a 'society is naturally composed not of disparate individuals but of associative units', and that the health of a society depends on the density of voluntary associations that constitute it; capitalist society is thus 'a society inherently poor in structure and growing visibly poorer every day'.[22] The strength of utopian socialism is that it addressed itself to the issue of 'a renewal of society through a renewal of its cell-tissue', and aimed to 'substitute society for State to the greatest degree possible'.[23] Buber argues that neither Marx nor Engels gave sufficient attention to the process of social restructuring, in spite of the assertion that the new society matures in the womb of the old. Organic restructuring necessitates the development of a network of cooperative settlements which go beyond simple consumer or producer cooperatives – as in the Israeli kibbutzim.

Buber's central concern recalls the aspect of alienation which is manifest in the relations between people, and whose transcendence is addressed elsewhere in his writings in terms of the 'I–Thou' relationship:

> and the most valuable of all goods – the life between man and man – gets lost in the process; the autonomous relationships become meaningless, personal relationships wither; and the very spirit of man hires himself out as a functionary.[24]

His arguments in favour of cooperative settlements rest upon a recognition that the social relations of production lie at the root of the character of society. His claim, however, is that the post-revolutionary leap and the dictatorship of the proletariat involve a contradiction between means and ends which is not present in utopian socialism. The so-called utopian does not believe in this post-revolutionary leap, but in 'continuity within which revolution is only the accomplishment, the setting free and extension of a reality that has already grown to its true possibilities'.[25] In Buber's view the 'utopian' approach to the problem is more realistic, since it is difficult to see how the centralisation of the first phase of socialism will give way to full communism. In other words, the expectation that the state will somehow wither away is itself utopian, i.e. unrealistic.

If Buber's arguments about the merits of the utopian socialists are open to debate, he quite correctly identifies the issue which separates them from Marx and Engels. For the judgements made by these two about utopian socialism are mixed, and their criticisms are not directed primarily at its speculative character but at the views of social change contained therein and its actual role in political developments.

Moreover these judgements change over time, not just with the development of the theoretical perspectives of Marx and Engels but with the place of the ideas and movements in the political scene. More attention was paid to them in the 1840s when the movements were still in a relatively flourishing state and, during this period, Engels's judgements in particular shift from a very positive appraisal, especially of Owenism, to a much more critical stance. This shift entails a changing political judgement about the possibility or otherwise of a peaceful transition to socialism. In the 1870s, utopian socialism again became a specific target for critical comment, but again it is the idealist approach to social change that is the key issue.

In praise of Owenism: the young Engels

The collaboration between Marx and Engels dates from 1844, the year in which Engels began writing *The Condition of the Working Class in England*. Prior to this Engels had been deeply influenced by Owenism since his arrival in England in 1842, and had commended it both as a goal and as a strategy. Indeed, his view that violent revolution was the only possible means of instituting communism was, for a time, overridden by a belief in gradual and peaceful change.[26] In 'Letters from London', despite the remark that 'Owen writes . . . like a German philosopher, i.e., very badly', Engels commends the role of Owenism in the political education of the working classes and particularly stresses its opposition to private property and to religion. The atheism of Owenism led Engels to assert that 'the English Socialists are far more principled and practical than the French'.[27] However, his views of utopian socialism of all kinds are sympathetic. Writing in the Owenite journal *The New Moral World* at the end of 1843, he explores the differences between socialist and communist movements in France, Germany and England. He concludes that:

> As to the particular doctrines of our party, we agree much more with the English Socialists than with any other party . . . in everything bearing upon practice, upon the *facts* of the present society, we find that the English Socialists are a long way before us, and have left very little to be done. I may say, besides, that I have met with English Socialists with whom I agreed upon almost every question.[28]

This agreement extended to writing a very positive 'Description of recently founded communist colonies still in existence', in which

Engels claimed that 'communism, social existence and activity based on community of goods, is not only possible but has actually already been realised in many communities in America and in one place in England, with the greatest success'. Many such groups were religiously motivated and the particular importance of the Owenite community at Harmony was that it was not; and even if Harmony should fail as a result of financial difficulties, or problems arising from government by non-members, it would still prove that community of property could not only work, but had obviously beneficial results:

> We . . . see that the people who are living communally live better with less work, have more leisure for the development of their minds, and that they are better, more moral people than their neighbours who have retained private property.[29]

A speech written shortly afterwards contains a long and frankly adulatory section on the merits of Owen's plans, particularly the labour-saving effects of communal living (although Engels does not suggest the abolition of the sexual division of labour in this context, observing of Harmony merely that 'the housekeeping is done for all of them together by some of the women, and this of course saves a great deal of expense, time and trouble').[30] Even the architectural detail of Owen's plans receives Engels's seal of approval.[31]

It is, however, the question of the transition which is particularly important here, and it is notable that Engels does not argue that revolution is inevitable or desirable. Rather, various possibilities exist for the peaceful introduction of communism – and if these steps are not taken, revolution will ensue. He suggests that 'the English will probably begin by setting up a number of colonies and leaving it to every individual whether to join or not; the French on the other hand will be likely to prepare and implement communism on a national basis'.[32] The prerequisites for the peaceful transition to communism – the only way of avoiding its violent and bloody introduction – were state education, reorganisation of the Poor Relief system on lines very similar to Owen's earliest proposals and progressive taxation.[33]

Engels's view of the meaning of communism and the nature of communist society seems to have been very much more prosaic than Marx's at this stage and this perhaps accounts in part for his favourable discussions of Owenism. At about the same time Marx was attacking the notion of 'crude communism' and arguing that true communism was the '*positive* transcendence of *private property* as *human self-estrangement*'; '*communism* is the necessary form and the dynamic principle of the immediate future, but communism is not as such the goal of human development, the form of human society'.[34] Marx too

48

saw the importance of Owenite atheism but did not credit it with as much significance as did Engels, for although 'communism begins with atheism (Owen) . . . atheism is initially far from being communism'.[35] But Marx shared Engels's views of some of the strengths of the utopian socialists in their criticisms of bourgeois society:

> They therefore declared *'progress'* (see *Fourier*) to be an inadequate abstract *phrase*; they assumed (see *Owen* among others) a fundamental flaw in the civilised world; that is why they subjected the *real* foundations of contemporary society to incisive *criticism*. This communist criticism had practically at once as its counterpart the movement of the *great mass*. . . . One must know the studiousness, the craving for knowledge, the moral energy and the unceasing urge for development of the French and English workers to be able to form an idea of the *human* nobility of this movement.[36]

Engels became increasingly critical of the Owenite movement. In *The Condition of the Working Class in England* he contrasted Owenism with Chartism, having apparently given up hope that the strengths of these movements would be combined. By this stage Engels saw Chartism as the genuinely working-class movement, and had a much more uncompromising view of class antagonisms; 'English Socialism', on the other hand, 'arose with Owen, a manufacturer, and proceeds therefore with great consideration towards the bourgeoisie and great injustice towards the proletariat'.[37] Engels criticised the lack of any view of historical development, the wish to create communism overnight and the reliance on winning public opinion as a means of doing this. He had resumed his earlier assumption that revolution was necessary; but 'in proportion, as the proletariat absorbs socialistic and communistic elements, will the revolution diminish in bloodshed, revenge and savagery. . . . If, indeed, it were possible to make the whole proletariat communistic before the war breaks out, the end would be very peaceful; but that is no longer possible, the time has gone by. . . . It is too late for a peaceful solution'.[38]

The critique of utopian socialism

'The time has gone by'. This lies at the heart of the subsequent critique of utopian socialism developed by Marx and Engels in which the insights of Owen, Fourier and Saint-Simon are praised and defended, while the movements consequent on them are attacked. It explains the ambivalence of this critique, as well as the centrality of the distinction between the movements and their founders. We shall follow the emergence of this critique through the comments of Marx and Engels to its culmination in Engels's *Socialism: Utopian and Scientific*.

Early in 1845, when Marx and Engels were planning to arrange the publication in German of a library of the works of the best foreign socialist writers, Engels suggested to Marx that:

> it would be better to sacrifice *theoretical* interest to practical
> effectiveness, and to start off with the things which have most
> to offer the Germans and are closest to our principles; the best,
> that is, of Fourier, Owen, the Saint-Simonists etc. Morelly might
> also appear fairly early on.[39]

(Godwin, on the other hand, was to be excluded on the grounds that his conclusion that man should emancipate himself as far as possible from society was essentially anti-*social*.) Engels was particularly anxious to see Fourier translated, 'omitting, of course, the cosmogonic nonsense',[40] and indeed the only practical outcome of the project was Engels's own translation of 'A Fragment of Fourier on Trade'. In his comments on this Engels asserts that 'Fourier speculatively constructs the future, after correctly understanding the past and the present'; he 'inexorably exposes the hypocrisy of respectable society'; he 'has criticised existing social relations so sharply, with such wit and humour that one readily forgives him for his cosmological fantasies'. German theorists, on the other hand, who pursued 'true' socialism adopted only the worst from the French and English socialists, 'the schematic plans of future societies' and ignored the best, 'the *criticism of existing society*'.[41]

Neither Marx nor Engels was ever as scathing about the utopian socialists as they were about the 'true socialists' in *The German Ideology*. Indeed, in this work the systems of the utopian socialists are to some extent defended against the attacks on them by the true socialists:

> Incidentally, as to the systems themselves, they nearly all
> appeared in the early days of the communist movement and had
> at that time propaganda value as popular novels, which
> corresponded perfectly to the still undeveloped consciousness of
> the proletarians, who were just then getting into their stride.

Again, Fourier's work is praised for containing 'a vein of true poetry', although the systems of Owen and Cabet are here said to show 'not a shred of imagination'. Whatever the inspirational qualities of various utopian writers, however, 'as the party develops, these systems lose all importance'.[42]

50

It was therefore not the originators of utopian socialism who attracted the greatest criticism, but the socialist movements which continued to adhere to their systems. Marx complained that both the Owenites and the Fourierists were opposed to combinations:

> the socialists want the workers to leave the old society alone, the better to be able to enter the new society which they have prepared for them with so much foresight. . . . In spite of both of them [economists and socialists], in spite of manuals and utopias, combination has not ceased . . . to . . . grow.[43]

Engels was also to express increasing exasperation:

> the Fourierist gents become daily more tedious. The *Phalange* is nothing but nonsense. The information contained in Fourier's posthumous work is confined entirely to the *mouvement aromal* and the mating of planets which would appear to take place *plus ou moins* from behind.[44]

The reconciliation of these ambivalent attitudes and the clarification of what was, for Engels at least, a distinct shift of position came in *Principles of Communism* and in the *Manifesto of the Communist Party*. Utopian socialism represents a stage of development which should by now have been surpassed. Thus:

> The significance of Critical–Utopian Socialism . . . bears an inverse relation to historical development. In proportion as the modern class struggle develops and takes definite shape, this fantastic standing apart from the contest, these fantastic attacks on it, lose all practical value and all theoretical justification. Therefore, although the originators of these systems were, in many respects, revolutionary, their disciples have, in every case, formed mere reactionary sects. They hold fast by the original views of their masters, in opposition to the progressive historical development of the proletariat. They, therefore, endeavour, and that consistently, to deaden the class struggle and to reconcile the class antagonisms. They still dream of experimental realisation of their social Utopias, of founding isolated 'phalanstères', of establishing 'Home Colonies', of setting up a 'Little Icaria' . . . and to realise all these castles in the air, they are compelled to appeal to the feelings and purses of the bourgeois.[45]

In so far as the practical proposals contained in the various schemes require the disappearance of the emerging class antagonisms, they are utopian in the sense of being unrealistic. But this is not a point which is of particular salience here for Marx and Engels. It is the way in which

51

the disciples of the utopian socialists oppose working class political action which is at issue, such as the fact that 'the Owenites in England, and the Fourierists in France, respectively oppose the Chartists and the *Réformistes*'.[46] The fundamental error of the utopian socialists which gives rise to this unacceptable political position is the expectation that society can be changed by the appeal to all classes on the basis of reason and justice, and the belief that their blueprints of the good society will be the cause of social transformation. It is this idealist, as opposed to materialist, concept of social change which is the real problem:

> Historical action is to yield to their personal inventive action, historically created conditions of emancipation to fantastic ones, and the gradual, spontaneous class-organisation of the proletariat to an organisation of society specially contrived by these inventors. Future history resolves itself, in their eyes, into the propaganda and the practical carrying out of their social plans.[47]

This judgement, if fully endorsed by Engels, is radically different from those he was making five years earlier. But this can be attributed only in part to a shift in his theoretical position and is also the result of changes taking place in the movements under discussion. Through the 1840s the Owenite movement increasingly took on the form of a millenarian sect, without the mass following that it had earlier had.[48] Nevertheless, even in these circumstances utopian socialism is seen as having some merits:

> Such fantastic pictures of future society, painted at a time when the proletariat is still in a very undeveloped state and has but a fantastic conception of its own position, correspond with the first instinctive yearnings of that class for a general reconstruction of society. But these Socialist and Communist publications contain also a critical element. They attack every principle of existing society. Hence they are full of the most valuable materials for the enlightenment of the working class.[49]

Utopian socialism is, in the *Manifesto of the Communist Party*, praised for its original criticisms of capitalism, patronised for its ineffectual solutions at a time when it was too young to know any better, and castigated for being effectively reactionary when its historical relevance was superseded.

There is little discussion of utopian socialism as such in Marx's or Engels's writing in the 1850s and 1860s. The critical references to utopian socialist movements dwindled, for as Engels wrote (not, as it happens, entirely accurately) in 1852, 'Owen's writings have been forgotten'.[50] However, the issues recur in different forms. Early in 1852

Marx observed that one response to political defeat was for the working class to retreat into essentially utopian schemes:

> In part [the proletariat] throws itself into *doctrinaire experiments, exchange banks and workers' associations, hence into a movement in which it renounces the revolutionising of the old world by means of the latter's own great, combined resources, and seeks, rather, to achieve its salvation behind society's back, in private fashion, within its limited conditions of existence, and hence necessarily suffers shipwreck.*[51]

He continued to criticise this withdrawal into utopian schemes, collaborating with Ernest Jones in arguing against the cooperative movement which was the main lasting legacy of Owenism; co-operation could not work in capitalist society, although cooperative production and trade might be one of the main features of a society run by the working class.[52]

The power of the utopian socialists as critics of capitalist society was something of which Marx and Engels never lost sight. In the *Grundrisse* Marx quotes Owen at length on the difference capital creates between workers and capitalists, and there are references to Owen (and, indeed, to Thomas More) in *Capital*. These, however, are not endorsements of Owen's proposed solutions, still less endorsements of utopian socialism as a political movement which was, in any case, largely defunct. In the 1870s, however, socialist ideas again began to proliferate and among these were views which Marx at any rate saw as dangerously utopian:

> Utopian socialism, in particular, which for decades we have been sweeping out of German workers' heads with so much effort and labour – their freedom from it making them theoretically (and thereby also practically) superior to the French and English – this utopian socialism, the chimerical game played with the future structure of society, is again spreading in a much more futile form; it is not to be compared with the great French and English utopians, but with – Weitling. It is natural that utopianism, which *before* the age of materialist–critical socialism concealed the latter within itself *in nuce*, coming now *post festum* can only be silly – silly, stale and basically reactionary.[53]

Shortly afterwards Engels wrote his most systematic critique of utopian socialism. This was originally part of *Anti-Dühring*, a much longer critique of the new German utopian socialism which Marx was complaining about. It differs little in its judgements of utopian socialism from the *Manifesto of the Communist Party*. Dühring, whom Engels was attacking, was contemptuous of Saint-Simon, Fourier and

Owen, dismissing them as 'social alchemists'. Engels replies by observing that alchemy was necessary in its epoch, and describes Dühring as an impertinent dwarf.[54] The substance of his defence is by now familiar; the three great utopians, like certain earlier ones (including Thomas More, Thomas Münzer and Morelly), were limited by their historical context. To all these 'socialism is the expression of absolute truth, reason and justice and has only to be discovered to conquer all the world by virtue of its own power. . . . To make a science of socialism, it had first to be placed upon a real basis'.[55]

With Marx's discovery of the materialist conception of history and the process of expropriation of surplus value under capitalism, socialism was put on a new footing.

> From that time forward socialism was no longer an accidental discovery of this or that ingenious brain, but the necessary outcome of the struggle between two historically developed classes – the proletariat and the bourgeoisie. Its task was no longer to manufacture a system of society as perfect as possible, but to . . . discover in the economic conditions . . . the means of ending the conflict. . . . The Socialism of earlier days certainly criticised the existing capitalistic mode of production and its consequences. But it could not explain them, and, therefore, could not get the mastery of them.[56]

Whereas the utopian socialists deduced from philosophy outlines of a new and more perfect social order and sought to impose these from without through propaganda and experiment, now the possibility of transformation could be found in economics.

Although he observes that the social systems proposed by the early socialists were utopian, and that 'the more completely they were worked out in detail, the more they could not avoid drifting off into pure fantasies',[57] Engels again stresses their critical content, and their initial political importance. Thus:

> We delight in the stupendously grand thoughts and germs of thoughts that everywhere break out through their fantastic covering, and to which these philistines are blind.[58]

More specifically, he praises Saint-Simon for possessing the breadth of view of a genius, 'a . . . breadth of view, by virtue of which almost all the ideas of later Socialists, that are not strictly economic, are found in him in embryo'. Fourier, besides being described as the greatest satirist of all time, is commended for his theory of history and for his 'masterly' critique of 'the bourgeois form of the relations between the sexes, and the position of women in bourgeois society'.

Engels observes that Fourier was 'the first to declare that in any given society the degree of woman's emancipation is the natural measure of the general emancipation'. Of Owen, he says that 'every social movement, every real advance in England on behalf of the workers links itself to the name of Robert Owen'.[59] In *Socialism: Utopian and Scientific* the criticisms of the various movements adhering to the ideas of Saint-Simon, Fourier and Owen which are contained in the *Manifesto of the Communist Party* are absent; the point is strongly made, however, that those who, like Dühring, continue to proceed by the construction of abstract socialist systems, are not merely irrelevant but effectively antagonistic to the development of the working-class movement which alone can construct socialism through the process of revolution.

The legacy of Marxism

It is clear that the basis of Marx's and Engels's criticisms of utopian socialism is not an objection to speculation about the future, but a difference of view about the process of transformation. As Vincent Geoghegan puts it, 'what is under attack here is not anticipation as such, but rather the failure to root this anticipation in a theoretical framework cognizant of the essential dynamics of capitalism'.[60] However, Geoghegan has also shown how, in the period of the Second International, the epithet 'utopian' not only became a real term of abuse (in much the way that Berneri describes) but was extended to a total rejection of all attempts to outline the nature of socialist society – even to the point of suggesting that it was a mark of the immaturity of women that they were attracted by such descriptions. Although early utopians from More through the English Civil War to Fourier were accorded respect and interest, contemporary specification of goals was regarded as a dangerous heresy; this position was shared by Karl Kautsky, Eduard Bernstein, Rosa Luxemburg and Georgii Plekhanov.

It was always a difficult position to maintain. The rejection of utopia and the need for goals were in constant tension and conflict, and the suppression and marginalisation of dreaming about a better future was never totally successful; it had a habit of creeping in at the back door, often in the disguised form of assertions about a past golden age. The tension is illustrated by Lenin's own ambivalence in rejecting utopianism unequivocally, while defending the practice (by then generally frowned upon) of dreaming about the future. On the one hand, he argued that 'Marxists . . . are hostile to any and every utopia', since 'utopia is a wish that can never come true . . . that is not based on social forces and not supported by the growth and development of political, class forces'. Further, 'there is no trace of utopianism in Marx, in the sense that he made up or invented a 'new' society'.[61] On the other hand, Lenin's *What is to be done?* borrowed the title of a utopian novel by Nikolai Chernyshevsky and contains a long quotation from Pisarev:

> 'There are rifts and rifts', wrote Pisarev concerning the rift between dreams and reality. 'My dream may run ahead of the natural march of events or may fly off at a tangent in a direction in which no natural march of events will ever proceed. In the first case my dream will not cause any harm; it may even support and augment the energy of the workingmen. . . . There is nothing in such dreams that would distort or paralyze labour power. On the contrary, if man were completely deprived of the ability to dream in this way, if he could not from time to time run ahead and mentally conceive, in an entire and completed picture, the product to which his hands are only just beginning to lend shape, then I cannot imagine what stimulus there would be to induce man to undertake and complete extensive and strenuous work in the sphere of art, science and practical endeavour. . . . The rift between dreams and reality causes no harm if only the person dreaming believes seriously in his dream, if he attentively observes life, compares his observations with his castles in the air and if, generally speaking, he works conscientiously for the achievement of his fantasies. If there is some connection between dreams and life then all is well.' Of this kind of dreaming there is unfortunately too little in our movement.[62]

Lenin's defence of dreaming was less influential than his reproduction of the dominant orientation to utopia as intrinsically unrealistic and in opposition to political analysis and action. The idea that utopia used to be defensible and even fruitful remained, alongside the insistence that it was superseded both in theory, and later in practice. Morton's comments on the end of utopia illustrate the way in which the Soviet Union itself became the focus for utopian hopes, an identification which fed the subsequent identification of Stalinism with Marxism with utopianism. The Cold War added a further twist, producing the equation between communism, fascism and utopia illustrated by Berneri's commentary. And the vacuum created by the Marxist fear of specifying goals continues to afflict the socialist project.

Utopia as function

The dominant meaning in Marxism thus identifies 'utopian' with 'unrealistic', and the term utopia embraces all speculation about future society. It is therefore a definition in terms of form and content, although utopia's function is construed in negative terms as necessarily counter-revolutionary. But this is a radical revision of the way in which Marx and Engels used the concept. It is abundantly clear that in their hands the term is indeed used in a way which emphasises the unrealistic nature of utopia, More's 'no place'. However, the imputed lack of realism applies less to the content of the utopian systems in question than to the models of social change associated with them. Since the primary concern of both Marx and Engels was with fostering such changes, the rejection of utopia is a rejection on the basis of its imputed social function – that of distracting the working classes from more suitable political activity, from 'conscious participation in the historical process revolutionising society before our very eyes'.[63] Utopian socialism draws up schemes for the future. Its main fault however is not that it does this, or that the schemes themselves outline the wrong sort of future, but that it entails an idealist model of social change, suggesting that the mere propagation of such schemes will have a transformative effect. Utopia here is effectively defined in terms of its function, which is seen as a negative, counter-revolutionary, one:

> The chief offence does not lie in having inscribed [a] specific nostrum in [a] programme, but in taking a retrograde step at all from the standpoint of a class movement to that of a sectarian movement.[64]

In their terms the key question is whether movements foster a deeper understanding of the class struggle, or whether they disguise it behind plans to persuade all classes to combine in the construction of a society based on harmony.

Form and content are not, however, totally irrelevant. It is also a defining characteristic of utopian socialism that it produces detailed blueprints of the future. Further, both Marx and Engels comment at times on the actual proposals contained in these and other schemes, sometimes in a negative and sometimes in a positive way. The term utopian is therefore also used more generally as a negative descriptor of unrealistic policies, and in these instances it is a judgement about content. Such a judgement can of course only be made from the standpoint of alternative assumptions about the nature of socialist society, assumptions which, as we have seen, are clearly present in their work. These however were quite deliberately never presented in the schematic form of utopian socialism. For this reason, and because of the materialist content of their theories, Marx and Engels would defend themselves against the charge of utopianism; and indeed they are not utopian in the sense in which they use the term, even if they may be so according to other definitions.

The pejorative meaning of utopia which is dominant in Marxism can thus be seen to have its roots in the critique of utopian socialism that runs through the writings of Marx and Engels. However, this critique does not justify a rejection of utopia defined in a broad sense of a mere description of aspirations for a good society, and cannot be automatically extrapolated to other forms of socialism that people may wish to discredit by the label utopian. It does not follow that all speculation about the nature of socialist society is equally culpable on the grounds of being idealist, counter-revolutionary and plain wrong. Not all visions of the good society are assumed to be self-creating, and it is only on these grounds that it can be argued that the presence of such an image within Marxism does not make it utopian in the same sense.

Establishing a 'correct' interpretation of the position adopted by Marx and Engels is not just a question of conceptual clarification or textual exegesis. The reason why the pejorative use of the term utopia is useful politically now, as then, is that it can be used as a weapon in the invalidation of opposing ideologies and policies. The issues raised here touch on a central political and theoretical debate within Marxism and beyond, namely that concerning the role of ideological processes in social change. For this reason, the place of utopia in Marxist thought has remained a controversial issue. Conceptual clarity is of crucial importance in this debate; for what Marx and Engels were rejecting as utopian, and thereby adding so substantially to the pejorative connotations of the term, is manifestly not the same as that dreaming which Lenin commended, or that which later Marxists have sought to re-insert into Marxism in the name of utopia.

3

Mobilising myths:
utopia and social change in Georges Sorel and Karl Mannheim

In the previous chapter, we saw how utopia came to be defined by Marxists as reactionary on the grounds that it sought to impose an ideal plan upon reality rather than seeking in that reality the means of social change. This view of utopia was shared by Sorel, but Sorel also argued that ideas, in the form of myths, could potentially perform a mobilising and transformative function. The distinction drawn by Sorel between myth and utopia is interesting in its own right, but doubly so when compared with the analysis offered by Karl Mannheim, probably the most well-known theorist of utopia; for Mannheim's argument similarly insists on this transformative potential, while attributing it to utopia. Part of the difference between the two is terminological, with Sorel's use of the term myth having strong similarities with Mannheim's definition of utopia. There are, however, also differences of substance, particularly concerning the emphasis on human will and the political evaluation of myth or utopia: Sorel celebrates the non-rationality of myth for its effectiveness; Mannheim fears the irrationality of utopia as well as the possibility of its extinction. The focus for both writers is, as in Chapter 2, on the role of ideas in social change; but whereas in Marxist hands utopia is defined in terms of the negative function of preventing social change, here myth and utopia, respectively, are defined in terms of the positive function of promoting it.

Revolutionary syndicalism

Georges Sorel is a difficult theorist to classify. He was born in France in 1847, and spent his early adult life as an engineer employed in the public service. Far from being a professional intellectual, he published his first works in 1889 before retiring from public employment and moving to Paris in 1892. For at least part of his subsequent career as a political commentator and analyst he saw himself as a revisionist Marxist, albeit with serious differences from Bernstein. His best-known work, *Reflections on Violence*, espouses revolutionary syndical-ism; but he subsequently became involved with the right-wing *Action Française*, adopted a religio-political stance that was both nationalistic and Catholic, and wrote some profoundly anti-semitic articles. This was not a straightforward shift to an essentially fascist position; Sorel ended his life an admirer of both Mussolini and Lenin, seeing bolshevism as a Russian version of syndicalism. This politically eccentric position led to his finding support from both the Left and the Right, including the contemporary New Right in France. Never-theless, it has been said of Sorel's views in later years that while 'it seems inappropriate to label Sorel's own writings in this period either openly or implicitly "fascist" . . . his attack upon the Jews, criticism of liberal democracy and evocation of the morally uplifting benefits of war coupled with an awareness of the power of the idea of the nation . . . certainly provides an intimation of some of the least attract-ive ideological developments of the later inter-war years'.[1]

Although Sorel's position was eccentric, it was not altogether erratic. A theme which was fundamental to both his syndicalist and traditionalist positions, and indeed preceded his conversion to a form of Marxism in 1892, was the emphasis on moral regeneration both of individuals and of society. This preoccupation has been argued to place Sorel firmly in the tradition of French social thought which is essentially concerned with morality, ethics and the ways of life embodying these.[2] Such a tradition would include such theorists as Emile Durkheim. But while Durkheim may be seen by some as a conservative thinker, his political leanings were far more democratic than those of Sorel, as is clear from their very different responses to the Dreyfus affair.[3] Sorel himself believed Durkheim's *Le Suicide* to consolidate historical materialism.[4]

The distinction between myth and utopia which principally con-cerns us here was developed in *Reflections on Violence* and other writings between 1905 and 1909, when the syndicalist movement in France was at its height, and Sorel at his most enthusiastic about it. Revolutionary syndicalism was for a brief period the dominant orientation of the *Confédération Générale du Travail* (CGT) which was formed in 1895. From 1902 the CGT brought into one organisation the *bourses du travail*, which were nominally labour exchanges, but in practice principally educational and propaganda institutions, and the

Fédération des Syndicats, the industrially based wing of the trade union movement. As in the British trade union movement, there were conflicting aims within the CGT – to pursue economic advantage within the capitalist system or to seek its destruction; unlike British trade unions in the late nineteenth century, the syndicates relied mainly upon direct industrial action, including not only strikes and walk-outs, but sabotage. Deaths and injuries, as well as defeats, in industrial disputes led to the rapid decline of revolutionary syndicalism within the CGT.[5]

There were three key elements in the version of syndicalism supported by Sorel: the syndicates themselves, which were to be both the means of change and the basic units of the ensuing social order; the proletarian general strike; and proletarian violence. The importance of all three lay in their capacity for moral regeneration and the fostering of the heroic spirit in the (male) proletariat. Class struggle was to be welcomed and intensified, partly because it revealed the conflicting interests of bourgeoisie and proletariat and might ultimately lead to the abolition of such antagonisms; but its greatest merit was that it produced an admirable psychology similar to that of pre-Socratic Greece. Richard Vernon stresses how, for Sorel, the value of institutions was measured by the extent to which they had 'an affinity with socialist aspirations' in terms of the psychological attitudes they reproduced. Whereas syndicates fostered responsibility, dignity and initiative, state socialism could only have retrograde effects.[6]

It is notable that Sorel did not share Marx's view of the alienating nature of work under capitalism. Rather, factory production as developed under capitalism was celebrated as the necessary foundation of socialism:

> Everything must proceed on the model of the factory running in an orderly manner, without capriciousness or waste of time. If the aim of socialism is to transfer the regime of the factory to society as a whole, one can scarcely exaggerate the importance of the progress that is taking place in work discipline, in the organization of collective effort, and in the efficiency of technical direction. The *good practices* of the factory are clearly the source of the justice of the future. Socialism will inherit not only the apparatus evolved by capitalism and the science created by technical progress, but also the co-operative procedures developed in the factories, over a long period, for making the best possible use of time and of human effort and capacity.[7]

Modern industry led to technical progress, with greater precision and fewer faults resulting in goods which were both more functional and more attractive. Revolutionary syndicalism would build on this potential and free producers would strive for constant improvement in the quality and quantity of production.

The moral and educational role of the syndicates was fundamental, for 'it would be criminal to encourage a social revolution which would result in imperiling what little morality exists' – and in any case, social transformation would not be possible unless the workers had already 'acquired a superior level of moral culture'. Sorel agreed with Durkheim that the question of whether a mechanism existed to develop this morality was crucial, but argued that the syndicate was superior in this respect to the professional associations favoured by Durkheim:

> the professional association in which the administrative spirit tends necessarily to dominate is definitely inferior, in this aspect, to the union in which are grouped workers who have given proof, to a particularly high degree, of productive capacities, of intellectual energies, and of devotion to comrades. In such a syndicate, liberty is encouraged and, by reason of the necessities of economic struggles, the will to solidarity is always firm. We have then good reason to think that syndicates could be powerful vehicles of moralization.[8]

The syndicate, it was suggested, was the best agency to deal with three fundamental moral problems: alcholism, the abuse of women by their husbands and of children by their fathers. Sorel argued that it was 'relatively easy' for the workers to police these problems, 'since the woman is an industrial worker and can thus be a member of a union which will help her when her husband treats her in a way that he himself would not want to be treated by his boss' and 'through the woman the union watches over the child, the hope of the proletariat, who should be introduced very young into socialist groups'. The development of the workers' syndicates must however be autonomous and exclude intellectuals 'whose leadership would have the effect of restoring hierarchies and dividing the proletariat'.[9] Modern industry, with the assistance of the syndicate, provided the institutional basis for the development of both technical skills and moral discipline.

Utopia and myth

Although there are intimations here of the kind of society which would follow revolutionary transformation, there is little elaboration. Sorel was more reluctant than Marx to comment on the shape of a future socialist society. He argued that:

> socialism is necessarily very obscure, since it deals with production, *i.e.*, with the most mysterious part of human activity, and since it proposes to bring about a radical transformation of that region which it is impossible to describe with the clearness that is to be found in more superficial regions.[10]

Indeed, it was possible to invent indefinitely 'ridiculous' utopias regarding production without readers (presumably less sophisticated than Sorel) finding them contrary to common sense.[11] Sorel argues that the major problem of the organisation of industry posed by the utopians (by which he appears to mean Saint-Simon, Owen and Fourier) has in practice been solved by capitalism.

Sorel's use of the term utopia is not particularly rigorous, and veers between references to form, content and function. The first of his three types of utopia elides all three: literary utopias, including More's, are described as devices to compare real and ideal life and are dismissed on the grounds that they seek to reverse economic history; such fictional exercises have 'a harmful influence on the formation of the revolutionary mind' through the extreme simplification of economic, political and psychological questions.[12] The second type of utopia includes Saint-Simonianism and Owenism, characterised by the fact that they seek an abrupt and accelerated transformation of society. Third, there are utopias which are incorporated into political programmes. All have in common that they define the present as bad, anticipate a sudden catastrophe and renewal and the creation of a perfect world based upon abstract ideas of justice. However, all that utopias can do is 'to express desires and regrets', for they have no grasp of the mechanisms of social transformation.[13] Sorel includes in the category of utopians 'all reformers who cannot ground their plans in the observation of the social mechanism'; and quotes with approval Plekhanov's edict that 'whoever seeks a perfect organization starting from an abstract principle is utopian'[14] – whether that principle be human nature, or a proletariat with a historic mission.

Sorel indeed argues that the *Manifesto of the Communist Party* 'offers the widest analogies to utopian literature',[15] and criticises Marx for allowing 'a quantity of old rubbish which he found in the Utopists to creep into his writings'.[16] However, he refrains from dismissing Marx as a utopian: the reference to the utopian nature of a belief in the historic role of the proletariat is directed at his own Marxist contemporaries rather than at Marx himself. Sorel saw Marx's great strength as the emphasis upon the social mechanism that made transformation possible, and although he thought Marx parlously ignorant about the organisation of the proletariat in England, he also thought him correct to see this class as a possible force for change. Marx, according to Sorel, was wrong in fact about the imminence of revolution, but right in principle. Social mechanisms are themselves historically variable, however, and Marxists who proceed from an 'abstract principle of the unique proletariat', rather than grounding their analysis and politics in observation of empirical reality, are castigated by Sorel as utopian.[17]

Utopia, as defined by Sorel, embodies several distinct characteristics which are presumed to be inseparable. It includes plans for a future society and failure to grasp the real possibilities and processes of social change, thus eliding in a familiar way two elements which have no intrinsic connection. Utopias are also condemned for being abstract, and for being essentially products of the intellect rather than the will. Nevertheless, although the future cannot be predicted, and although it is dangerous to think about the future in a utopian way, some vision of the future is necessary because without this we cannot act at all. There is also a moral requirement to consider the future, although this again is not a matter of predicting the survival, demise or creation of particular practices and institutions, but of 'knowing whether or not the *preparation is sufficient* for the struggle not to end in a destruction of civilization'.[18] To escape the charge of utopianism, these visions must take a particular form:

> Experience shows that the *framing of a future, in some indeterminate time*, may . . . be very effective and have very few inconveniences; this happens when the anticipations of the future take the form of those myths, which enclose with them all the strongest inclinations of a people, of a party or of a class, inclinations which recur to the mind with the insistence of instincts in all the circumstances of life; and which give an aspect of complete reality to the hopes of immediate action by which, more easily than by any other method, men can reform their desires, passions and mental activity.[19]

The particular myth which is central to revolutionary syndicalism is the myth of the proletarian general strike, construed both as a possible actual event in the future and more importantly as a myth which mobilises people to action. Sorel observes that 'men who are participating in a great social movement always picture their coming action as a battle in which their cause is certain to triumph'; it is to these images that he applies the term myth.[20] The function of any such myth is to facilitate action and it must therefore be judged in these terms, not in terms of its empirical accuracy, so that it should not be taken seriously as a prediction. It operates intuitively rather than intellectually, and thus is fundamentally different from a utopia. The myth of the general strike is 'a body of images capable of evoking instinctively all the sentiments which correspond to the different manifestations of the war undertaken by Socialism against modern society'.[21]

Revolutionary myths are thus expressions of will rather than descriptions of the future and as such 'lead men to prepare themselves for a combat which will destroy the existing state of things'. A myth cannot be separated into its constituent parts and judged against reality, for it only operates as a whole, and it is not susceptible to refutation by empirical evidence:

> A myth cannot be refuted since it is, at bottom, identical with the convictions of a group, being the expression of these convictions in the language of movement; and it is, in consequence, unanalysable into parts which could be placed on the plane of historical descriptions.[22]

In contrast, in Sorel's view, the whole point of a utopia is to furnish a model with which the existing society can be compared and found wanting. Utopias do not have to be treated as generic wholes in the same way as myths, since their elements are at least in theory separable and reforms may be carried out piecemeal; they may be dismembered and their elements are subject to potential refutation by facts. However, if utopia and myth may be contrasted at the level of definition and analysis, in practice they may be interwoven; these are ideal types in Max Weber's sense, so that actual utopias may contain myths, and myths may contain utopian elements.

Sorel argues, however, that utopia is being eliminated from socialism, which is progressively less concerned with a beautiful future and has become 'the preparation of the masses employed in great industries for the suppression of the State and property'.[23] His identification of socialism as a movement rather than a state of society to be treated as a historical goal recalls Marx's assertion that communism is the real movement which abolishes the present state of things:

> Socialism is the workers' movement, the revolt of the proletariat against ruling institutions. It is the organization which is both economic and ethical at the same time, which we see forming before our eyes, and whose purpose is to struggle against bourgeois traditions.[24]

The myth of the general strike is thus virtually unadulterated by utopia. It operates in terms of feeling, intuition and instinct rather than intellect, and promotes action rather than contemplation or reflection. The function of utopia is criticism, but an impotent criticism; the function of myth is transformation and change.

The superiority of myth over utopia is not just that it is more effective at changing the world. Myth is morally superior because of the state of mind which it induces and the action which it gives rise to. Sorel's ethical standard is the heroic individual – a distinctly male individual modelled on soldiers fighting for noble causes. The image of virility is epitomised in Sorel's extolling action over thought in the phrase 'words are female and only acts are male'.[25] And it is in action – specifically in revolutionary action – that the individual possesses the greatest freedom and thus most completely himself. In this context, Sorel quotes Bergson's claim that *'moments in which we are fully in possession of ourselves are rare* and that is why we are rarely free. . . . To act freely is to regain possession of ourselves'. The moments which have this character are described rather vaguely by Bergson as those in which we make serious decisions and which are unique; for Sorel 'it is quite obvious that we enjoy this liberty above all when we try to create a new man in ourselves for the purpose of shattering the historical framework which encloses us'.[26] The proletarian general strike is a myth which produces the heroic state of mind, a 'striking manifestation of *individualistic force*' with 'each working with the greatest possible zeal, each acting on his own account, and not troubling himself much to subordinate his conduct to a great and scientifically combined plan'.[26] Such a state can only be produced through struggle, through conflict and indeed through proletarian violence.

Sorel makes a distinction between violence and force, force being used by the state to maintain the status quo. The function of proletarian violence, of violence during strikes and for the syndicalist cause is quite different. It serves to emphasise the division between classes, to clarify the conflict of interests in society, to demarcate the lines of the struggle through which not only the proletariat but also the decadent middle class may gain energy and vigour. Sorel's justification of proletarian violence is essentially an argument for moral courage rather than an apology for general thuggery.[28] He was concerned that beyond a certain limit, violence could have the effect of reducing economic output and could also be a threat to morality; but he did not believe that this limit would be breached, largely because of the moral effects of syndicalism. The need to limit violence for both economic and moral reasons led Sorel to oppose sabotage as a tactic – a position which was far from universally shared in the syndicalist movement;

but proletarian violence expressed the soul of the revolutionary proletariat and as such was the ultimate means of salvation:

> the idea of the general strike (constantly rejuvenated by the feelings roused by proletarian violence) produces an entirely epic state of mind, and at the same time bends all the energies of the mind to that condition necessary to the realisation of a workshop carried on by free men, eagerly seeking the betterment of industry. . . . It is to violence that socialism owes those high ethical values by which it brings *salvation* to the modern world.[29]

Myths are necessary because without them, revolts will not provoke revolution. Whether they bear any relation to future history is irrelevant to their power and their value. At the centre of the myth lies the experience of grasping the inner self, of becoming and possessing oneself more intensely than is possible in normal life. Utopias, on the other hand, are cognitive constructs, products of the intellect, of reason. As such they are divorced from the soul of the proletariat, have no real connection with anything, are at best impotent and at worst diversionary and reactionary. Myths emphasise process, utopias portray ends. Thus 'syndicalism is free of all utopianism in the sense that it subordinates prospects for its triumph to the complex of conditions, and while waiting it performs the role of a cleansing agent in the world'.[30]

Ideology and utopia

For Sorel there existed systems of beliefs which, because they were expressive of the will of a social group, could lead to action which would have the effect of shattering the status quo, and it was to these that he applied the term myths. Karl Mannheim also held that transformation could be brought about through the operation of deeply held and intensely willed beliefs; but he called such ideas utopias. Sorel's concept of myth is however not quite the same as Mannheim's concept of utopia, despite the existence of illuminating similarities; concepts take their meaning in part from the framework of analysis within which they are employed, and the questions addressed by Sorel and Mannheim, and their general approaches, were very different.

Almost every aspect of Mannheim's life and thought contrasts with that of Sorel. Sorel had a successful career in the employ of the French Civil Service; he was neither a marginal member of French society nor a professional intellectual; *Reflections on Violence* is generally read as a celebration of the irrational in human action; and Sorel was markedly anti-semitic. Mannheim, on the other hand, was a Jew, born in Budapest, exiled from Hungary to the Weimar Republic in 1919 where he was Professor of Sociology at Frankfurt from 1928; and then exiled to England in 1933 when the Nazis gained power. In England he continued his academic career, but in a context where his interests and approach were idiosyncratic.

Mannheim's work lies firmly in the interpretative tradition of sociology established by Weber, although he was clearly influenced by both Marx and Georg Lukács. His discussion of utopia forms part of his best-known book *Ideology and Utopia*, which was published in German in 1929 and in English in 1936. As the title of the book implies, Mannheim makes a distinction between ideologies and utopias, and it is a distinction based upon their social function. Both ideologies and utopias are ideas, and are ideas which are 'incongruous with' and transcend the reality within which they occur, being oriented towards objects which do not exist in the actual situation. The difference is that ideologies operate to sustain the existing state of affairs, while utopias operate to change it:

> Only those orientations transcending reality will be referred to by us as utopian which, when they pass over into conduct, tend to shatter, either partially or wholly, the order of things prevailing at the time.[31]

> Utopias . . . are not ideologies in the measure and in so far as they succeed through counteractivity in transforming the existing historical reality into one more in accord with their own conceptions.[32]

Mannheim is quite clear that form and content are not the defining characteristics of utopia. He argues that 'the utopian element in our consciousness is subject to changes in content and form' and 'it is not always the same forces, substances, or images which can take on a utopian function, i.e. the function of bursting the bonds of the existing order'.[33] Because of this focus on function rather than form or content in the definition of utopia, Mannheim's object of analysis differs from that conventionally assumed in the liberal–humanist tradition. He is not concerned with a literary genre, or even with the somewhat wider category of visions of ideal societies. Indeed such visions may be ideological rather than utopian, that is they may act as forces to maintain rather than to transform the status quo. He points out that the medieval idea of paradise, while located outside of society in an otherwordly sphere, was an integral part of the maintenance of that society. It is only when such images take on a revolutionary function, as in such millennial sects as the Anabaptists, that they become utopian rather than ideological.

The use of the term utopia to refer to a category of social fictions is rejected by Mannheim as historically naïve and descriptive rather than analytical. Literary works commonly designated utopias are, at least initially, only individual expressions; they can become truly utopian only if and when they become the expression of the will of a social group, and the inspiration of successful social action in pursuit of change. Much of what is conventionally (and sometimes pejoratively) regarded as utopian is therefore excluded on this definition and consigned to the realm of ideology:

> Wishful thinking has always figured in human affairs. When the imagination finds no satisfaction in existing reality, it seeks refuge in wishfully constructed places and periods. Myths, fairy-tales, other-worldly promises of religion, humanistic fantasies, travel romances, have been continually changing expressions of that which was lacking in actual life. They were more nearly complementary colours in the picture of the reality existing at the time that utopias working in opposition to the *status quo* and disintegrating it.[34]

While the form and content of utopia may be historically variable, its defining characteristic is the capacity to transform the situation and realise itself. Ideologies, on the other hand, are those 'situationally transcendent ideas which never succeed *de facto* in the realization of their projected contents'.[35] Mannheim recognises the difficulty in applying this dichotomy. One reason why it is difficult is that ideologies and utopias are by definition tied up in struggles for social power and in these struggles groups have a vested interest in declaring each other's ideas incongruous with reality. Political discourse consists precisely of the attempt to invalidate opposing views and legitimate one's own. As Mannheim puts it, subordinate groups have an interest in unmasking the ideas of the dominant as ideological, and dominant groups have an interest in labelling ideas which challenge their authority as utopian (in the colloquial sense of unrealistic) as a means of invalidating them. Mannheim stresses that he is not using the term utopia in this sense; clearly, he is not suggesting that utopian ideas are incongruous because they are in principle unrealisable. He is referring to relative, rather than absolute utopias, that is to utopias which seem 'to be unrealizable only from the point of view of a given social order which is already in existence';[36] and indeed, to be truly utopian, they must turn out to be realisable. As a result, the distinction between ideology and utopia can, as Mannheim recognises, only really be applied with hindsight:

> Ideas which later turned out to have been only distorted representations of a past or potential social order were ideological, while those which were adequately realized in the succeeding social order were relative utopias.[37]

Further, since the concepts of ideology and utopia are ideal types in Weber's sense, in the real world ideologies may contain utopian elements and utopias may contain ideological ones, so that distinguishing between the two becomes even more difficult.

Utopian mentalities

There are many weaknesses in Mannheim's distinction between ideology and utopia besides those on which he himself comments and we shall return to these presently. However, his attempt to differentiate between the two was not an end in itself but a prelude to developing a typology of utopias. The typology implies both a historical development of the form and content of utopia and the coexistence of the different forms in mutual opposition as an integral part of the process of class conflict and historical change. Mannheim distinguishes four types of utopia: chiliasm; the liberal–humanist idea; the conservative idea; and the socialist–communist utopia. Each of these is characterised by a different orientation to, and experience of, time; and it is the treatment of historical time which Mannheim sees as the organising principle of the utopian mentality.

Mannheim's discussion of chiliasm owes much to an early work by Ernst Bloch, *Thomas Münzer als Theologe der Revolution*. He says that 'an inner affinity between Munzer and [Bloch] has made possible a very adequate exposition of the essence of the phenomenon of Chiliasm'. This essence is an experiential one, for in chiliastic or millennial groups Mannheim argues that action is not inspired by ideas, but by something much more deeply rooted in the 'vital and elemental levels of the psyche'. Whereas millennialism appears to be orientated to the future, Mannheim argues that the chiliast 'is not actually concerned with the millennium that is to come', but with a leap over into ecstasy.[38]

> The only true, perhaps the only direct, identifying characteristic of Chiliastic experience is absolute presentness. . . . For the real Chiliast, the present becomes the breach through which what

70

was previously inward bursts out suddenly, takes hold of the outer world and transforms it.[39]

Chiliasm is therefore implicity hostile to all actually existing conditions and processes of becoming, as it seeks this breaking through into a qualitatively different kind of existence, and what it seeks 'can only be adequately satisfied in Kairos'. Kairos is a theological term, whose meaning is explained by Paul Tillich as 'fulfilled time, the moment of time which is invaded by eternity', and distinguished from 'perfection or completion in time'.[40]

The idea of breaking through into an experience of fulfilment, of wholeness, appears in different ways in both Sorel and Bloch. For Sorel the importance of proletarian violence is precisely that it generates an experience of freedom and full possession of the self, and it is the heroic state of mind produced that is important, rather than the actions that flow from it. Sorel's debt to Bergson is explicit. Mannheim and Bloch are both critical of Sorel (and of Bergson) and particularly of the ease with which Sorel's approach was incorporated into fascism. Yet both identify *experience* as an important element in utopia. Mannheim's emphasis on kairos as the defining principle of chiliasm has parallels also in the less active, more contemplative, but perhaps equally ecstatic (in the literal sense of standing outside) experience of the fulfilled moment discussed by Bloch (see Chapter 4 below).

Mannheim argues that while there may be chiliastic elements remaining in twentieth-century political beliefs (particularly in anarchism), it is a mentality which emerged with the disintegration of medieval society. The chiliastic experience was characteristic of the lowest strata of society, and 'underlying it is a mental structure peculiar to oppressed peasants, journeymen, an incipient *Lumpenproletariat*, fanatically emotional preachers, etc.'[41] If this seems a rather catholic collection of groups to share a specific 'mental structure', it is widely accepted that millenarian movements are generally rooted in oppressed strata. Mannheim's own analysis here draws less on Bloch than on Engels's discussion of Thomas Münzer in *The Peasant War in Germany*.

In this discussion it is clear that Engels made a very positive evaluation of ideas which could be seen as forerunners of revolutionary communism, in spite of the fact that they were expressed in theological language and lacked an understanding of what was possible in the particular historical context. Münzer had the additional merit of being caught up in the real class struggles of his time. Engels describes Münzer as a 'magnificent figure' who 'went far beyond the immediate ideas and demands of the plebeians and peasants, and organised a party of the elite of the then existing revolutionary elements'. He argues that in the teachings of Münzer, communist ideas, while based on visions of early Christianity, expressed the real aspirations of a section of society. His programme was 'a brilliant anticipation of the conditions for the emancipation of the proletarian element that had scarcely begun to develop'. He demanded the immediate establishment of the Kingdom of God on earth – by which, according to Engels, he meant a 'society with no class differences, no private property and no state authority independent of and foreign to, the members of society'.[42]

That Münzer is not regarded by Engels as a utopian in any derogatory sense reinforces the point that to some extent the difference between his definition and Mannheim's is a semantic one. Mannheim does regard Münzer as a utopian, precisely because his ideas were not only incongruous with reality but produced revolutionary activity and real social change, even if they did not succeed in transforming the world in their own image. Engels sees Münzer as a revolutionary rather than a utopian for similar reasons, although his approval depends not just on the function of Münzer's ideas in their own historical location but on the parallel between their content and Engels's own view of the proper content of a communist programme. He would only describe them as utopian ideas, despite their transcendence of reality, if their social function had been to preserve the status quo, to prevent transformation – if, in Mannheim's terms, they were ideological. There are major differences between their interpretations of Münzer, however, since Mannheim argues that the most important aspect of chiliasm is the pursuit of ecstasy rather than acting as midwife to the Kingdom of God.

Mannheim's second type of utopia is the liberal–humanitarian idea. Unlike chiliasm it is an essential feature of this type that ideas do guide activity, and there is an emphasis on reason and on free will. The gap between the existing state of things and the ideal world constructed by bourgeois liberalism was bridged by 'the belief that reality moves continually towards an even closer approximation to the rational' – a belief of which Mannheim is acutely critical in this context, although it later emerges as an essential element in his own argument.[43] Whereas in chiliasm utopia must break in abruptly from outside, in this mode utopia becomes a goal set in the future, towards which existing processes are moving – a view common among the commentators discussed in Chapter 1 above. The world-view embodied here represents not the oppressed strata, but 'the middle stratum that was disciplining itself through conscious self-cultivation and which regarded ethics and intellectual culture as its principal self-justification (against the nobility) and unwittingly shifted the bases of experience from an ecstatic to an educational plane'.[44] Its characteristic time-orientation involves progress rather than kairos.

The liberal–humanist utopia is followed by that of conservatism. In many ways it seems inappropriate, on Mannheim's own definitions, to describe this as a utopia rather than as an ideology. For the conservative utopia emerges in response to the liberal utopia, in opposition to it in order to protect the social position of the dominant class, and is dedicated to re-enacting the past and preserving tradition. It celebrates the past as immanent in the present, and time is perceived as duration. Mannheim's characterisation of conservatism applies with uncanny accuracy to neo-conservatism as it developed during the 1980s, some fifty years after he was writing; it is correct even in that neo-conservatism (at least in British politics) emerged as a reaction to the growth of economic liberalism within the Conservative Party.[45] But if Mannheim's description of the nature and function of conservatism is correct, why does he call it a utopia?

Mannheim is aware of the paradox here. He argues that the 'conservative mentality as such has no utopia'. However:

> the counter-attack of opposing classes and their tendency to break through the limits of the existing order causes the conservative mentality to question the basis of its own dominance, and necessarily brings about among the conservatives historical–philosophical reflections concerning themselves. Thus, there arises a counter-utopia which serves as a means of self-orientation and defence.[46]

But because he is examining the shifting constellation of the utopias of different social groups in their conflicts with one another, it becomes necessary to describe this mode of 'incongruous' thought as a utopia as well, in spite of the fact that his description makes it more properly an ideology than a utopia. What this illustrates above all is the problematic nature of the distinction between ideology and utopia in the first place, for when conservatism is provoked by its opponents into the need for political legitimation it may also find it necessary to do this by the affirmation of a particular form of society, even if it is a form deemed to be represented by the survivals of the past in the present, whose preservation for the future becomes the overriding concern.

Mannheim's fourth form of utopian mentality is the socialist–communist utopia. Like conservatism this derives its preoccupations from the need to counter the other forms of utopia. Time here is seen as a series of strategic points in history, rather than a gradual progress as in the liberal–humanist idea; socialism shares with the liberal idea the location of a perfect world in the future, but here it occupies a much more specific point in time, the collapse of capitalism. It shares also the liberal opposition to the status quo, to the conservative affirmation of existing reality and to the chiliastic mentality, especially as it is expressed in anarchism.

Mannheim's most interesting claim about the socialist–communist utopia relates to the fact that he perceives it as not only less incongruous with reality than the preceding forms, but as progressively so. 'Socialist mentality . . . represents a redefinition of utopia in terms of reality'. Not only does the utopian idea (by definition) transform reality in its own image, but in the case of the socialist–communist idea this is possible precisely because the idea continually adjusts itself to what is possible, and 'corrects itself' against the present.

> The socialist 'idea', in its interaction with 'actual' events, operates not as a purely formal and transcendent principle which regulates the event from the outside, but rather as a 'tendency' within the matrix of this reality which continuously corrects itself with reference to this context.[47]

This has the effect of reducing the utopianism of utopia and leaves Mannheim with the problem that utopia may disappear. For Mannheim, the historical progress through the dominant forms of the utopian mentality involves a 'general subsidence of utopian intensity', 'a gradual descent and a closer approximation to real life of a utopia that at one time completely transcended history'.[48]

> Thus, after a long tortuous, but heroic development, just at the highest stage of awareness, when history is ceasing to be blind fate, and is becoming more and more man's own creation, with the relinquishment of utopias, man would lose his will to shape history and therewith his ability to understand it.[49]

Utopia and history

Mannheim's treatment of the distinction between ideology and utopia and his discussion of the various utopian mentalities involve an attempt to grasp as a totality the process of historical development and the interplay of groups and ideas within it. His approach is, however, subject to inadequacies and inconsistences. The dichotomy between ideology and utopia is functional rather than formal; it links utopia to the future as an anticipation and catalyst of emergent reality, while ideology is bound to the past and attempts to stabilise and preserve the status quo. Further, ideology is linked to dominant but declining classes, utopia to oppressed (or at least subordinate) and rising ones. Neither portrays reality accurately, but utopia succeeds in reshaping the world in its own image and thus becomes true – although the process of convergence between utopia and reality results in the potential extinction of utopia altogether.

There are four different objections which can be levelled at the dichotomy between ideology and utopia. Firstly, the categorisation of ideas into those which change and those which support the existing state of affairs is extremely crude. It leaves no space for ideas which may be neutral, or whose relationship to the present is ambiguous or paradoxical. In Mannheim's view, almost all ideas are situationally transcendent and are thus either ideologies or utopias: 'Ideas which correspond to the concretely existing and *de facto* order are . . . relatively rare and only a state of mind that has been sociologically fully clarified operates with situationally congruous ideas and motives'.[50] Further, Mannheim's schema elides the dominant with the residual in the concept of ideology, and the subordinate with the emergent in the concept of utopia, implying a unilinear and deterministic view of history. In the definition of utopia as that which is adequately realised in the future, it consigns to ideology ideas (and social forces) which may be oppositional but defeated.

The second and third problems, namely the notion of 'adequate realisation' and the issue of causality, relate to the criterion of success as a defining characteristic of utopia. The idea of adequate realisation implies that one would not expect a utopia to be implemented in all its details; since these are ideal-typical concepts, actual utopias are contaminated with ideological elements. But what degree of realisation will be deemed to be adequate, and who is to make this judgement? Here, Mannheim's concept of utopia is radically different from Sorel's concept of myth, for Sorel does not require any correspondence between the content of a mobilising myth and the state of affairs which it brings about; its function is merely to mobilise people to action to overthrow the existing state of affairs.

The issue of causality is a further difficulty: it is not merely a matter of utopia anticipating the future – of wanting something which the future turns out to hold – but of utopia creating the future. A utopia is an idea which is acted on (passes over into conduct), changes the situation (shatters the prevailing order) and realises itself. Yet the fact that a change is desired and anticipated, and that change comes about, does not demonstrate that the change occurs because of the desire or any action flowing from it; Bellamy's invention of credit cards in

Looking Backward was not remotely connected with their introduction in reality. To identify an idea as a utopia, we have therefore to establish not only that a change has occurred sufficiently in line with its content, but also that the idea was instrumental in effecting the change, which in practice is very difficult to do even with the benefit of hindsight.

This difficulty has led both Mannheim and subsequent commentators to offer weaker versions of the definition of utopia. Thus Mannheim suggests that we should 'regard as utopian all situationally transcendent ideas (not only wish-projections) which in any way have a transforming effect upon the existing historical–social order'.[51] This does not deal with the problem of causality but does reduce the difficulties of assessing adequate realisation, since the position implied here is much closer to Sorel's. The distinction between ideology and utopia is glossed in an even weaker form in Louis Wirth's preface to the English edition of *Ideology and Utopia*: here, ideologies become 'those complexes of ideas which direct activity toward the maintenance of the existing order', while utopias are 'complexes of ideas which tend to generate activities toward changes of the prevailing order'.[52] The criterion of success has now been interpreted out altogether. However, while this might seem to leave something more usable (albeit still fraught with difficulty), it is not what Mannheim said.

A similar re-interpretation of Mannheim is offered by Paul Ricoeur in *Lectures on Ideology and Utopia*. Ricoeur argues that both ideology and utopia are centrally concerned with the problems of power and authority and they can be contrasted on three levels. The function of ideology is always legitimation, the best aspect of this being an integrative function, the worst being distortion; the function of utopia is challenge, the best aspect being the exploration of the possible, the worst being unrealisable fancy bordering on madness. If the 'pathology of ideology is dissimulation . . . the pathology of utopia is escape'. In this instance, the connection between ideas and actions has weakened almost to the point of disappearance. Moreover, the perceived function of utopia has been transformed from change to criticism; for Ricoeur, the function of utopia is 'to expose the credibility gap wherein all systems of authority exceed . . . both our confidence in them and our belief in their legitimacy'.[53]

Ricoeur, however, does make some extremely pertinent criticisms relating to our fourth area of difficulty, Mannheim's view of reality. Ricoeur points out that in Mannheim's analysis the differences between ideology and utopia are in some ways less important than the characteristic which they share, that of being incongruous with or transcending reality, or orientated to objects which do not exist in the actual situation; yet this is to beg the question of what is real. Mannheim treats this as unproblematic:

The nature of 'reality' or 'existence as such' is a problem which belongs to philosophy, and is of no concern here. However, what is to be regarded as 'real' historically or sociologically at a given time is of importance to us and fortunately can be definitely ascertained.[54]

Ricoeur argues that Mannheim's notion of reality is inadequate; it is assumed to be something fixed and 'out there', of which objective knowledge is possible in a seemingly unproblematic way and which can be contrasted to the symbolic realm of ideas. Mannheim does not perceive that social reality is always and essentially socially mediated, rendering the opposition between ideas and reality, and hence the judgement of (non)congruence, untenable. Ricoeur's project is to rescue and develop the distinction between ideology and utopia while abandoning the criterion of non-congruence and thus preserving the status of the symbolic realm as an integral part of reality.

The criticism of Mannheim's view of reality is correct, but Ricoeur's own reformulation loses two important elements which are present, if inadequately so, in Mannheim. The first is the sense of connection between ideologies, utopias and social classes, and their integral role in class conflict. The second is the temporal dimension represented by the idea of residual and emergent groups and ideas which is embodied in the original dichotomy. The complexity of the process with which both Mannheim and Ricoeur are inadequately grappling is presented with customary lucidity in Raymond Williams's 'Base and Super-structure in Marxist Cultural Theory'.

Williams argues that the idea of society as a totality consisting of symbolic and cultural as well as economic practices (which both Ricoeur and Mannheim are employing) has certain advantages in that it represents the complexity of reality. On the other hand, the danger is that any notion of economic or class determination is lost. Only by simultaneously using Gramsci's concept of hegemony is it possible to grasp both the class character of society and the role of ideas, meanings and values within an essentially dynamic social process. We can then locate a 'central, effective and dominant system of meanings and values, which are not merely abstract but which are organized and lived'.[55] This dominant culture is not homogeneous; it contains alternatives within it (so that the much vaunted diversity of choice of both products and life-styles proffered by advanced capitalism may represent both an economic benefit of market segmentation and an ideological advantage). However, there are also 'practices, experiences, meanings, values which are not part of the effective dominant culture', which may be alternative or oppositional.[56] The difference between alternative and oppositional modes depends on whether the intention is to be left alone to live alongside the dominant culture or, in the case of oppositional forms and practices, to transform it. This formulation goes beyond Mannheim's simple dichotomy between ideology and utopia. Moreover, Williams posits the existence of residual and emergent forms as part of a process which cuts across the categories of dominant, alternative and oppositional modes, rather than being elided with them; both residual and emergent practices may be either alternative or oppositional, but are commonly subject to a process of incorporation into the dominant sphere. Thus an idea or practice which at one juncture is oppositional may subsequently become merely an alternative within the range of dominant options made available within society. Even with hindsight, then, it would be difficult to say whether, for example, Owenism was ideological or utopian in Mannheim's terms; Engels's judgement that at one stage it was genuinely oppositional, later a diversion, could be entirely accurate. What we have is a much more complex system in which class interest remains central, but the process of legitimation and challenge is both more dynamic and more clearly rooted in lived experiences, rather than being an abstract battle between disembodied ideas.

Ideas and action

It is central to Williams's argument that ideas are deeply rooted in the practices of everyday life. Mannheim also maintains that ideas are rooted in social groups and are weapons in the conflicts and struggles between classes. However, Mannheim does not succeed in sustaining this perspective with any degree of consistency. His ambivalence to utopia as the viewpoint of the rising class leads him to a contradiction between active and contemplative views of knowledge – the first similar to, the second different from, Sorel.

We have already seen that Mannheim was alarmed at the possible disappearance of utopia, since it represented the will to change the world. On the other hand he was deeply ambivalent to the irrational aspects of utopian mentalities. The idea of a utopian mentality goes beyond a cognitive belief in a set of propositions; Mannheim confines the term to those situations where the utopian elements in a belief system are dominant and therefore lead to an overall view of the world which is 'incongruous with reality' – i.e. a perspective which is therefore incapable of assimilating empirical facts about the world which do not fit in with the dominant orientation. Some of his comments on utopia itself are less than enthusiastic, and indeed far more critical than those on ideology. This is particularly marked in the introduction to the English edition of *Ideology and Utopia*, where he writes:

> The concept 'ideology' reflects the one discovery that emerged from political conflict, namely, that ruling groups can in their thinking become so intensively interest-bound to a situation that they are simply no longer able to see certain facts which would undermine their sense of domination. There is implicit in the word 'ideology' the insight that in certain situations the collective unconscious of certain groups obscures the real condition of society both to itself and to others and thereby stabilizes it.

In contrast,

> The concept of *utopian* thinking reflects the opposite discovery of the political struggle, namely that certain oppressed groups are intellectually so strongly interested in the destruction and transformation of a given condition of society that they unwittingly see only those elements in the situation which tend to negate it. Their thinking is incapable of correctly diagnosing an existing condition of society. They are not at all concerned with what really exists. . . . Their thought is never a diagnosis of the situation; it can only be used as a direction for action. In the utopian mentality, the collective unconscious, guided by wishful representation and the will to action, hides certain aspects of reality. It turns its back on everything which would shake its belief or paralyse its desire to change things.[57]

Mannheim's discussion of utopia here is at its closest to Sorel's concept of myth. There is the element of the collective unconscious, which can be compared with Sorel's emphasis on the non-rational 'strongest inclinations' or 'sentiments' which mobilise people instinctively. And, importantly, there is the emphasis on will and on collective action. Mannheim's claim that 'the collective unconscious and the activity impelled by it serve to disguise . . . social reality',[58] together with the implication that such refusal to recognise all of reality is necessary to action in pursuit of the group's interests, is similar to Sorel's claim that myths are important because they mobilise groups to action and that the historical accuracy of the content of the myth is of little relevance; there are times when one cannot afford to see the other point of view. However, Mannheim's evaluation seems to be far less positive than Sorel's.

In this preliminary chapter, Mannheim makes a strong argument about the connection between knowledge and action. The overall project of *Ideology and Utopia* is the development of the sociology of knowledge and Mannheim stresses two principles. First, it deals not with individuals but with styles of thought characteristic of particular groups in specific historical circumstance. Mannheim goes so far as to say that 'strictly speaking it is incorrect to say that the single individual thinks. Rather . . . he participates in thinking further what other men have thought before him' – and this in a specific situation which is, from the point of view of the individual, predetermined.[59] Secondly, and more importantly, he makes the point that thought is not a process of contemplation but is intrinsically bound up with action; this action is collective; and its guiding principle is the will to preserve or to change existing conditions. It is an insistence which fits well with his contention that ideology and utopia are forms of thought which can be understood only in terms of the projects of the social groups concerned; and much less well with his discussion of the potential role of intellectuals in resolving the conflicts of perception between social classes.

The main project of *Ideology and Utopia* is to explore the implications of the fact that all knowledge, and particularly all knowledge of the social world, is partial, selective and dependent upon the social location of the observer. The concept of ideology has undergone a change on two dimensions, from particular to total and from special to general. Particular theories of ideology are those which see only certain aspects of world views as distorted by the social position of the holder; total theories see the whole world-view as so influenced. Special theories attribute this distortion to the points of view only of certain selected groups; a general theory sees all viewpoints as influenced by the interests and position of the observer. With the move to a general, total view of ideology, we leave the realm of unmasking the deceptions of specific interest groups and enter the new space of the sociology of knowledge. We enter too into a new problem (or rather, a new version of an old one), the problem of relativism. For if all knowledge is the product of the social position of the observer, how are we to evaluate competing versions of the state of the world?

Whereas Lukács deals with this problem by positing the proletariat as a universal class which, freed from false consciousness, will abolish class society and hence class determined knowledge, Mannheim shies away from such a partisan view (and its revolutionary implications). Rather, the understanding of the general thesis of the socially situated nature of knowledge, and of the partial and class-related character of all world-views, calls for a synthesis which will transcend them. The class called upon to transcend the problem is not the proletariat but the intelligentsia, since they are relatively free from class determination. At a superficial reading, Mannheim's position is clearly absurd; the intelligentsia obviously is not free from class determinations and intellectuals are, like everyone else, embedded in social relationships and social structures, although they and others may sometimes be deluded about this. Thus Adorno castigates Mannheim:

> The answer to Mannheim's reverence for the intelligentsia as 'free-floating' is to be found not in the reactionary postulate of its 'rootedness in Being' but rather in the reminder that the very intelligentsia that pretends to float freely is fundamentally rooted in the very being that must be changed and which it merely pretends to criticize.[60]

In Mannheim's defence it should perhaps be said that he only refers to the 'socially unattached intelligentsia' as a *relatively* classless stratum, which is less clearly identified with particular interests than those who participate more directly in the economic process. Furthermore, he held this to be true only of an intelligentsia which was widely recruited from different social origins. To some extent, the characteristic of being relatively unattached and capable of and motivated to see several points of view was a product of the nature of intellectual life itself; but it was also the product of highly specific social conditions (which have never actually existed). It remained perfectly possible that intellectuals might put their energies into furnishing theories for particular social groups – conservative theorists in particular needed to be recruited in this way – although Mannheim judged this to be a 'negative misuse of a peculiar social position'.[61] In so far as there was any hope of a synthesis and thus of progress in social understanding, it lay with the intellectuals:

> We owe the possibility of mutual interpenetration and understanding of existent currents of thought to the presence of such a relatively unattached middle stratum which is open to the constant influx of individuals from the most diverse social classes and groups with all possible points of view. Only under such conditions can the incessantly fresh and broadening synthesis . . . arise.[62]

In this discussion of the role of intellectuals Mannheim's view of knowledge, while still dependent on social conditions, is far more contemplative and less bound up with action. It also gives a far greater priority to the role of ideas and of rationality in the social process. It is the very nature of intellectual life, as well as the social location of intellectuals, which motivates and makes possible the broad, synthesising view which will be the basis of a better future through a better grasp of reality.

There is a disjunction between Mannheim's discussion of utopia and his discussion of the role of intellectuals, which involves a shift away from seeing knowledge as an active component of social practice. Some commentators argue that the contradictory position that results is the product of considerable differences between the German and English versions of *Ideology and Utopia*, arising not just from problems of translation but from changes in Mannheim's own theoretical position between 1929 and 1936. (The English translation was approved by Mannheim himself.) The transformation of theoretical vocabulary between the two editions results in a less active and more contemplative orientation, together with a more negative attitude towards utopia than is found in the original version.[63] The implication of this is that the similarity between Mannheim's concept of utopia and Sorel's concept of myth is closer in the earlier formulation than in the later.

The similarities are perhaps more obvious than the differences. Both myth and utopia are defined in terms of their transformative function, although utopia transforms society in its own image while myth merely mobilises people to effect a transformation; the myth is mobilising but not anticipatory, while utopia is both. However, Mannheim refuses both Sorel's confidence in the proletariat and his celebration of irrationality, demanding salvation from a progressive synthesis provided by intellectuals. Neither writer resolves the tension between reason and passion: Sorel cheerfully surrenders reason to passion and ends up legitimising fascism; Mannheim, exiled by fascism, painfully surrenders passion and commitment to reason and ends in confusion.

4

Utopian hope:
Ernst Bloch and reclaiming the future

A very different attempt to define utopia in terms of its function can be found in the work of Ernst Bloch. Bloch's work is much less well known in the English-speaking world than Mannheim's, since translations have only very recently become available. Assimilation is also inhibited by problems of style and substance: his complexity is universally acknowledged, while his claim to reintegrate Marxism and utopia leads to suspicion on the part of both non-Marxists and Marxists. The 1400 pages of his *The Principle of Hope*, constituting as they do the most sustained and wide-ranging attempt to rehabilitate the concept of utopia within Marxism, cannot properly be ignored in any discussion of utopia: there are implications here both for how we define the utopian object and the boundaries of the field of study, and for how we approach material within that field.

Bloch's relationship to Marxism is more problematic. Like William Morris, discussed in the next chapter, Bloch stands at the juncture of Marxism and Romanticism. His project can therefore be seen as an attempt to import into Marxism a concept of utopia deriving from a mixture of mysticism and the Romantic tradition and thus as a contamination or dilution of Marxism itself, or it can be seen in Bloch's own terms, as an attempt to reinstate Marx's own intentions within Marxism through the fundamental but neglected *Marxist* concept of utopia. Both Bloch's success in forging such a synthesis between utopia and Marxism and the orthodoxy or otherwise of the result are matters on which disagreement is inevitable. The history and reception of *The Principle of Hope* illustrate that this has not been a purely academic matter.

Bloch was born in 1885, eight years before Mannheim and two

years before the death of Marx. His interest in utopia preceded that in Marx, with the key concept of the 'Not Yet' which runs through his argument dating from 1906. By 1921 he had written two major works on utopia: *Geist der Utopie* and the study of Münzer which so influenced Mannheim (and which Bloch himself was later to describe as a work of revolutionary Romanticism). His subsequent development as a Marxist involved close relationships with both Lukács and Walter Benjamin. Like many other radical German intellectuals Bloch was of Jewish origin, and was forced into exile in the thirties. He spent the years from 1938 to 1949 in the USA, but unlike such people as Theodor Adorno, Herbert Marcuse and Erich Fromm, he did not become integrated into American academic life. These years were spent working on drafts of *The Principle of Hope* and in 1949 Bloch returned to the German Democratic Republic as Professor of Philosophy at Leipzig University.

Bloch's return to the GDR emphasises the fact that since the early twenties he had been a committed communist, believed the Soviet Union to be building the communist utopia to which he aspired and saw an opportunity to participate in the construction of a new and better society; hope was a practical as well as a theoretical matter. When the first two volumes of *The Principle of Hope* were published in 1955 Bloch was awarded the National Prize. However, in 1956 there was a marked change in the political climate and the theoretical orthodoxy of Bloch and his pupils was called into question; Bloch was compulsorily retired from teaching. The third, most mystical, and from a Marxist point of view, much more questionable, volume of *The Principle of Hope* was published in a small edition in 1959, but was hardly greeted with acclaim. When the Berlin Wall was built in 1961 Bloch, currently on holiday in West Germany, decided to stay there; he was offered a post at Tubingen, where he remained until his death in 1977. It is clear from this changing response to Bloch's work that it is possible to regard it either as a major development of Marxist philosophy, which is how Bloch intended it, or as potentially dangerous revisionism.

The ubiquity of utopia

At a descriptive level, utopia is defined far more broadly by Bloch than by the commentators we have hitherto considered. He includes daydreams, myths and fairy-tales as well as travellers' tales and literary utopias. More surprisingly, such diverse topics as the sea voyages of medieval Irish monks and alchemical attempts to synthesise gold are discussed. The creative arts, particularly literature, architecture and music, are also important vehicles of utopia. Bloch refuses the identification of utopia with a literary genre:

> to limit the utopian to the Thomas More variety, or simply to
> orientate it in that direction, would be like trying to reduce
> electricity to the amber from which it gets its Greek name and in
> which it was first noticed. Indeed, the utopian coincides so
> little with the novel of an ideal state that the whole total of
> *philosophy* becomes necessary . . . to do justice to the content of
> that designated by utopia.[1]

Explorations of the vast field which Bloch regards as utopian occupy four of the five sections of *The Principle of Hope*. The first, very short, section is concerned with day-dreams which are part of everyday life for people of all ages, although the preoccupations of children, adolescents and adults differ. They include dreams of revenge, of sexual conquest, of financial success and its consequences:

> Most people in the street look as if they are thinking about
> something else entirely. The something else is predominantly
> money, but also what it could be changed into.[2]

Included here are the fantasies with which people help themselves through the day. Bloch agrees that these are essentially 'escape attempts',[3] involving the wish to break out of the world or change one's place within it, rather than to change to world itself. Nevertheless, they form part of the spectrum of utopian wishes.

The second section, which occupies the bulk of the first of the three volumes, is concerned less with the external manifestations of utopia than with its essence, anticipatory consciousness, and will be discussed separately. Part three returns to expressions of utopia as 'wishful images in the mirror', where the forms include circuses, fairs and fairy-tales, the lure of travel, and dance, film and theatre. The wishful images discussed here are seen as a transition to the construction of 'outlines of a better world', the substance of part four. Even here the field is broader than that commonly perceived as utopian, although this section does include much of the more traditional material. The survey of social utopias includes Plato, Campanella and much of utopian socialism, besides Zionism and the women's movement, both of which are treated with disdain, as is William Morris. Social utopias are followed by technological, architectural and geographical utopias and by 'wishful landscapes' described in literature or portrayed in art. Part five occupies the whole of the third volume and is subtitled 'identity' or 'wishful images of the fulfilled moment'. It explores the goal and experience of authentic humanity as reflected in or diffracted through literature, music and religion.

Only part four corresponds in any way to what is normally seen as utopian, because it lies closest to utopia defined in terms of form as an ideal commonwealth. What binds the broad content of this section to the even more wide-ranging material of parts one, three and five, is that all constitute 'dreams of a better life'.[4] Bloch thus traces a path through 'the little waking dreams to the strong ones, via the wavering dreams that can be abused to the rigorous ones, via the shifting castles in the air to the One Thing that is outstanding and needful'.[5] All merit inclusion as utopian, because all are examples of wishful thinking. The notion of wishful thinking does not here carry its usual pejorative connotations. Bloch would agree with Mannheim that 'wishful thinking has always figured in human affairs' and that 'myths, fairy-tales, other-worldly promises of religion, humanistic fantasies, travel romances, have been continually changing expressions of what was lacking in actual life'. He would agree too that they have a compensatory aspect and even that they are susceptible to manipulation: the mirror in which wishful images are reflected is 'a beautifying mirror which often only reflects how the ruling class wishes the wishes of the weak to be'.[6] However, the compensatory aspect of wishful thinking does not in itself mean that it operates, as Mannheim supposes, to sustain the status quo. It is not merely fictitious compensation for the discomforts of experienced reality, but a venturing beyond that reality which is essential to the inauguration of a transformed future. Utopia contains compensation, but also anticipation.

Not Yet

The designation of utopia as 'anticipatory consciousness', which is the subtitle of part two of *The Principle of Hope*, depends upon Bloch's central concept, the Not Yet. It has two aspects, the Not-Yet-Conscious and the Not-Yet-Become – its ideological and material, or subjective and objective aspects. The idea of the Not-Yet-Conscious is developed through a critique of Sigmund Freud. In Bloch's view, Freud regarded the unconscious as a kind of rubbish bin of repressed material that was no longer conscious; this overly negative approach on Freud's part disregarded the additional and countervailing characteristic of the unconscious, that of being a creative source of material on the verge of coming to consciousness. The unconscious is also the pre-conscious, is intrinsically creative and the source of the utopian impulse, which Bloch appears to regard as a fundamental human propensity. The expression of the Not-Yet-Conscious is of course subject to social determination and thus varies with individual and historical circumstances; hence the variation in utopian expression demonstrated in the rest of *The Principle of Hope*. The Not-Yet-Conscious is at its strongest in youth, is expressed *par excellence* in the creative arts and is intensely present in times of change, particularly revolutionary change. Thus 'all times of change are filled with Not-Yet-Conscious, even overfilled; a Not-Yet-Conscious which is carried by a rising class'.[7]

What prevents the Not-Yet-Conscious from being a purely psychoanalytic or ontological category is that it is the subjective correlate of the Not-Yet-Become, a category which applies to material reality. It is fundamental to Bloch's argument and to the concept of the Not-Yet-Become that the material world is essentially unfinished, the future is indeterminate and therefore that the future constitutes a realm of possibility. Once the world is seen as in a constant state of process, but a process whose direction and outcome is not predetermined, there are always many possible futures – futures which are real possibilities, rather than merely formal possibilities. Not all projected futures are real possibilities; there are of course constraints, and Bloch's model is not one of pure voluntarism. Nor are all real possibilities desirable: they include 'devastatingly, possible fascist Nothing' as well as 'finally feasible and overdue, socialism'.[8] These possible futures must be seen as part of, rather than outside, reality despite the fact that the indeterminacy of the future means that there is no necessary development from potentiality to actuality, and despite the fact that not all real possibilities will in fact be realised. Utopia, as the expression of the Not-Yet-Conscious, is vindicated in so far as it reaches forward to the real possibility of the Not-Yet-Become; it is thus actively bound up in the process of the world's becoming, as an anticipation of the future (rather than merely a compensation in the present) and, through its effects on human purpose and action, as a catalyst of the future. Human activity, informed by imagination, has a decisive role to play: 'the hinge in human history is its producer'.[9] Utopia is the expression of hope, a hope construed 'not . . . *only as emotion* . . ., but *more essentially as a directing act of a cognitive kind*'.[10]

Through the Not Yet, utopia is shifted from a descriptive to an analytic concept, defined in terms of a function which is simultaneously expressive and instrumental. The Not Yet itself carries multiple meanings, the two dominant ones emphasising the necessity of utopian expression. The German phrase *noch nicht* can be translated both as 'not yet' and as 'still not'. It may thus carry the meaning of something that is not *yet*, but is expected, stressing a future presence or actuality; or something that is still *not*, stressing an absense or lack in the present. Wayne Hudson comments that Bloch fails to distinguish these meanings,[11] but this 'failure' is essential to Bloch's purpose, which is to convey simultaneous lack and hope of fulfilment, absence and potential presence, longing and potential satisfaction. The ambiguity expresses Bloch's recognition that it is very difficult to experience a lack and impossible to articulate it without some sense of what is lacked, the satisfaction that would meet the need. All wishful thinking thus draws attention to the shortcomings of reality, a necessary step on the way to change. In addition, the Not Yet is intended to convey not just the interdependence of want and satisfaction, but the drive from one to the other, towards change – not just wishful, but will-full thinking.

Abstract and concrete utopia

If the assertion that utopia is anticipatory is not to imply a wholly idealist and voluntarist view of the future, the distinction must be made between those dreams of a better life that constitute real possibilities and those that do not; Bloch is therefore driven to make a distinction between abstract and concrete utopia. Anticipatory elements are identified with concrete utopia (and, as we shall see, with Marxism), compensatory elements with abstract utopia; thus Bloch refers to 'the power of anticipation, which we [call] concrete utopia . . . (as distinct from the utopistic and from merely abstract utopian-izing)'.[12] It is not a question of dividing the mass of material outlined above into concrete and abstract examples, as a division of sheep from goats. Just as Mannheim pointed out that ideology and utopia are ideal types and appear in reality interwoven with one another, so too Bloch sees abstract and concrete utopia, compensation and anticipation, as interwoven in the objects of his study. Unlike Mannheim, Bloch carries this to its logical conclusion: the task is to reveal and recover the anticipatory essence from the dross of contingent and compensatory elements in which utopia is dressed up in particular historical circumstances. Abstract utopia means that the derogatory sense of the term remains, and rightly so, but should not outweigh the positive sense that pertains to the function of concrete utopia: 'the category of the Utopian, beside the usual, justifiably pejorative sense, possesses the other, in no way necessarily abstract or unworldly sense, much more centrally turned towards the world: of overtaking the natural course of events'.[13]

Again, as for Mannheim, the essential distinction between abstract and concrete utopia is one of function although the dichotomy is less sharp. Although Bloch's concrete utopia, like Mannheim's utopia, is defined by its anticipatory and transformative function and is linked to the future, abstract utopia does not constitute ideology in Mannheim's sense and is not necessarily linked to the past. Whereas Mannheim's dichotomy suggests that those who are not with us are against us, Bloch is adamant that even the most abstract of utopian venturing beyond is better than pessimism or bourgeois philistinism because it contains the intention towards a better life; if the utopian function of reaching towards a transformed future is only immaturely present, at least it is vestigially so.

There are other contrasts which should be noted. Firstly, there is an epistomological difference. Mannheim's conceptualisation of reality sets both ideology and utopia in opposition to this and simultaneously confines them to the realm of ideas. For Bloch, the unfinished nature of reality locates concrete utopia as a possible future within the real; and while it may be anticipated as a subjective experience, it also has objective status. Secondly, there is a political difference: while Mannheim fears the irrationality of utopia and its revolutionary implications, Bloch welcomes the 'red dream' and the proletarian revolution, identifying utopia with the ultimate good. There are, however, problems which are common to both Bloch and Mannheim; in both cases, the criteria for the distinction seem to involve subjective judgements which are necessarily contentious, and in both cases, history must be the final arbiter, although in Bloch's case the history which arbitrates is not a pre-determined one.

Bloch's celebration of the anticipatory element present even in vestigial or contaminated forms across the range of human culture, and his simultaneously ruthless attitude to utopia's abstract trappings, recall Engels's response to utopian socialism; it is a celebration of the thoughts that break out through fantastic coverings, coupled with a rejection of the coverings themselves – and implying that it is a greater blindness to reject the former than to be deluded by the latter. Nevertheless, the distinction between abstract and concrete utopia is fundamental to Bloch's project. The rehabilitation of utopia depends upon the removal of the abstract elements which clutter up the concrete core. Concrete utopia must be winnowed out, stripping wishful thinking of that which is purely fantastic, compensatory and escapist: the process entails:

knowledge and removal of the finished *utopistic element*, with knowledge and removal of *abstract utopia*. But what then remains: the unfinished forward dream, the docta spes which can only be discredited by the bourgeoisie – this seriously deserves the name utopia in carefully considered and carefully applied contrast to utopianism; in its brevity and new clarity, this expression then means the same as: *a methodical organ for the New, an objective aggregate state of what is coming up.*[14]

What can then happen is that the utopian function 'tears the concerns of human culture away from . . . an idle bed of contemplation' and 'opens up, on truly attained summits, the ideologically unobstructed view of the content of human hope'.[15] As Habermas puts it, 'within the ideological shell Bloch discovers the Utopian core, within the yet false consciousness the true consciousness'.[16]

Cultural surplus and the fulfilled moment

A large part of the substance of *The Principle of Hope* consists of Bloch's attempt to demonstrate the core of concrete utopia in a range of cultural forms, including both religion and bourgeois culture. The reclamation of these as more than repressive ideology is justified by the idea of cultural surplus. Bloch does not dispute the view that the ruling ideas in any age are the ideas of the ruling class, or that ruling class ideologies justify social conditions by disguising their own economic roots and the system of economic exploitation. However, many cultural productions outlast the conditions that give rise to them: they 'reproduce themselves in cultural consciousness even after the disappearance of their social bases'.[17] This formulation is unsatisfactory in that it ignores the fact that cultural productions do not reproduce themselves, but are reproduced within historical contexts, even if these differ in some respects from those in which they originate. However, Bloch argues that ideology would be unable to carry out its most important function, 'namely premature harmonization of social contradictions', if it consisted only of deception and false consciousness;[18] and those elements which are detachable from the immediate conditions of creation are designated cultural surplus. This surplus is differentially distributed between different cultural forms, being more prevalent in architecture than philosophy, and particularly so in music; it is this that creates continuing culture; and this which must be reclaimed. Cultural surplus is equated with concrete utopia: 'it becomes clear that this very surplus is produced by nothing other than the *effect of the utopian function* in the ideological creations of the cultural side'.[19] A similar process of 'reclamation' is applied to the history of natural law in *Natural Law and Human Dignity*, identifying the common concern with dignity – 'the fundamental right not to be treated as scum' – that forms its essence, despite the limitations of its expression and the frequently apologetic trappings that surround it.[20]

If the essence of natural law is dignity, the essence of utopia is the pursuit of happiness. This includes a quest for an ontological state (as well as a social state which underpins it). The experience sought is described, among other things, as a 'homeland of identity' or the 'highest good' and can be prefigured in art through the experience of the 'fulfilled moment'. The goal, or One Thing Needful, is plainly the transcendence of alienation, construed here as a subjective experience which is anticipated in and communicated through art. Great music, particularly that of Beethoven and Brahms, conveys this experience both as aspiration and anticipation and Bloch's descriptions of major works by these composers convey his conception of the direction of the utopian impulse. Of Beethoven's *Fidelio* he writes:

> Every future storming of the Bastille is intended in Fidelio . . . Beethoven's music is chiliastic . . . more than anywhere else music here becomes morning red, militant-religious, whose day becomes as audible as if it were already more than mere hope. It shines as pure work of man. . . . Thus music as a whole stands at the frontiers of mankind, but at those where mankind, with new language and the *call-aura around captured intensity, attained We-World* is still only forming. And precisely the order in musical expression intends a house, indeed a crystal, but from future freedom, a star, but as a new earth.[21]

Even music which is ostensibly connected primarily with death carries this utopian function, and in a particularly intense way. Thus Bloch writes of Brahm's Requiem:

> all music of annihilation points towards a robust core which, because it has not yet blossomed, cannot pass away either; it points to a *non omnis confundar*. In the darkness of this music gleam the treasures which will not be corrupted by moth and rust, the lasting treasures in which will and goal, hope and its content, virtue and happiness could be united as in a world without frustration, as in the highest good; – *the requiem circles the landscape of the highest good*.[22]

Although the passion and poetry of Bloch's writing, particularly at points like these, is seductive, the criteria by which the utopian essence is extracted, or abstract and concrete utopia distinguished, remain obscure. It often seems as if what Bloch is doing is reading his own concerns back into the history of culture or law in a way which is both subjective and teleological. Indeed, the teleology is explicit: '*True genesis is not at the beginning but at the end*', and 'the world is full of propensity towards something, tendency towards something, latency of something, and this intended something means fulfilment of the intending'.[23] There is a goal, and one whose content Bloch is sure of, even though he seeks to define utopia in terms of its function in anticipating and approaching this goal. Ultimately, as we shall see, the distinction between abstract and concrete utopia can only be made by reference to this content; but first we must consider the relationship between utopia and Marxism.

Concrete utopia and Marxism

Bloch's project was not simply the rehabilitation of the concept of utopia but its rehabilitation within Marxism as a neglected Marxist category. The distinction between abstract and concrete utopia is essential to the argument that utopia is a necessary element in Marxist analysis, since concrete utopia is embodied in Marxism where real change and aspirations are interwoven, and were human will and social process meet. Utopia refers not just to anticipatory consciousness, the product of the Not-Yet-Conscious, but to the Not-Yet-Become which is anticipated. Bloch argues that Marxism, far from negating utopia, rescues it, and does so in two ways: first, by the recognition of the importance of what is becoming, as an aspect of reality, in the concept of tendency; and secondly, by revealing the process by which utopia is possible. Possibility – *real* rather than merely formal possibility – provides the link between utopia and Marxism. Bloch is critical of interpretations of Marxism which see it as a deterministic philosophy:

> It is not sufficient to speak of dialectical process and then to treat history as a series of sequential Fixa or even closed 'totalities'. A narrowing and diminishing of reality threatens here, a turning away from 'efficacy and seed' in reality; and that is not Marxism.[24]

Bloch's assertions about what Marxism is reveal much about his own position, as well as constituting a claim to orthodoxy. He argues that there are two strands in Marxism. A 'cold' and a 'warm' stream. These are, or should be, interwoven, and the consequence of their separation is precisely the dangerous separation between means and ends which concerned Buber:

> Only coldness and warmth of concrete anticipation together therefore ensure that neither the path in itself nor the goal in itself are held apart from one another undialectically and so become reified and isolated.[25]

The cold stream is that of analysis; through this, 'Marxist materialism becomes not only the science of conditions', but also a process of disenchantment, as 'the science of struggle and opposition against all ideological inhibitions and concealments of the ultimately decisive conditions, which are always economic'. The warm stream represents the passionate pursuit of unalienated experience, which remains the ultimate purpose of that analysis:

> To the *warm stream* of Marxism . . . belong liberating intention and materialistically humane, humanely materialistic real tendency, towards whose goal all these disenchantments are undertaken. From here the strong appeal to the debased, enslaved, abandoned, belittled human being, from here the appeal to the proletariat as the turntable towards emancipation. The goal remains the naturalization of man, humanization of nature which is inherent in developing matter. . . . Marxism as a doctrine of warmth is thus solely related to that positive Being-in-possibility, not subject to any disenchantment, which embraces the growing realization of the realizing element, primarily in the human sphere. And which, inside this sphere, signifies the utopian Totum, in fact that freedom, that homeland of identity, in which neither man behaves towards the world, nor the world behaves towards man, as if towards a stranger.[26]

Both the idea and the reality of concrete utopia become possible through Marxism, not just as theory, but as practice:

> This final matter or the content of the realm of freedom first approaches in the construction of communism, its only space, has never before been present; that is beyond doubt. But it is also beyond doubt that this content lies within the historical process and that Marxism represents its strongest consciousness, its highest practical mindfulness.[27]

And yet, if Marxism is the embodiment of concrete utopia, it does not follow that the goal has previously been utterly inconceivable. It is precisely this which has been foreshadowed – or perhaps forelighted – throughout history in the cultural forms expressing the Not-Yet-

Conscious. Human longing has always involved an inkling of what was really longed for, but only with Marxism has it been possible for this to become simultaneously fully graspable in the imagination and in reality. Bloch claims orthodoxy for this position by reference to a letter from Marx to Arnold Ruge, dated 1843, which he quotes repeatedly:

> Our motto must therefore be: reform of consciousness not through dogmas, but through analysis of mystical consciousness which is still unclear to itself. It will then become apparent that the world has long possessed the dream of a matter, of which it must only possess the consciousness order to possess it in reality. It will become apparent that it is not a question of a great thought-dash between past and future, but of the *carrying-through* of the thoughts of the past.[28]

This passage is important to Bloch for two reasons. First, it stresses the centrality of human vision in social transformation, in support of which Bloch also cites another, more well-known, passage about the distinguishing characteristic of the human species:

> We are assuming work in a form in which it belongs exclusively *to man*. A spider carries out operations which resemble those of a weaver, and a bee puts many human builders to shame with the building of its wax cells. But what distinguishes the worst builder from the best bee from the outset, is that he has built the cell in his head before he builds it in wax, at the end of the work process there is a result which already existed in the *imagination of the worker* at the beginning of that process, i.e. already existed *ideally*. Not that he only *effects* a formal change in the real; he also *realizes his purpose* in the natural world.[29]

Secondly, the claim that 'mankind has long possessed the dream of a matter' is invoked as a justification of utopian imaginings and Bloch's interest in them: the dream of a matter to which Marx refers is identified by Bloch with the dreams and aspirations emanating from the Not-Yet-Conscious and constituting the broad field of utopia itself. In support of dreaming as a legitimate and indeed necessary activity for Marxists, Bloch also repeats Lenin's quotation from Pisarev (see above, p. 56). It is a passage, says Bloch, 'which has come to be very much praised over the years, but not so eagerly taken to heart'.[30] Utopia, as forward dreaming, is neither an esoteric by-way of culture, nor a distraction from the real business of class struggle, but a central and crucially important element in the production of the future.

Beyond alienation

Bloch's defence of dreaming does not mean, however, that he provides us with a description of what socialist society will be like, or even that such an image can be pieced together from his writings as it can with Marx and Engels. This is not because Bloch shared the orthodox opposition to such depiction: in discussion with Adorno in 1964, he pointed out that Marx's strictures against such imaginings were historically specific judgements, and argued that in spite of the dangers of drawing up blueprints, Marx had cast too little of a picture of the future. In Bloch's case, the absence of description of the institutional nature of socialism seems to have more to do with his general emphasis on individual experience, despite the fact that he is quite clear that this experience is dependent upon socio-economic conditions. In 1972, he described 'the essence of what is due to be realised' as 'the individual who is no longer to be humiliated, enslaved, forsaken, scorned, estranged, annihilated, and deprived of identity'.[31] The quest is for the transcendence of alienation, the overcoming of antagonism between humanity and the world, for feeling at home in the world. The image of home or homeland is a recurrent one, forming the conclusion to *The Principle of Hope*:

> But the root of history is the working, creating human being who reshapes and overhauls the given facts. Once he has grasped himself and established what is his, without expropriation and alienation, in real democracy, there arises in the world something which shines into the childhood of all and in which no-one has yet been: homeland.[32]

Bloch's view of the nature of utopia, expressed elsewhere in more Marxist terms as the end of alienation and the realm of freedom, owes much to the definition of communism preferred by the young Marx, so that one might say that *utopia* . . .

> as fully developed naturalism, equals humanism, and as fully developed humanism equals naturalism; it is the *genuine* resolution of the conflict between man and nature, and between man and man – the true resolution of the strife between existence and essence, between objectification and self-affirmation, between freedom and necessity, between the individual and the species. [It] is the riddle of history solved, and it knows itself to be this solution.[33]

The critical element in the function of utopia means that some specification of content is necessary: utopia 'first and foremost . . .

provides the *standard* to measure . . . facticity . . . as departure from the right.'[34] It is necessary too to the distinction between abstract and concrete utopia. Although this content is only specified at an abstract level there is a clear identification between concrete utopia and Marxism as both means and end, function and goal. The goal is happiness and dignity, the abolition of both suffering and degradation. 'Becoming happy was always what was sought after in the dreams of a better life, and only Marxism can initiate it'.[35] Indeed, Bloch argues that all utopias have in one way or another been directed towards socialism, although in view of his frame of reference this may be tautological; 'socialism . . . is the practice of concrete utopia'.[36]

Bloch does make clear in *Natural Law and Human Dignity* that the goal of the 'unalienated *humanum*' depends upon the achievement of a 'future classless society'.[37] The references to Marxism in this work suggest that Bloch does not depart very far from the model of revolution followed by socialism followed by full communism, which alone permits unalienated living. The goals are freedom, equality and fraternity, but in a more complete form than has hitherto been possible:

> freedom is liberation from oppression, and oppression is brought about by economic inequality and its effects. In its uniquely concrete sense as a freedom from oppression, as a freedom of passing from the self to the we without alienation, freedom is the alpha of revolution, and it furnishes the revolutionary impulse an unprecedented allegory. . . . Freedom is equally an omega of revolution, that is, it opens the door to the identity of men with themselves, an identity in which there is no longer anything alien, no alienation, no reification, no unmediated nature, no destiny. *Equality*, on the other hand, provides neither a suitable allegory of the revolutionary impetus, nor an adequate symbol of the content of the revolutionary goal. In exchange, *equality* provides *the stable substance of revolution*; it marks the seriousness of that revolution which is distinguished from all previous revolutions by its ultimately classless content. In its material totality, equality is nothing other than the constructive idea, if not the socialistic construction then in the communistic construction that immediately follows it.[38]

Both equality and fraternity involve the overcoming of alienation between individuals. The object of equality is 'the inclination toward the *human identity* that has yet to arrive . . . [and] . . . which . . . always glimmers, like the harmony of men with the image they have of the *humanum*, a harmony in which they are postulated as one'. Fraternity, differentiated from limitless fraternisation, is 'the affect of the union of purpose, the affect of the recognition that the communality of all one's worth and all that others value is provided by the communality of purpose'.[39]

Bloch refers repeatedly to the principle of production according to ability, consumption according to need. Much of his argument recalls Marx's comments in the *Critique of the Gotha Programme*; Bloch is clear that this becomes possible only after the transformation of the productive base of society and of work itself, entailing 'the discarding of dependencies and the introduction of human work that creates history'.[40] Marx refers to the transcendence of bourgeois right; Bloch's argument elaborates this point, concluding that the principle 'renders superfluous the right to the fruits of one's labor, but of course only in that it has . . . abolished all relations of equivalence in a life beyond labor, a life that becomes possible for everyone'.[41] One prerequisite for this is the abolition of private ownership of the means of production; another is solidarity. None of this constitutes a proposal for immediate action, although the suggested time-scale is very short:

> It takes much time before wages, the state, and classes are
> surpassed. Rome was not built in a day, anti-Rome or
> no-longer-Rome is hardly to be expected in less than one or two
> generations.[42]

Yet the general direction is clear. Moreover, the goal involves the withering away of the state and a necessary connection between socialism and democracy: Bloch quotes Rosa Luxemburg in asserting that 'no democracy without socialism, no socialism without democracy . . . is the formula of an interaction that will decide the future'.[43]

If it is possible to extract these elements of Bloch's view of the social conditions that make unalienated experience possible, it is also true that they are present at best in a very sketchy form and are almost entirely absent from *The Principle of Hope*. The emphasis is not, as it was for Marx, upon the mode of production and the labour process which objectively involve alienated labour, and consequently result in alienation from self and from others (an alienation which itself is an objective condition and only secondarily, if at all, a subjective state). There is a tendency in Bloch for these aspects of alienation to appear solely as subjective experience. The utopian function is largely carried by art and culture – although *Natural Law and Human Dignity* concludes with the words 'Art is not alone in holding the dignity of humanity in its hands'.[44] The prefiguring of utopia in art operates through the provision of glimpses of unalienated experience, especially in the form of the fulfilled moment. The anticipation of the future is thus experienced through a process of contemplation or even of consumption, rather than through a process of production. If this is more appealing than Sorel's suggestion that individuals are somehow most in possession of themselves, least subject to alienation, when inspired to acts of proletarian violence, it is at least equally divorced from the process of the material production of everyday life. It is quite clear from Bloch's argument in *Natural Law and Human Dignity* that he does not intend this fracture between the objective and subjective aspects of alienation, but it is easy to see how his position can be construed as idealist. This is true to an even greater extent of his treatment of religion.

The repossession of the Kingdom of God

Given the overt biblical reference which Bloch uses in his discussion of Brahms's Requiem to convey the profundity of the utopian quest and the prefiguring of its goal in artistic achievement, it can be no surprise that he treats religion, and particularly the Judao–Christian tradition, with considerably more respect than is general among Marxists. It is the mystical rather than didactic elements of religion which appeal to him and he argues that the biblical tradition is the major source of utopian striving in the Western world. 'Utopian unconditionality comes from the Bible and the idea of the kingdom, and the latter remained the apse of every New Moral World'.[45] In Bloch's view, this is not simply because the ideological supremacy of institutionalised Christianity made the Bible an available cultural resource which could be extensively drawn on by architects of the utopian tradition: in the third volume of *The Principle of Hope* Bloch makes far more radical claims about the importance of the Christian concept of the Kingdom of God.

Bloch's overall project has been described as an intention to fill the gap into which the Gods were imagined.[46] He refuses to belittle the importance of the gap or to underestimate the richness of the way in which it has been filled by religion. Again, he denies that this involves any departure from Marx, who observed not only that religion was the opiate of the people but that it was the heart of a heartless world and the spirit of spiritless conditions. For Bloch it is also therefore an anticipation of a world no longer heartless, conditions no longer spiritless. Religion carried utopia as goal and as aspiration and would continue to do so as long as reality fell short of the conditions for a truly human existence. In demonstrating the positive religious input into constructive utopianism, Bloch cites not only Joachim of Fiore, and as one would expect Thomas Münzer, but also the young Engels:

> The self-confidence of humanity, the new Grail around whose throne the nations jubilantly gather. . . . This is our vocation: to become the Templars of this Grail, to gird our swords about our loins for its sake and cheerfully risk our lives in the last holy war, which will be followed by the millennium of freedom.[47]

It is of course possible to argue, as Christopher Hill has done in relation to Gerrard Winstanley, that this use of religious language is of far less significance than Bloch makes out. However, this is tangential to the main argument. Bloch suggests that the idea of the Kingdom carries the vision of utopia which Marxism makes a real possibility. This is a complex claim, for he is not suggesting that the idea of the Kingdom can be reduced to a plan for a social utopia; had he been doing this his impact upon theologians would have been rather less. But then Bloch's view of Marxism does not involve simply the assertion that the conditions for communism as a better mode of social organisation exist, although this was part of his thesis. What is prefigured in all utopian traces is the overcoming of antagonism between humanity and the world – a state which begins to be really conceivable and approachable through Marxism, in communism. The resolution of antagonisms that is represented in the image of the Kingdom is more profound than could be imagined in any currently conceivable social state for it, like Brahms's Requiem, involves the overcoming of death, the most profound problem of human existence and the most profound anti-utopia.

What Bloch argues is that for religion to become unnecessary (for his is an atheistic position, if one that can only be misunderstood by merely describing it as atheistic), Marxism must absorb the field of hope represented by the Kingdom. Or, to put it another way, the idea of God must be separated from that of the Kingdom, and repossessed as at least a potential embodiment of true humanness, the *humanum*. It can then be reinserted into the space occupied by the Kingdom, as a goal whose possession in consciousness is essential to its possession in reality:

> But *religion as inheritance* (meta religion) becomes conscience of the final utopian function in toto: this is human venturing beyond self, is the act of transcending in league with the dialectically transcending tendency of history made by men, is *the act of transcending without any heavenly transcendence but with an understanding of it: as a hypostatized anticipation of being-for-itself.*[48]

The Marxist inheritance of religion involves the abolition of religion, but it also involves the affirmation of faith in a redeemed future which Bloch sees as religion's positive aspect.

Form, function, content

If we consider Bloch's use of the concept of utopia in terms of form, function and content, a number of issues emerge about Bloch's approach and about the general problem of the definition of utopia. With no other writer is the rejection of form as a defining characteristic of utopia as consistent and explicit as it is with Bloch. The reason for this rejection is simultaneously political and theoretical: Bloch's Marxism, unorthodox though it may be, means that his central preoccupation is change. The assumption that dreams of a better life may play a part in this leads Bloch to define utopia in analytic terms, as an element in this process, rather than in descriptive terms; hence the overt emphasis on function rather than form or content. Since the function of expressing, anticipating and effecting the future can be identified in a vast range of cultural forms, the subject matter of utopia is identified in terms of the common charateristic of the intention towards a better life.

There are problems with this approach. The first, which is a weakness in Bloch's treatment rather than a difficulty inherent in the approach itself, is that there is very little discussion of the significance of utopia's appearance in particular cultural forms – a fact remarked on critically by Lukács. In theory, it would be possible to incorporate much greater consideration of the way in which particular forms provide the vehicle for the utopian function in different historical circumstances. Although the task is more than daunting, the theoretical possibility of such explorations is one of the strengths of Bloch's approach. The second problem, while related to the first, is also more insuperable. If the field of utopian striving is virtually limitless, selection within it is necessary; and of course Bloch is selective, choosing those elements in culture which, particularly before Marxism made utopia possible, are most imbued with concrete utopia. The abandonment of form as a criterion leads to a broadening of the field of study – which is then narrowed again by the distinction between abstract and concrete utopia. This distinction, while ostensibly made in terms of function, in practice relies upon content.

The preoccupation with change makes the function of utopia its central characteristic. This was true for Marx and Engels, although for them utopia was defined largely in terms of its negative function of obstructing the revolution. Bloch abandons these negative conno- tations, and (like Mannheim), defines utopia in terms of the positive function of effecting transformation. The process of change is a complex one, and consequently the function of utopia has several aspects. Hudson identifies four of these:

> its *cognitive function* as a mode of operation of constructive reason, its *educative function* as a mythography which instructs men to will and desire more and better, its *anticipatory function* as a futurology of possibilities which later become actual, and its *causal function* as an agent of historical change.[49]

One might add a fifth, which precedes all of these: its expressive function, as an articulation of dissatisfaction. These are properly read not as separate functions, but as different facets of a unified utopian function. This model of utopia, which is later reasserted in the work of Zygmunt Bauman,[50] confronts many of the usual objections to utopia. These include the claims that utopia is unrealistic because it refuses to respect the constraints of external conditions, as well as dangerous since the pursuit of utopia leads inexorably to totalitarianism. It is essential to Bloch's view of utopia that he rebuts both claims. With the Not-Yet-Become, the emphasis on process and tendency, he denies not the existence of constraints but the degree of constraint implied in an essentially 'finished', closed and static world. The space that is opened up in Bloch's cosmology *requires* utopia in order that humanity may be able to imagine, will and effect the future.

Yet it is only concrete utopia which has this transformative function. The distinction between abstract and concrete utopia cannot be made in terms of function other than in a completely tautological way. The content of utopia – as the transcendence of alienation – is the effective arbiter; the criteria are both abstract and unspecified. There is a conflict between Bloch's insistence on the future as a realm of possibility and the teleology which posits socialism and disalienation as goal. On one hand, Bloch recognises that 'the Nothing', as a possible future, 'is a utopian category': 'Nothing and All . . . are still in no way decided as utopian characters, as threatening or fulfilling result-definitions of the world'.[51] On the other hand, the propensity of which the world is full 'means a world which is more adequate for us, without degrading suffering, anxiety, self-alienation, nothingness'.[52] This conflict can be resolved only by the supposition that utopia is, as Bloch's argument suggests, rooted in human beings as an ontological category, a fundamental propensity; but Bloch also points out that Marxism insists on the social determination and historical transformation of human nature, and thus the absence of a 'fixed generic essence' of humanity. Bloch therefore fails to sustain the definition of utopia in terms of function, appealing to content to identify the elements in culture which represent humanity's deepest aspirations and the truth of tomorrow.

Legacies

Although Bloch's view of utopia has not to date had much influence on the field of utopian scholarship, his work was extremely influential in two areas. The first of these is what has come to be called Western Marxism, an overly hegemonic term for that strand in Western Marxism which has been concerned with the analysis of culture and the role of ideology in social transformation. Bloch, together with Lukács and Karl Korsch, was one of the key figures in this development and was thus an important influence upon the group of intellectuals (including Fromm, Marcuse, Tillich and Adorno) centred on the Institute of Social Research in the 1930s. In Western Marxism, and particularly in the work of the Frankfurt School, there is a tendency to use the term utopia in a positive sense, as a glimpse of a longed-for condition, rather than in the strongly negative sense that has become characteristic of the dominant interpretation of Marxism.

The sense that art has at least the intention towards utopia is not confined to Bloch, but can also be found in the work of Lukács and Adorno, as well as Marcuse. Yet Bloch was alone in his almost unqualified optimism. Lukács, whose views diverged sharply from Bloch's in the twenties, saw art as incapable of raising experience to the level Bloch implied. The later Frankfurt School, reinforced in pessimism by the Holocaust and also by the strong theoretical influence of Weber, similarly lacked Bloch's faith in the future. The position is exemplified by Adorno:

> Art's Utopia, the counterfactual yet-to-come, is draped in black. It goes on being a recollection of the possible with a critical edge against the real; it is a kind of imaginary restitution of that catastrophe, which is world history; it is freedom which did not come to pass under the spell of necessity and which may well not come to pass ever at all.[53]

Faith, however, is the raison d'être of theologians, and it is upon their thinking that Bloch's analysis of utopia has had the greatest impact. The use of Bloch's ideas within the Christian–Marxist dialogue shows how the theological interpretation diverged from his intentions, and also highlights problems of Bloch's own anthropology and cosmology. The two theologians most heavily influenced by Bloch were Paul Tillich and Jurgen Moltmann. Tillich was involved in the Frankfurt School in the thirties, and before Bloch's return to the GDR tried unsuccessfully to arrange for the publication of *The Principle of Hope* in Oxford. Tillich's view of utopia is summed up in a short article which shows his debt to Bloch both in terms of the concept and the language.

Tillich opens with three assertions about the status of utopia. First, utopia 'is rooted in the nature of man himself'. Secondly, it is not possible to understand history without reference to utopia, since human consciousness and action are meaningless without reference to utopia as beginning and end. Thirdly, with clear dependence on Bloch, he argues that 'all utopias strive to negate the negative . . . in human existence; it is the negative in that existence which makes the idea of utopia necessary'.[54] Utopia has both positive and negative characteristics: it contains truth, in so far as it contains the telos, the goal and purpose of existence; but it also contains untruth, in that it forgets that estrangement is a condition of human existence. Utopia is fruitful in that it opens up possibilities which would have been lost without utopian anticipation; but it is unfruitful in that it is in the nature of the wish to describe impossibilities as real possibilities. Utopia contains power, the power of transformation, and the 'root of its power is the essential – the ontological – discontent of man in every direction of his being';[55] but utopia is also impotent in that its negative content inevitably leads to failure and disillusion. This contradictory nature of utopia – again defined in terms of function and implicit content – calls for its transcendence. Tillich sees this as accomplished by reference to two orders, the horizontal and the vertical. The horizontal is that of the political and social, of immanent utopia. The vertical is that of radical transcendence, the divine, which continually breaks through. In this breaking through, the Kingdom of God actualises itself in history; but it is always resisted and suppressed, so that fulfilment in the horizontal is only ever partial.

Although Tillich's debt to Bloch is obvious there is also a radical departure here. Bloch did not see estrangement as a necessary feature of the human condition, but as a contingent one. As we have seen, despite the suggestion that utopianising is a fundamental human propensity, Bloch denied the existence of a fixed human nature which would make it possible to posit estrangement as a necessary and universal condition. 'There is', he says, 'no fixed generic essence of man . . .; rather the entire course of human history is evidence of a progressive transformation of human nature'.[56] Bloch saw in communism a way out of estrangement, so that utopia was a real possibility. Although there are similarities between Tillich's notion of radical transcendence and Bloch's discussion of the fulfilled moment, there is no doubt that Bloch believed more strongly in the possibility of the full actualisation of utopia – at least if the abstract content (which corresponds to Tillich's negative aspects) were to be eliminated.

A similar divergence is apparent between Bloch and Moltmann. It was through Moltmann's *Theology of Hope* that Bloch had his greatest impact on Christianity, although Moltmann's concern with eschatology which led him to be so receptive to *The Principle of Hope* itself derived from the work of Karl Barth. Following Bloch, Moltmann developed a concept of 'creative expectation' which he defined as 'hope which sets about criticizing and transforming the present because it is open towards the universal future of the kingdom'.[57] The radical implication of this was that the Kingdom was, as for Tillich, not merely transcendent but something which demanded social transformation. Thus 'the social overthrowing of unjust relationships is the immanent reverse-side of the transcendent hope of resurrection'.[58] Bloch, however, had no concept of resurrection. He recognised death as the ultimate problem of reconciling humanity to the conditions of existence, the ultimate obstacle to the achieving of utopia; but he did not adopt a religious solution. Moltmann argued that Bloch sought in vain for 'a *concept of history without a concept of transcendence*, an *eschatology of the world without the resurrection*'.[59] In the face of the problem of death Bloch has no substitute for God; but he remains an atheist.

The fact that Bloch's insistence upon the transformative function of utopia was imported into radical theology only made Marxists more suspicious. George Lichtheim referred to Bloch's views as 'a species of gnosticism or pantheism' which appealed 'only to that section of the New Left which is eternally in search of a Weltanschauung to bolster its instinctive rejection of the modern world'.[60] Similar criticisms of the whole of Western Marxism (with the grudging exception of Gramsci) as representing an alarming wave of irrationalism have been made more recently.[61] In the end, there is no doubt that Bloch's view of utopia rests on anthropological claims about the nature of human beings and human consciousness, embodied in the concept of the Not-Yet-Conscious, as well as on cosmological claims about the unfinishedness of the world and real possibility embodied in the Not-Yet-Become. These, as well as the political claim that Marxism makes concrete utopia a real possibility, are contestable, but there are other reasons why Bloch's work has not had more impact outside the realms of theology.

For most readers the problem of whether or not Bloch is orthodoxly Marxist is not a burning issue, and rightly so; the question of whether his position is right, or at least useful, is of much greater importance. Yet problems remain for Marxists and non-Marxists alike and Bloch remains difficult to assimilate to either a Marxist or a liberal–humanist tradition. For Marxists, there is a suspicion that Bloch's Romanticism and mysticism render him fundamentally anti-materialist (although this judgement is far too simple). Even if one accepts the proposition that there are warm and cold streams in Marxism whose integration must be sustained, the absence of attention to economic and social forces suggests that the cold stream has in this case received too little attention. Further, within both Marxist and liberal–humanist traditions in the Anglo–American academic world the predominantly positivist orientation is at odds with the non-verifiable nature of the argument. If Bloch is not hopelessly mystical, he is at least irredeemably evaluative. From the point of view of both these traditions there are major weaknesses in Bloch's argument: the positing of transcended alienation as a goal disconnected from the process of material production; the emphasis on subjective experience; the failure or refusal to provide clear or verifiable criteria for his distinctions; and a teleology which suggests that history has a goal rather than simply that human beings have purposes. These weaknesses make it difficult to assimilate Bloch's strengths, which in the end may be more important. Besides the fact that Bloch brings into focus both the question of the function of utopia and the boundaries, if any, of the field of its subject matter, his work transcends the limits of purely intellectual enquiry. He reminds us that utopia involves fundamental questions about the human condition and its future, and he refuses to abandon faith in the possibilities of that future. His legacy is therefore too important to be left solely to theologians.

5

The education of desire:
the rediscovery of William Morris

The relationship between Marxism and utopia also comes under
scrutiny in discussions of the work of William Morris, and particularly
of the significance of his utopian novel *News from Nowhere*. The absence
of reference to Bloch in recent re-evaluations of Morris is surprising;
themes and issues in Bloch's work can be compared both to Morris's
work itself and to the later debates arising from it. Both Bloch and
Morris attempted an integration of Romanticism and Marxism, transforming both in the process: in Bloch's case, this took place within the
field of academic philosophy; for Morris it was the outcome of an
aesthetic, moral and economic critique of capitalism, linked in his later
life to a practical commitment to communism. The transcendence of
alienation and the centrality of art were issues common to both.
Subsequent debates share with Bloch a focus on the relationship
between reason and passion, or the cold and warm streams, which
reappears as the relationship between knowledge and desire; the
definition of utopia is once again in terms of a function which is
simultaneously educative and transformative. The question of the
significance of dreaming occurs in all three contexts.

News from Nowhere

Morris was, of course, writing much earlier than Bloch. He was born in
1834 and died in 1896, thus being more nearly contemporary with Marx
himself. His rejection of capitalism began as an aesthetic rejection of
the sheer ugliness of Victorian artefacts and architecture, but did not

106

end there; strongly influenced by John Ruskin, Morris was to develop his own theories about the relationship between artistic production and its social base, and in 1881 declared himself a socialist. In 1883 he joined the Social Democratic Federation. This split in 1884 and Morris became one of the founder members of the seceding body, the Socialist League. Further political conflicts led to his leaving the League in 1890 to set up the Hammersmith Socialist Society. Despite the political turmoil of these years, he remained active in these explicitly Marxist organisations. His writings during the last fifteen years of his life include a number of lectures on aspects of socialism, *A Dream of John Ball* and *News from Nowhere*.

News from Nowhere was written in 1890 and has always been by far the most widely known of Morris's socialist writings. It had a large circulation and was translated into several languages including German and Russian; Lenin is said to have had a copy of the Russian translation, but there is no record of what he thought of it, if indeed he read it. The novel therefore formed the basis of many people's interpretations and misinterpretations of Morris's political position. Subtitled *An Epoch of Rest*, it is an account of England in the twenty-second century, to which Morris travels in a dream, waking up on the site of his own house by the Thames at Hammersmith. The first part of the book describes a journey from here to meet 'Old Hammond' at the British Museum. The second part is a long conversation with Hammond (who, it is whimsically implied, is Morris's grandson), explaining both how society works and the revolution by which the change came about. The third part is a journey up the Thames from Hammersmith to Kelmscott in Oxfordshire (where Morris had his country home) for haymaking. The world portrayed in the first and third sections is compatible, at least on a superficial reading, with a view of Morris as woolly, well-meaning and fundamentally im-practical; but this is substantially belied by the insistence on the need for revolutionary change and for the building and growth of the new society.

In this future England, most of London has disappeared to be replaced by fields and gardens: the distinction between town and country had been abolished. Villages remain, with communal meeting places, and markets where produce is brought for distribution, but no money is used; one simply asks for what one wants. Schools no longer exist, and children learn practical skills through both play and participation in society. The Houses of Parliament are used to store manure – 'dung is not the worst kind of corruption'.[1] The ugliness of industrialism has been superseded by an ecologically sustainable system largely based on craft production. However, in spite of the apparent dominance of handwork there is machinery available, and power which can be used as fuel for transport as well as supplied as required to small workshops, making large factories unnecessary. The central theme is of work as pleasure, and the separation between mental and manual labour has been overcome. It is a dream from which Morris wakes to the reality of industrial capitalism and political struggle; but the book ends with the words 'if others can see it as I have seen it, then it may be called a vision rather than a dream'.[2]

Despite the fact that *News from Nowhere* contains a long section on 'how the change came about', which takes the form of a proletarian revolution followed by the withering way of the state, the dominant mood of the book remains anti-industrial and the society presented by Morris is one of much greater simplicity than can be regarded as feasible. Nevertheless, the specific reason for the writing of *News from Nowhere*, the broader context of Morris's socialist writings as a whole, as well as the concluding words of the book itself, emphasise that it is far more than a reactionary and medievalist romance. It was written, in fact, in response to Edward Bellamy's *Looking Backward*, published in 1888. This novel, which also enjoyed massive sales, portrays a centralised socialist society emerging without conflict from monopoly capitalism. Production is based on 'industrial armies' organised with an efficiency that would have delighted Sorel, although he would have been less enthusiastic about the centralised organisations of production and consumption. Although both leisure and consumption are greatly increased in Bellamy's latter-day Boston, the life aspired to is that of the suburban middle classes of the time. Morris referred to it as a Cockney paradise; his published review was remarkably restrained, but made his position and his reasons for writing his own utopia clear. The counterview of socialism set out here must be read as the underlying intention of *News from Nowhere*:

> I believe that the ideal of the future does not point to the
> lessening of men's energy by the reduction of labour to a
> minimum, but rather to the reduction of *pain in labour* to a
> minimum, so small that it will cease to be a pain; a gain to
> humanity which can only be dreamed of till men are more
> completely equal than Mr. Bellamy's Utopia would allow them
> to be, but will most assuredly come about when men are really
> equal in condition . . . the true incentive to useful and happy
> labour is and must be pleasure in the work itself . . .[3]

Thus the transformation of work lies at the heart of socialism. Moreover, this is not something that can be brought about by massive centralisation, but requires the active participation of individuals in all aspects of the social process:

> there are some Socialists who do not think that the problem of the organization of life and necessary labour can be dealt with by a huge national centralisation, working by a kind of magic for which no-one feels himself responsible; that on the contrary it will be necessary for the unit of administration to be small enough for every citizen to feel himself responsible for its details, and be interested in them; that individual men cannot shuffle off the business of life on to the shoulders of some abstraction called the State, but must deal with it in conscious association with each other; that variety of life is as much an aim of true Communism as equality of condition, and that nothing but a union of these two will bring about real freedom: that modern nationalities are mere artificial devices for the commercial war that we seek to put an end to, and will disappear with it. And finally, that art, using that word in its widest and due signification, is not a mere adjunct of life which free and happy men can do without, but the necessary expression and indispensable instrument of human happiness.[4]

The comparison between *Looking Backward* and *News from Nowhere* is a common one, arising both from the fact that Morris was responding directly to Bellamy's novel and from the fact that the two books can be seen to embody two models of socialism which have more generally competed with one another. The contrasts between the two books are striking. A less obvious comparison can be made between both these novels and *Herland*, written by Charlotte Perkins Gilman in 1915. Such a comparison emphasises the failure of both Morris and Bellamy to give any serious attention to the questions of the position of women or the care of children. In both male utopias the sexual division of labour persists, and although both claim to give real respect to women, both as mothers and as household managers, both simultaneously make this the main role of women and fail to discuss it at any length: women are, as usual, largely invisible. *Herland*, in contrast, has motherhood as a central theme. This entirely female society, reproduced by parthenogenesis, can be read as an exploration of the kind of society that might emerge if the needs of children (and their mothers) were genuinely prioritised. Morris's concern with alienated labour then appears to address only some of the issues about work in capitalist and communist society.

Art, work and alienation

Morris's central theme in *News from Nowhere* is the condition of full equality that makes it possible for work to become pleasurable and to take on its proper role as the ground of human self-actualisation – that is, the overcoming of alienated labour. Other aspects of alienation concern Morris too, particularly relationships between individuals, and *A Dream of John Ball* emphasises the theme of fellowship:

> he who doeth well in fellowship, and because of fellowship, shall not fail though he seem to fail today, but in days hereafter shall he and his work yet be alive, and men be holpen by them to strive again and yet again.[5]

Not that fellowship was an end in itself, in the way that creative work is: 'it is for him that is lonely or in prison to dream of fellowship, but for him that is of a fellowship to do and not to dream'.[6] Morris's goal, like Bloch's, can therefore be seen as the transcendence of alienation. However, Morris's approach to the issue is, arguably, more authentically Marxist, concentrating as it does on the transformation of the labour process and the abolition of the market which governs it; Morris's alternative involves the combination of mental and manual labour characteristics of craft production, but the simultaneous abolition of commodity production since there is no buying and selling of goods. There are markets in *News from Nowhere*, but they are simply collection and distribution points; there is no assigning of exchange values.

For Morris, as for Bloch, the transcendence of alienation involves the sphere of art. While a full exploration of their aesthetic theories is beyond the scope of this discussion it is worth noting that their views of the role of art differ; and, paradoxically, while Morris focuses on the production rather than the consumption of art, it is Bloch who attributes to it the more active utopian function. Morris, as a creative artist, concentrates on the process of artistic production; in contrast, when Bloch, as a cultural critic, talks of the utopian function of art and refers, for example, to the experience of the fulfilled moment, the focus is on consumption, not production. It is an important contrast, but a dangerous one. Bloch himself was at pains to distinguish 'contemplation (and . . . passive enjoyment)' as features of bourgeois aesthetics from 'hope (and . . . the aroused will)' which are the essence of the utopian function of art, and which imply an active and involved response – but a response nonetheless.[7] Conversely, as Edward Thompson points out, Morris's idea of 'beauty' implies 'sweet, easeful, decorative, soothing' in a manner characteristic of precisely the contemplative attitude Bloch seeks to distance himself from.[8]

What is meant by the term 'art' differs somewhat between Morris and Bloch. Morris was concerned primarily with architecture and the visual, especially decorative, arts; he distinguished these from the 'intellectual arts' which are addressed 'wholly to our mental needs', rather than being aspects of things 'intended primarily for the use of the body'.[9] Bloch would not make such a distinction, since he attributes the utopian function to culture in its widest sense; nevertheless, his discussions place far more emphasis on the intellectual than the decorative arts. The difference between the two on the role of art is even more marked.

For Morris, art is primarily product. It is the 'expression of . . . joy in labour'.[10] The unalienated activity of communist society will produce more and better art and the activity of artistic production itself epitomises the transcendence of alienation. Yet art itself plays little role in the transition to communist society; indeed, Morris finds it thinkable that art may have to die awhile until the conditions conducive to its flourishing are created.[11] Again, the position should not be overstated: Morris also argued that the ugliness of industrial society stunted the human personality, and *News from Nowhere* was written because he believed it could inspire people to work for a form of socialism worth having. It was, he said, 'essential that the ideal of the new society should always be kept before the eyes of the working classes, lest the *continuity* of the demands of the people should be broken, or lest they should be misdirected'.[12] If the arts are the 'expression of the value of life', it is also true that 'the production of them makes [our] life of value'.[13] And Bloch would surely agree that 'all the greater arts appeal directly to that intricate combination of intuitive perceptions, feelings, experience and memory which is called imagination', and that 'all worthy schools of art . . . [are] the outcome of the aspirations of the people towards the beauty and true pleasure of life'.[14] Nevertheless, Thompson's judgement stands: 'Morris has not emphasised sufficiently the ideological role of art, its active agency in changing human beings, its agency in man's class-divided history.'[15] Nor, therefore, does Morris attribute active agency to art in the realisation of utopia.

For Bloch, on the other hand, the utopian function of art is more active. It nourishes the sense that 'something's missing', and is a necessary inspiration to social transformation. Without art to embody the dream of a matter, we will not be able to possess it in reality. Bloch has little to say about how social conditions impinge on the artist; he is a philosopher, not a sociologist, of art. Yet Bloch's insistence that hunger is the most fundamental human drive qualifies the priority assigned to art: 'people must first fill their stomachs, and then they can dance'.[16] Similarly, Morris wrote that 'any one who professes to think that the question of art and cultivation must go before that of the knife and fork . . . does not understand what art means'.[17] Thus the contrast, while significant, should not be overdrawn; it is perhaps more a difference of emphasis within arguments that are complementary. A properly dialectical approach would need to combine these perspectives.

William Morris reconsidered

Although it is suggested here that *News from Nowhere* should be read as a critique of alienation the interpretation of this book remains contentious. It finds its place in most, though not all, compendia of utopias, but is usually then discussed without reference to Morris's political writings and activities. For many Marxists, its form as a utopian novel has long been sufficient to prevent it receiving serious attention, even where it has been read. Many Marxists would still not give it the time of day, although arguably the rise of 'green' issues in contemporary politics makes it more relevant than ever. In the years following its publication, the very wide circulation of the book, combined with the deliberate suppression of Morris's political activities and writings by his biographers and the strongly anti-utopian attitudes characterising Marxism, led to the propagation of two myths about Morris. In one, the 'bourgeois myth', his socialism was ignored and denied altogether; in the other, the 'Menshevik myth', he was portrayed as a gentle, eccentric and above all anti-Marxist, English socialist. The latter myth was the one most prevalent among Marxists, even after Robin Page Arnot both named the myths and attempted to reclaim Morris for Marxism in the 1930s.[18]

Bloch, who dismisses Morris in less than two pages, subscribes to the same myth: 'capitalism is fought by Morris not so much because of its inhumanity as because of its ugliness, and this is measured against the old craftmanship'.[19] Even the revolutionary transition fails to redeem Morris in Bloch's eyes:

> Morris prophesies the revolution as the fruit and self-destruction of 'unnatural' industrialism, and he welcomes the revolution, though only as an act of annihilation. For once it has died down, not only the capitalists, but also the factories will be destroyed, in fact the whole plague of civilisation in the modern age will have been removed. Revolution thus appears to this machine-

wrecker to be a sheer turning back of history or a dismantling; once it has done its work, the world of craftmanship will return, people will stand – after the modern age has disappeared – on the colourful ground of native Gothic, which was only disguised in the English renaissance.[20]

Bloch is said not to have been greatly at ease with the English language and presumably had only limited access to Morris's writings. His judgement, which appears to be based solely on a reading of *News from Nowhere* and an ignorance of its context, is understandable. Nevertheless, the dismissal is ironic given subsequent debates: if there are common issues raised by Bloch and Morris, there are even more striking similarities between Bloch's work and the themes taken up by Morris's recent commentators.

The beginning of the general re-evaluation of Morris came not with Arnot's 'vindication', but with three books published in the 1950s – that is, at approximately the same time as *The Principle of Hope*. The first was Morton's *The English Utopia*. As we have seen, Morton's subject matter was largely the history of utopian literature in England, and utopia was defined with reference to form as a literary genre, although Morton did set out to trace the connections between these utopias and the circumstances of their production. It was a major departure for a Marxist to address the history of utopias at all and there is no doubt that Morton's analysis was, by and large, orthodox. Perhaps the most interesting aspect of the book, however, is that he accords the greatest positive value to the medieval folk utopia of *The Land of Cokaygne* and to *News from Nowhere*. Cokaygne is a land of plenty, of clement weather, of ease, of absence of conflict, where 'the larks that are so couth fly right down into man's mouth'.[21] In spite of the fantasy which characterises the poem, Morton claims significance for it as a genuine folk utopia which represents the beginning of hope – just as Bloch claims utopian significance for expressions of wishful thinking.

Morton's account is more historical than Bloch's, for he sees this hope not as an ontological constant whose form of expression varies, but as a product of the decline of serfdom in fourteenth-century England: 'what had formerly been so universally endured without question or hope was at last beginning to be felt as a burden', and therefore could be contradicted, at least in fantasy, and sometimes in outright rebellion.[22] *News from Nowhere*, over five hundred years later, is for Morton the culmination of the utopian tradition, synthesising with the literary tradition the aspirations expressed in *The Land of Cokaygne* so that Morris's 'Nowhere' is Cokaygne – but Cokaygne transformed and, most importantly, presented as the outcome of class struggle and revolution, as communism achieved. It is, says Morton, 'not only the one Utopia in whose possibility we can believe, but the one in which we could wish to live'[23] – although given the persistence of the sexual division of labour in Nowhere, some of us might give only qualified support to this sentiment.

Arguably both Arnot and Morton did much to try to create another myth, a Marxist myth which reads *News from Nowhere* as an account of the goal of communism *tout court*; 1955, however, saw the publication of Edward Thompson's *William Morris: Romantic to Revolutionary*. Thompson was not concerned primarily with the interpretation of *News from Nowhere*; his central project was the analysis of Morris's transition from the Romantic tradition of Carlyle and Ruskin to a revolutionary socialist position. What was important about Morris, in Thompson's view, was not that he made this move but that in the process of so doing he effected a synthesis between Romanticism and Marxism which enriched and transformed both. Marxists were not culpable for failing to recognise that Morris was really a Marxist, but for ignoring the element of 'moral realism' in Morris's work which would add to Marxism itself. Yet Thompson shared Morton's assertion that *News from Nowhere* was 'the first Utopia that is not Utopian', and called it a 'Scientific Utopia' – thus still hesitating to declare it both fully utopian and valuable but seeking to argue, as Perry Anderson puts it, that 'there was no significant contradiction or even tension' between showing the 'extraordinary originality of Morris's moral and political imagination' and reclaiming him 'for Revolutionary Marxism'.[24]

The sheer lack of understanding by Marxists of the importance of Morris (and indeed of the whole radical Romantic tradition) is emphasised by the lack of impact of this remarkable book. That lack of understanding was fractured by Raymond Williams's *Culture and Society* published in 1958. This book was much broader in scope, addressing the development of the idea of culture in Britian between 1780 and 1950. It was focused neither on utopianism nor on Morris and was not written from a Marxist perspective. Indeed, Thompson has located Williams's work as stemming from the same radical Romantic tradition as that of Morris: 'Williams' own writing, over two decades, had exemplified how tough a mutation of that tradition can still be, and how congruent to the thought of Marx'.[25] In *Culture and Society* Williams, who had read Thompson's book, as Thompson had read Morton's, advanced a substantially similar argument about the significance of Morris's work. Morris, he argued, had both a backward and a forward reference, drawing from Ruskin 'a right understanding . . . of what kinds of labour are good for men, raising them, and making them happy',[26] but applying this under new circumstances. Not only did the arts define a 'quality of living which it was the whole purpose of political change to make possible'; the significance of Morris in this essentially Romantic tradition was that he 'sought to attach its general values to an actual and growing social force: that of the organized working class'.[27] So that while Morris's socialism was indeed revolutionary and Marxist, it was integrated into an existing rejection of capitalist industrial society: 'The economic reasoning, and the political promise, came to him from Marxism; the general rebellion was in older terms'.[28]

Because of this synthesis, the reference back and the reference forward, Williams saw Morris as a 'pivotal figure'.[28] It was a judgement made, however, in spite of, not because of, *News from Nowhere*. Williams saw the novel as contributing to the later dilution by others of Morris's position, highlighting the weakness of his rejection of machinery and his essentially regressive longing for a non-industrial society, rather than the strength of his opposition to capitalism; Williams also contended both then and later that any future socialist society would necessarily be more, rather than less, complex than our own.[30] Morris's utopia was therefore relegated to a position of lesser importance than his political writings (although that judgement was later qualified):

> For my own part, I would willingly lose *The Dream of John Ball* and the romantic socialist songs and even *News from Nowhere* – in all of which the weaknesses of Morris's general poetry are active and disabling, if to do so were the price of retaining and getting people to read such smaller things as *How we Live and How we might Live, The Aims of Art, Useful Work versus Useless Toil,* and *A Factory as it might be.* The change in emphasis would involve a change in Morris's status as a writer, but such a change is critically inevitable. There is more life in the lectures, where one feels that the whole man is engaged in the writing, than in any of the prose and verse romances. These seem so clearly the product of a fragmentary consciousness – of that state of mind which Morris was always trying to analyse. Morris is a fine political writer, in the broadest sense, and it is on that, finally, that his reputation will rest. The other and larger part of his literary work bears witness only to the disorder which he felt so acutely.[31]

The purpose of quoting this passage is not to take issue with its content although, as we shall see, quite different judgements are possible. Rather, it is to demonstrate that while Williams was concerned to present a re-evaluation of Morris, and to demonstrate the synthesis of Romanticism and Marxism which Morris achieved, this did not constitute a defence of utopian fiction. Both Williams and (particularly at this stage) Thompson were concerned with a much broader reading of Morris's work, and particularly with his political essays. The rehabilitation of Morris does not therefore necessarily imply a rehabilitation of the utopian form, if by that we understand a fictional description of the desired society. It does, however, imply a recognition of the utopian function, of venturing beyond, which is a general characteristic of Morris's political writing. This remained largely implicit, however, until the reissue of Thompson's book in 1977, with its now well-known postscript which discusses the development since the 1950s of the debate about the significance of Morris. This debate is here shown to have far wider implications than the proper evaluation of Morris's work *per se*; it addresses precisely that relationship between Marxism and utopia which is Bloch's central problematic.

Claims and counterclaims

Whereas the first edition of *William Morris: Romantic to Revolutionary*, had, as Thompson observes, appeared as the height of the Cold War when Marxist sympathies were disreputable, circumstances in the late seventies were very different. Those twenty years saw a number of changes: the circulation of parts of Marx's own work which had previously been unavailable; an expansion of higher education, a growing respectability of Marxism and a consequent expansion of Marxist scholarship; a weakening of the assumed link between Marxism and pro-Soviet political views. They also saw an increase in interest in 'cultural studies' and in theories of ideology and culture. Partly through the influence of Gramsci's work, which itself became more extensively available during this period, but partly because of the general shift in the political and intellectual climate, Marxists were more receptive to the view that ideas had an important role to play in political struggle. If ideology was an important element in the maintance of the status quo then, conversely, a counter-culture or alternative common sense was an integral element in social change. Such a climate was clearly one in which potential audiences were likely to be more receptive to Thompson's ideas than they had been in the fifties. In addition, the development of Thompson's own ideas meant that a much clearer argument was set out about the relationship

116

between Marxism and utopia. This argument is developed largely through a debate with two French scholars, Paul Meier and Miguel Abensour, whose work on Morris superseded the original publication of Thompson's book.

Thompson reiterates that his book was an argument about the Romantic tradition and its transformation by Morris: Morris did not simply superimpose Marxist ideas on Romanticism, but integrated them into it 'in such a way as to constitute a rupture in the older tradition and to signal its transformation'. Nevertheless, 'the Romantic tradition had possibilities of antagonism to capitalist common-sense a good deal tougher than it is usual to attribute to it'. Morris took these antagonisms further in a direction in which they already tended: 'the moral critique of capitalist process was pressing forward to conclusions consonant with Marx's critique, and it was Morris's particular genius to think through this transformation, effect its juncture, and seal it with action'.[32] In rejecting Morris's socialism as regressive, 'orthodox Marxism turned its back upon a juncture which it neglected to its own peril and subsequent disgrace'.[33] On the other hand, Thompson takes issue with the creation of a third myth, the 'Marxist myth', which simply assimilates the whole of Morris's critique to Marxism. Such an assimilation is implied both in Arnot's 'vindication' and in Morton's discussion, as well as being wrongly interpreted as Thompson's own position; the result is not merely wrong but 'repressive . . . distancing and boring'.[34]

The specific target for this attack was a long study by the French Marxist Paul Meier, *La Pensée Utopique de William Morris* (translated into English as *William Morris: The Marxist Dreamer*). Meier's central concern is an explication of *News from Nowhere*, thus giving the utopian novel a centrality which at first sight seems curious for a Marxist. The oddity disappears as Meier's position emerges. He takes the text of *News from Nowhere*, elaborated by the political writings, as a description of Morris's goal; he then compares the critique of capitalism, the transition and the details of the projected society with those implied by Marx and claims that they are virtually identical. He notes in particular the two stages (of socialism and communism) as a central element in Morris's thought, and the parallel between the principles embodied in *News from Nowhere* and those set out in the *Critique of the Gotha Programme*. In so far as Meier vindicates Morris's utopianism (by which he means not just *News from Nowhere* but all the images of future society which can be found in the later writings), he does so by suggesting that the goal coincides in content with that pursued by Marx and Engels:

While Marx and Engels did not venture into the details of anticipation, they set out the markers, and Morris's utopia is based upon these primary data with astonishing consistency.[35]

It is, he says, 'ridiculous . . . to put William Morris into the last generation of Romantic writers' since 'the main inspiration and starting point of Morris's utopia are to be sought in Marxism'.[36]

Some of Thompson's objections to Meier's approach are well-founded. Firstly, it is undoubtedly true that Meier understates both the importance of the Romantic tradition in the development of Morris's thought, and Morris's independent contribution. Sometimes this leads to speculation verging on the absurd: Meier surmises that since Morris could not have read the *Critique of the Gotha Programme*, its contents must have been communicated to him by Engels, possibly through the intermediary of Belfort Bax, from the manuscript copy in his possession; Morris cannot be credited at arriving at similar conclusions himself.[37] Secondly, it involves evaluating Morris's ideas in terms of the approximation to a definition of Marxist orthodoxy; on the whole, Morris is seen to conform, but points of departure are characterised as weaknesses. More importantly, however, Meier's approach reinforces precisely that dichotomous division between Marxism and Romanticism which Thompson and Williams argue that Morris has overcome. Finally, in the wholly literal approach to Morris's speculations about the future, particularly where *News from Nowhere* is concerned, Meier's treatment misunderstands the function of dreaming and the function of utopia.

Before moving on to an alternative to Meier's approach, it should be noted that the Marxism to which Meier assimilates Morris is not the same as that of Arnot or Morton. Meier argues that while it is tempting to attribute Morris's 'humanism' to Ruskin's influence, and his economic and social thought to that of Marx, to do so 'betrays an ignorance . . . of the fact that Marxism is humanism, totally different from traditional abstract humanism, but real and fertile . . . it is this materialist humanism, and not speculative humanism, which is at the base of Morris's utopia'.[38] This is congruent with the beginning and end of Meier's book, which point to an interpretation of utopian thought and writing very different from the literalism which dominates most of the text. There is an early reference (echoing Bloch) to 'anticipatory thinking', a claim that 'utopia is primarily negation' (which connects with Marcuse) and, yet again, the quotation of the long passage from Pisarev on the rift between dreams and reality.[39] Indeed, despite Meier's meticulous attention to the detail of Morris's utopia, he also points out that Morris was not setting out a blueprint for future society:

All his writings show that he is dealing with a hypothesis, one that seems most logical and pleasing to him; but more than once

118

The education of desire

he stops himself making a doctrine out of it. He deliberately leaves obscure the answers to various problems and is not afraid of allowing imprecision, even inconsequence, to creep in now and then. He is careful not to draw up a detailed plan of future society and aims above all to suggest a utopian scale of values.[40]

In the final paragraph, Meier argues that it is the humanism of *News from Nowhere* as a 'tissue of possibilities' that gives it lasting significance; and the function of utopia in general is precisely that it 'supports a scale of values'.[41] These claims point towards a much less literal interpretation than Meier in fact provides, and it is to just such a reading that Thompson inclines, following Miguel Abensour and John Goode – a reading based on its status as dream.

Dreaming the future

In the first part of *The Principle of Hope* Bloch argues that dreams constitute an expression of anticipatory consciousness, whose utopian function is ultimately the transformation of reality and the attainment of unalienated being. Goode's discussion of the significance of the dream form in Morris's writing (particularly *A Dream of John Ball*, but also *News from Nowhere*) contains a similar argument. The function of the dream form is neither to posit a goal nor to construct a compensatory fantasy, but to emphasise the role of vision and will in the process of social transformation:

> Morris . . . invents new worlds or reinvokes dream versions of old worlds, not in order to escape the exigencies of the depressing actuality but in order to insist on a whole structure of values and perspectives which must emerge in the conscious mind in order to assert the inner truth of that actuality, and give man the knowledge of his own participation in the historical process that dissolves that actuality.[42]

Of course, Goode is here referring to the use of the dream as a literary device, whereas Bloch is talking about the sleeping and waking dreams of myriad individuals. But the arguments connect. Morris wrote in the opening paragraph of *A Dream of John Ball*: 'all this have I seen in the dreams of the night clearer than I can force myself to see them in dreams of the day'.[43] Goode comments:

> 'Force' suggests that dream, though an alienated activity, is one

119

which is open to discipline, and 'clearer' implies that the relief which is sought still has a responsibility to truth. Dream is given a positive intellectual role. More importantly, however, the sentence makes an important distinction between the involuntary dream of the night and the willed 'dream of the day': not only do dreams have specific responsibilities, but these responsibilities are fulfilled better by the proper assessment of the involuntary invasion of consciousness than by the conscious effort to bring those values to mind. The fullest possibility of vision is available only to the dream that is beyond the individual will.[44]

Bloch also made a distinction between day-dreams and night-dreams, claiming that nocturnal dreams feed on the past and are a space in which 'very early wishes circulate'; day-dreams are subject to direction and therefore contain more anticipation, less compensation.[45] The judgement is the opposite of Goode's, yet both distinguish between sleeping and waking dreams on the basis of the element of intentionality in day-dreaming. Goode's interpretation may require qualification. The dreams to which Morris was referring were those containing strong visual (particularly architectural) images – images which might well have been drawn from his childhood. And while Morris employs the nocturnal dream as an aspect of the form and content of his novels, what is actually involved in their composition is precisely the constructive process of day-dreaming to which Bloch refers – and which he prefers, precisely because of its subjection to discipline and its potential for responsibility to truth.

The function, as for Bloch, is not compensation, but anticipation and transformation. Goode's most important point is that the vision set out in the dream is not a literal goal but the vehicle for the communication of the values on which a socialist society would be based. The merit of *News from Nowhere* lies precisely in the fact that it does not set out 'to become objective by creating a social system of a totality of institutions', and that it therefore avoids becoming 'gratuitous and dehumanized' like Bellamy's *Looking Backward*: 'What it sets out to portray is not what the future will be like, but how a nineteenth-century socialist might conceive of it in order to communicate the rationale of his faith in his socialist activity'.[46] (Again, for Bloch, communicability is one of the key features distinguishing the day-dream from the nocturnal dream.) Utopia, says Goode, is 'the collectivization of dream', the dream made public.[47] In the end he argues that *News from Nowhere* fails to fulfil this role because, despite the revolutionary transition, the connection to political activity in Morris's own time is absent. The transition is not therefore adequately explained and 'the collectivity of the dream is not brought into relationship with the possible collectivity of the present'; but that is what utopia should do.[48] Similar sentiments on the role of literature are contained in Gert Ueding's exposition of Bloch's position:

Literature as utopia is generally encroachment of the power of the imagination on new realities of experience. . . . In addition, its temporal point of reference is the future. However, it does not withdraw from the reality principle merely to place an ethereal and empty realm of freedom in place of the oppressive realm of necessity. Rather it does this intentionally to test human possibilities, to conserve human demands for happiness and playfully to anticipate what in reality has not at all been produced but what dreams and religious or profane wish-images of humans are full of. On this definition, literary activity becomes a special form of dream work.[49]

Goode's final judgement on *News from Nowhere* is critical and echoes Williams's reservations. The weakness of the transition means that while it conveys a real sense of the values that would characterise communist society, these are 'not so much a picture of enacted values as a reversal of the rejected values of modern life'.[50] In the end, the book is 'much less a Utopia than an account of the agony of holding the mind together' in the face of seemingly insuperable difficulties and unattainable aspirations.[51]

Abensour shares with Goode the central argument that the importance of *News from Nowhere*, and of all utopias, lies not in the descriptions of social arrangements, or in some cases the vagueness or absence of these, but in the exploration of values that is undertaken. He rejects the opposition between science and utopia asserted by Engels, and yet again the point is made that the criticisms made by Marx and Engels of 'utopian socialism' are specific political judgements, which are not necessarily relevant to the utopian mode in general. Morris is claimed as a utopian communist and attempts (like Meier's) to reduce his thought to an illustration of Marxist truth are rejected as an exercise in closure and theoretical repression. For Abensour, the real question about the relationship between Morris and Marxism is not whether Marxists should criticise Morris, but whether they should criticise Marxism.[52]

Abensour further argues that from 1850 the nature of utopian writing became 'heuristic' rather than 'systematic' – that is, it shifted from the construction of literal blueprints to more open and more exploratory projects focused on values rather than institutions. The purpose of *News from Nowhere*, then, is to 'embody in the forms of fantasy alternative values sketched in an alternative way of life'[53] – a purpose which is neither Marxist nor non-Marxist but, as an imaginative construction, a-Marxist. It does not purport to offer a model of society, as goal or anything else. The point is not whether one agrees or disagrees with the institutional arrangements, but rather that the utopian experiment disrupts the taken-for-granted nature of the present:

> And in such an adventure two things happen: our habitual values (the 'commonsense' of bourgeois society) are thrown into disarray. And we enter Utopia's proper and new-found space: *the education of desire*. This is not the same as 'a moral education' towards a given end: it is rather, to open a way to aspiration, to 'teach desire to desire, to desire better, to desire more, and above all to desire in a different way'. [54]

What is claimed here as the key function of utopia is exactly the educative aspect which Bloch also stressed. The education of desire is part of the process of allowing the abstract elements of utopia to be gradually replaced by the concrete, allowing anticipation to dominate compensation. Utopia does not express desire, but enables people to work towards an understanding of what is necessary for human fulfilment, a broadening, deepening and raising of aspirations in terms quite different from those of their everyday life. Thus *News from Nowhere*, as a critique of alienation, does not just ask us to think about an alternative society, but invites us to experience what it would mean to be fully in possession of our own humanity – an experience which Bloch claims is offered to us through artistic works in the 'fulfilled moment'.

In his 1976 Postscript, Thompson drew heavily upon Abensour and Goode, but particularly the former, to clarify and develop both his interpretation of Morris and the general relationship between Marxism and utopia. The debate became much more than a question of the right evaluation of Morris, but opened out into a large and general question:

> what may be involved . . . is the whole problem of the subordination of the imaginative utopian faculties within the later Marxist tradition: its lack of a moral self-consciousness or even a vocabulary of desire, its inability to project any images of the future, or even its tendency to fall back in lieu of these upon the Utilitarian's earthly paradise – the maximisation of economic growth . . . to vindicate Morris's Utopianism may be at the same time to vindicate Utopianism itself, and set it free to walk the world once more without shame and without accusations of bad faith.[55]

Bloch evinced a similar concern:

Vulgar Marxism is already haunting the world in a kind of petit bourgeois communism, or, to put it in a less paradoxical way, it sees the main goal of communism in triviality such as an electric refrigerator for everyone, or art for everyone. It is exactly against such red philistinism that the new surplus, free of ideology, establishes and launches its utopian essence, its most central concern.[56]

Thompson's conclusion is that Marxism and utopia are complementary and mutually necessary. The precise nature of the relationship is subtly different from that posited by Bloch. Thompson wishes to recognise Morris as a utopian and as a Marxist, without 'either a hyphen or a sense of contradiction . . . between the two terms'.[57] Whereas Bloch argues that utopia is an existing but neglected Marxist category, Thompson argues that 'Morris may be assimilated to Marxism only in the course of a re-ordering of Marxism itself' – a re-ordering, that is, away from economism.[58] Of course, it is precisely such a re-ordering of Marxism that Bloch's thesis demands. But for Thompson there can be no total assimilation to even a re-ordered Marxism, because the 'operative principles' of utopia and Marxism are different. Utopia is the realm of desire, Marxism of knowledge, and 'one may not assimilate desire to knowledge'.[59] Utopia and Marxism need to be dialectically related. This of course is exactly what Bloch said about the warm and cold streams of Marxism, the streams of passion and analysis. The distinction is reiterated when Thompson writes of the need for Marxism to 'cease dispensing potions of analysis to cure the maladies of desire'.[60] For Bloch the problematic relationship is located within Marxism, for Thompson it is between Marxism and utopia; but it is the same problem and the same relationship.

Form, function and content

Throughout these debates on the significance of Morris, and even where Thompson ultimately confronts the general issue of the relationship between Marxism and utopia, the term utopia is used in a loose and undefined way. What identifies Morris as a utopian is primarily that he wrote *News from Nowhere*. This is true both for those who value the book and for those who regard it as a 'piece of pie-eyed sentimentality' – these latter not just Marxists, for the epithet comes from the arch-conservative ideologue Roger Scruton.[61] To some extent, then, utopia is being identified with a particular form. Meier, indeed, remarks that 'utopia is, to a certain extent, a literary genre with a set form', and for this reason examines the impact of that form on Morris.[62] Generally, though, the term is used rather more broadly, to refer to the images of future society found throughout Morris's socialist writings. Thompson, too, seems to treat utopia as the construction of images of the future, but also more essentially as a projection of desire – so there is reference not just to form, but to an ontological source.

The clearest argument, however, concerns the function of utopia, which is not just the expression, but the education of desire. Utopia entails not just the fictional depiction of a better society, but the assertion of a radically different set of values; these values are communicated indirectly through their implications for a whole way of life in order for utopia to operate at the level of experience, not merely cognition, encouraging the sense that it does not have to be like this, it could be otherwise. Utopia contradicts bourgeois common sense and facilitates a 'leap out of the kingdom of necessity into an imagined kingdom of freedom in which desire may actually indicate choices or impose itself as need'.[63] In these discussions, however, the ultimate function of utopia is left implicit. There is no assertion here, as in Mannheim, that the utopian is that which, when it passes over into conduct, tends to shatter the order of things prevailing at the time. However, there is plainly no point in the education of desire for its own sake, and if the function of utopia is the education of desire, the function of the education of desire is the realisation of utopia. As for Bloch, utopia has simultaneously expressive, educative and transformative functions. The issue becomes explicit in an essay by Williams, dating from about the same time as Thompson's postscript and similarly drawing on Abensour. Here, Williams argues that what makes something utopian is not just a quality of otherness but the element of transformation, requiring a continuity and connectedness to the present. And the transformation in utopia 'proper', as opposed to science fiction, is a willed transformation, not one which comes about by technological change or the alteration of external circumstances.[64]

But again the preoccupation with change that is characteristic of Marxist analyses presents the same problem. Some dreams may aid the processes of struggle, others may inhibit it. Thus Williams, like Mannheim, argues that images of paradise and tales of the Isles of the Blessed are not utopian, nor is most science fiction, while Cokaygne, which Morton sees as so important, is only latently so. What Williams sees as valuable in Morris's utopia (and in Rudolf Bahro's *The Alternative in Eastern Europe*) is the recognition of the long process of development of new needs, conditions and social relationships.

However, Williams does not quite define utopia in terms of function, since not all utopias are transformative, even if the best of them are. There are both systematic and heuristic utopias (*News from Nowhere* being an example of the latter). Both have strengths and weaknesses, and the potential weakness of the heuristic utopia is that it 'can settle into isolated and sentimental 'desire', a mode of living with alienation'.[65] Utopia may indeed have a transformative and emancipatory function, but it may also be merely compensatory; wishful, but not will-full, thinking. Similarly, just as Bloch does not accord equal value to abstract and concrete utopia, Thompson is adamant that not all utopian speculation is useful:

> To vindicate Utopianism . . . does not, of course, mean that *any* . . . utopian work is as good as any other. The 'education of desire' is not beyond the criticism of sense and of feeling, although the procedures of criticism must be closer to those of creative literature than those of political theory. There are disciplined and undisciplined ways of 'dreaming', but the discipline is of the imagination and not of science.[66]

This need to distinguish between the compensatory and transformative functions of utopia leads to an ambivalent and sometimes downright contradictory position. For example Williams, having argued that the transformative impulse is characteristic of utopia, also claimed that Bahro was not a utopian because he thought through 'the processes of transformation of conditions and needs'.[67] Perry Anderson concurs in the positive evaluation of Bahro, but not in the judgement that he is not a utopian:

> Bahro's thought can be described without derogation as utopian. In general, the historical capacity to project a future qualitatively beyond the confines of the present has typically involved overshooting the limits of the realizable, in transforming the conditions of the conceivable – a condition in turn of other and later liberations . . . In that sense, all creative socialist thought is likely to possess a utopian direction.[68]

The distinction between the 'positive' and 'negative' functions of utopia usually comes back to questions of content. The term utopia is retained in its derogatory sense for images of the future which, either because of their content or because of their failure to explicate the possibility of transition, can have no transforming power.

There is still a tendency, in making these evaluations, for Marxists to treat projected futures as blueprints rather than as explorations of values and to assess them accordingly, and also to neglect the experiential aspect of the education of desire. Consequently, while there has been something of a rapprochement between Marxism and utopia through the rediscovery of Morris, there remains a fear that utopian projections may divert and mislead, rather than encourage political activity. Morris himself was acutely aware of the problem. On the one hand he argued, as we have seen, that the vision of socialist society should be kept in view to give direction to popular demands. On the other hand, he was aware that the vision itself might lead aspirations and political struggle astray, or become detached from struggle altogether and 'be left on the barren shore of Utopianism'.[69] He was clear that *News from Nowhere* could not be a plan for the future, as it was not possible to gain sufficient imaginative distance from the present: 'It is impossible to build a scheme for the society of the future, for no man can really think himself out of his own days'. For this reason, 'his palace of days to come can only be constructed by the aspirations forced on him by his present surroundings, and from his dreams of the life of the past, which themselves cannot fail to be more or less unsubstantial imaginings'.[70] Any utopia, including his own, carried with it the danger that it would be taken literally – a danger to both those who would pursue it and those who would reject it as goal. He took issue with *Looking Backward* not just from distaste for the content, but because it was presented as the true nature and goal of socialism. The point is made as a general one:

> there is a certain danger in books such as this: a twofold danger; for there will be some temperaments to whom the answer given to the question, How shall we live then? will be pleasing and satisfactory, others to whom it will be displeasing and unsatisfactory. The danger to the first is that they will accept it with all its necessary errors and fallacies (which such a book *must* abound in) as conclusive statements of facts and rules of action, which will warp their efforts into futile directions. The danger to the second . . . is that they also accepting its speculations as facts will be inclined to say, If *that* is Socialism, we won't help its advent, as it holds out no hope to us. [71]

The ambivalence between the need for a vision to inspire and mobilise, not simply to articulate desire but to express and create hope, and the danger that such a vision may mislead and disable by expressing the wish without the will and power to effect change, lies at the heart of the Marxist response to utopia. Utopia is speculation about the socialist future, whether in literary or other form. Its function at best is to aid the transition to that future, at worst inadvertently to prevent it. Hence the need to distinguish between good and bad

126

utopias, to subject desire to discipline (Thompson), or to separate abstract from concrete utopia (Bloch). Through both Bloch's work and Thompson's, the traditional Marxist rejection of utopia is weakened. In both cases, it is argued that dreaming is an activity necessary to transcending our present sorry state, and that such dreams have both an educative and a transformative function; that the goal of the transformation is the transcendence of alienation; that art can prefigure that experience (Bloch) and will be fundamental to its realisation (Morris); and that these claims are, if not already contained within Marxism, at least compatible with and a necessary adjunct to it.

Marxism, Romanticism and utopia

The rehabilitation of utopia as outlined above depends on the assumption that the education of desire and the consequent development of an alternative common sense are necessary to social transformation, and indeed an integral part of it. While the influence of Gramsci on contemporary Marxism means that there is much sympathy for this view it is not, of course, a position without its critics. Marxists of an economistic persuasion are likely to find the Marxism/utopia debate so much idealistic hogwash and to prefer the bracing waters of the cold stream. And there are some real problems, raised (if perhaps overstated) by Perry Anderson in *Arguments Within English Marxism*. Anderson agrees that 'Morris's utopianism represents a feat of moral imagination without equivalent in the work of Marx, ignored without reason by Engels, and abandoned without sequel or echo in much later Marxism';[72] but he is critical of Thompson's account of this, of the distinction between desire and knowledge and the notion of the education of desire.

Anderson offers a historical explanation of Morris's utopianism and its poor reception by Marxists. In the first place, Morris's work not only represents the juncture between Romanticism and Marxism, but is the outcome of specific features of Morris's life – namely, secure wealth, polymathic skills and creative work – so that *News from Nowhere* represents a 'collective transvaluation of Morris's personal life situation'.[73] However, it is one which operates by inverting the present, elevating manual over mental labour, marginalising intellectual life and, above all, projecting the future in a way which involves 'consistent repression of the history of capitalism'.[74] Anderson, like Meier, reads *News from Nowhere* literally, measures it against Marxism, and finds it wanting. The reasons for Morris's lack of influence lie not with the limitations of Marxism but with the content, form and timing of his work. In particular, after 1917 'the construction of a communist society was no longer a matter of speculative theory, but of experimental practice' and 'the deep longing for another human order which had found expression in the utopias of the 19th century was now fastened to the – often scarcely less imaginary – society in the USSR'.[75] (Thus Anderson echoes Morton, but recognising the illusions involved in the identification.) Not only did this remain the case until the 1950s, but Morris's work rendered itself effectively irrelevant by its opposition to the prevailing emphasis on technology and economic growth. It was thus the historical context which led to a neglect of Morris, not an incapacity on the part of Marxism to confront utopianism *per se*. Anderson attempts, not very convincingly, to argue that Marxism has not been antipathetic to utopianism, citing as examples Marcuse and Adorno (but not Bloch) and particularly Bahro, whose work is described as 'a socialist figuration of the future beyond the antithesis between Romanticism and Utilitarianism'.[76]

It is arguable that it was precisely the historical circumstances which Anderson describes which led to the development of a kind of Marxism which was peculiarly insensitive to fundamental questions about the social basis of individual fulfilment. However, Thompson claims that there is a fundamental difference between the operative principles of utopia and Marxism, such that they remain distinct in spite of possible 're-orderings' of Marxism, and this gives weight to Anderson's claim that this is an ontological, rather than historical, argument. It is true that both Thompson and Bloch treat utopianism as arising from an ontological given, albeit one which is expressed in socially conditioned forms. Although the manifestations of hope and desire are various and are historically determined, their roots lie in the essential characteristics of human nature. This argument is not necessarily illegitimate, even from a Marxist viewpoint; even Marx worked with a model of human nature which assumed some aspects as given. The consequence, however, is that the basic force behind utopia is not open to historical explanation, even if the form and content of utopia undoubtedly are.

Anderson therefore criticises Thompson for positing a fundamental opposition between desire and knowledge as a necessary and a-historical aspect of human culture; in the same way, he says, in *The Poverty of Theory*, Thompson links values and feelings in opposition to ideas. It is the category of desire to which Anderson objects most strongly, and he rejects the phrase 'to teach desire to desire, to desire more, but above all to desire in a different way' as 'Parisian irrationalism' (although, as we have seen, it is scarcely exclusively Parisian).[77]

Behind this xenophobic epithet there are objections which merit serious consideration, for while it may not be irrational, it is plainly non-rational; the whole point is that the 'rational' categories of knowledge and analysis cannot contain human experience and one must also take account of its non-rational aspects. Yet the non-rational and the irrational may be difficult to distinguish. Desire does not necessarily lead in a utopian direction, as the anti-utopian lobby has pointed out with greater insistence than acuity. The emphasis on experience and feeling, common to Bloch's fulfilled moment, Mannheim's chiliastic ecstasy, Abensour's education of desire and Sorel's heroic possession of the self, does have real dangers; in Sorel's case, the affinity with fascism was all too real. But the problem is clearly recognised by both Bloch and Thompson: it is the reason why utopia is not simply about the expression and pursuit of desire, but entails its education; the emphasis upon the importance of experience and feeling that runs through the work of both Thompson and Williams presents this less as a goal to be sought than as data to be understood and subjected to the discipline of reason. As the Prophet said, passion should be directed with reason.[78] Indeed, while one can conceive of a dialectical relationship between the rational and the non-rational, it is hard (despite Hegel) to envisage any such relationship between the rational and the irrational.

More interestingly, Anderson argues that the polarisation of thought and feeling is itself historically determined: the distinction between the operative principles of desire and knowledge thus reiterates the antithesis between Romanticism and utilitarianism which he sees as embodied in *News from Nowhere*, and which is undoubtedly reflected in the contrast between *News from Nowhere* and *Looking Backward*. For Anderson, the real advance would be the supersession of this conflict – which at the time he saw as provided by Bahro's *The Alternative in Eastern Europe*, a judgement difficult to sustain in the light of Bahro's subsequent intellectual trajectory. However Anderson criticises Thompson, he is essentially concurring in the view that synthesis is necessary – and, since the opposition is historically contingent rather than ontologically given, possible.

It is the focus on experience, as well as the regressive elements in Morris's utopia, which opens not only Morris, but Thompson, Abensour, Goode and Bloch to charges of Romanticism. But why 'charges'? Romantic anti-capitalism was a major source not only of Morris's revolutionary commitment but of Marx's, and the concept of alienation provides the connection between the analysis of economic structures and human experience. It is hardly possible to argue that alienation is not a Marxist concept, although it may cease to be so when it is interpreted in ways which sever this link. Thus Michael Löwy argues that:

Marx's own view is neither Romantic nor Utilitarian, but the dialectical *Aufhebung* of both in a new, critical and revolutionary weltanschauung. Neither apologetic of bourgeois civilization nor blind to its achievements, he aims at a higher form of social organization, which would integrate both the technical advances of modern society *and* some of the human qualities of pre-capitalist societies – as well as opening a new and boundless field for the development and enrichment of human life. A new conception of labor as a free, non-alienated, and creative activity – as against the dull and narrow toil of mechanical industrial work – is a central feature of his socialist utopia.[79]

It seems that in so far as there is a problematic relationship between Marxism and utopia, it does not hang on the question of whether or not we should think about the future. Although it often arises in this form, this is based on a misunderstanding and is relatively easily dealt with. The real problem is how we should think about the future and, specifically, how we should think about feelings and about experience. The problem of Marxism versus utopia manifests as a problem of Utilitarianism versus Romanticism, knowledge versus desire, thought versus feeling. In the form of Romanticism versus utilitarianism, Löwy and Anderson argue that Marx overcomes this antithesis, Thompson that Morris does so, Anderson that Bahro does so. In the form of knowledge versus desire and the cold and warm streams, Thompson and Bloch propose their dialectical relationship, stopping short of a synthesis which overcomes the difference and tension between them. If some writers manage to synthesise the two it is a fragile synthesis, constantly in danger of disintegrating into its component parts.

6

An American dream:
Herbert Marcuse and the
transformation of the psyche

The most widely known attempt to reconcile Marxism and utopia occurs in the work of Herbert Marcuse. As with Bloch and Thompson, the issue of the education of desire is central, but it appears here as a question of the transformation of needs – the replacement of false needs by true needs, whose satisfaction demands the transcendence of alienated labour. For Marcuse this involves an embracing and cele-bration of the possibilities of technology, rather than its rejection in favour of craft production. Technology makes possible the abolition of scarcity and consequently renders utopia no longer an impossible dream but a possible future; it is the key to concrete utopia. The distinction between true and false needs is as problematic as that between concrete and abstract utopia and again requires recourse to a model of human nature – a model which Marcuse draws from Freud and spells out explicitly. Marcuse's use of the term utopia is more elusive and less consistent than Bloch's; but the general goal remains the same, the pursuit of a society in which unalienated experience will be possible.

Origins

Marcuse was born in 1898 into a middle-class German Jewish family. His early intellectual development was strongly influenced by Heidegger, although his political sympathies were radically different. Whereas Heidegger joined the Nazi party in 1933, and there is current controversy about the extent of his involvement in implementing the policy of the exclusion of Jews from academic posts, Marcuse was a

131

communist sympathiser (though not a party member) and was led to the study of Marxism by the rise of fascism. In 1932, when the Nazis came to power, Marcuse joined the Institute of Social Research; in 1934 he moved with the Institute to the United States, became a US citizen and remained there until his death in 1979.

In America, the Frankfurt School was dependent upon support from American institutions and, according to Douglas Kellner, this led to a collective decision to use code words for Marxist concepts and to tone down overtly political language.[1] The 'critical theory' which the school developed, and in which Marcuse played a central part, was essentially a form of Hegelian Marxism which, in the difficult political circumstances, dared not speak its name. This may account in part for the fact that Marcuse makes very little reference to Marx in many of his writings and derives much of his argument from Freud. The absence of reference to Bloch is less easily explicable. If the attempts by Bloch and Morris's commentators to reintegrate Marxism and utopia were independent of one another, the same should not have been true of Marcuse and Bloch. It was hardly possible, given Bloch's closeness to the Frankfurt School, for Marcuse to be ignorant of his work. Yet despite the occasional direct and indirect occurrence of the concepts of the Not Yet and anticipation in Marcuse's writing, there is little direct reference. In large part, Marcuse's approach to the problem of Marxism and utopia forms a third independent yet contemporaneous strand, albeit one arising initially from the same intellectual tradition as Bloch's.

Kellner describes Marcuse as 'a visionary utopian animated by the sense that life could be like it exists in art and dreams'.[2] If this could equally well be applied to Bloch, Marcuse's project was far less abstract – and arguably, like William Morris's, more orthodoxly Marxist because of the centrality given to the concept and process of labour. Marcuse's understanding of critical theory was that it aimed not only to comprehend existing conditions, but to do this through concepts which simultaneously embodied criticism of those conditions and their transcendence in the construction of an alternative; these concepts were thus intended to be descriptive, normative and anticipatory at the same time:

> Critical theory . . . makes explicit what was always the foundation of its categories: the demand that through the abolition of previously existing material conditions of existence the totality of human relations be liberated. If critical theory, amidst today's desperation, indicates that the reality it intends must comprise the freedom and happiness of individuals, it is only following the direction given by its economic concepts.

They are constructive concepts, which comprehend not only the given reality but, simultaneously, its abolition and the new reality that is to follow.[3]

The conjunction of analysis and anticipation (Bloch's warm and cold streams) accounts for both the strong negative and the strong positive that are to be found in Marcuse's work. Although Marcuse's formulation of the task of critical theory implies more than a dialectical relationship between analysis and transcendence, in that they are embodied in one another, he does not sustain this integration but fluctuates between optimism and pessimism. He insists, however, that critical theory intends material transformation rather than merely theoretical analysis. The goal is human happiness, only possible if radical change occurs, and the purpose of analysis is the direction and facilitation of this change:

The theory of society is an economic, not a philosophical, system. There are two basic elements linking materialism to correct social theory: concern with human happiness, and the conviction that it can be attained only through a transformation of the material conditions of existence. The actual course of the transformation and the fundamental measures to be taken in order to arrive at a rational organization of society are prescribed by analysis of economic and political conditions in the given historical situation.[4]

The centrality of 'human happiness' reflects Heidegger's pre-occupation with the possibility of authentic existence. In his transition to Marxism, Marcuse gives this a more concrete formulation; alienation replaces authenticity as the key concept, shifting the focus from philosophy and ontology to economics. This shift is, however, not complete; for alienation, as used by Marcuse (and, arguably, as used by Marx), is both an economic concept and an ontological one. Indeed, one of its strengths is precisely that it articulates the connection between economics and ontology. Marcuse's early concern with authenticity is retained in a concern with human essence and this is apparent not only in his interpretation of Marx, but in his adaptation of Freud, set out in *Eros and Civilization* and published in 1955.

Human nature and repression

Marcuse, like Bloch, relies on a concept of essential human nature, both to argue that the world should be otherwise and to locate the forces capable of transforming it. Bloch, as we have seen, does this by engaging with Freud in order to posit an intrinsic creative impulse in the unconscious, *contra* Freud's definition of it as a repository for the repressed. Marcuse both interprets Marx's *Economic and Philosophical Manuscripts* as providing a basis for the view that there are elements in human nature driving towards liberation, and finds foundation for a similar argument in Freud's theories. Marcuse regards himself as drawing out implications that already exist within Freud's work; in practice, however, this involves a greater adaptation of Freud than he admits. The result is that Marcuse, like Bloch, accords a central and positive role to fantasy, imagination and art in the potential transformation of society, ignoring the essentially regressive role which Freud accords to fantasy.[5]

If both Bloch and Marcuse incline to psychoanalytic and essentialist model of human nature, this is more dominant in Marcuse's work. It is a problematic approach to social theory, particularly where this theory entails a socialist commitment. It can be argued that the identification of basic human drives is intrinsically individualistic, and this in conflict with the intersubjective nature of social processes;[6] it is difficult to reconcile the psychoanalytic approach with Marx's claim that the human essence 'is no abstraction inherent in each single individual', but rather 'the ensemble of the social relations'.[7] Marcuse's project, though, was to establish that capitalist society was, from the point of view of individual human beings, thoroughly dystopian; to explicate how and why this was the case; and to examine the forces for and against its transformation. The argument requires a model of human nature as a measure of the good society, which Freud provided in much greater detail than Marx.

Freud, as understood by Marcuse, argued that the individual psyche was governed orginally (both individually and phylogenetically) by two instincts, Eros, the life instinct, and Thanatos, the death instinct. These give rise on the one hand to the pleasure principle and on the other hand to the Nirvana principle, the desire for oblivion. The two instincts are modified in interaction with one another, but decisively so in interaction with the external force of the environment. Thanatos must be conquered by Eros for the life to be possible at all; its destructive energy is diverted towards the outside world 'in the form of socially useful aggression', or 'used by the superego for the socially useful mastery of one's own drives'.[8] This involves the transformation of Eros itself, from an all-encompassing sexuality where 'the organism in its totality and in all its activities and relationships is a potential field for sexuality, dominated by the pleasure principle' to the 'special function' of genital sexuality.[9]

134

The suppression and limitation of Eros is necessary because the environment impinges in the form of the reality principle. The conflict between the pleasure principle and the reality principle, and the consequent suppression and transformation of Eros, are the foundation of civilisation. Civilisation is thus built on necessary repression, and repression which is entailed in the necessity of labour:

> This biological–psychological transformation determines the fundamental experience of human existence and the goal of human life. Life is experienced as a struggle with one's self and the environment; it is suffered and won by conquests. Its substance is unpleasure, not pleasure. Happiness is a reward, relaxation, coincidence, a moment – in any case, not the goal of existence. That goal is rather *labor*. And labor is essentially alienated labor.[10]

So Marcuse construes Freud. But whereas Freud argues that the conflict between the pleasure principle and the reality principle results in necessary repression and thence in civilisation, Marcuse argues that this depends upon the premise of scarcity. Scarcity however is, says Marcuse, a historical condition, not an unchanging natural one. While scarcity plainly still exists, the reason for this is not that it is impossible to produce an ample sufficiency for the world's population. Poverty exists now not because of absolute scarcity, but because of the way in which resources are distributed and used. And if scarcity is not necessary, but historically variable and now contingent upon particular social conditions, then the repression which is argued to derive from it cannot be entirely necessary either:

> The excuse of scarcity, which has justified institutionalized repression since its inception, weakens as man's knowledge and control over nature enhances the means for fulfilling human needs with a minimum of toil. The still prevailing impoverishment of vast areas of the world is no longer due chiefly to the poverty of human and natural resources but to the manner in which they are distributed and utilized. This difference may be irrelevant to politics and to politicians but it is of decisive importance to a theory of civilization which derives the need for repression from the 'natural' and perpetual disproportion between human desires and the environment in which they must be satisfied. If such a 'natural' condition . . . provides the rationale for repression, then it has become irrational.[11]

135

Marcuse also points out that what confronts individuals in any society is not the degree of scarcity which pertains as a 'natural' fact, but scarcity in a socially mediated and socially organised form; Freud's argument is therefore fallacious. Throughout civilisation 'the prevalent scarcity has . . . been organized in such a way that it has not been distributed collectively in accordance with individual needs' but has reflected the interests of dominant groups: 'the *distribution* of scarcity as well as the effort of overcoming it, the mode of work, have been *imposed* upon individuals – first by mere violence, subsequently by a more rational utilization of power'.[12]

Two things follow from Marcuse's argument. One is that in general, the reality principle (which itself varies historically) contains both an element of repression which is necessary and an element of repression whose role is simply to maintain the domination of particular groups and institutions. 'These additional controls arising from the specific institutions of domination are what we denote as *surplus-repression*.'[13] Secondly, the element of surplus repression increases as scarcity decreases. As technological progress makes possible the virtual abolition of scarcity, the proportion of surplus repression to necessary repression increases:

> The larger the discrepancy between the potential and the actual human conditions, the greater the social need for . . . 'surplus-repression', that is, repression necessitated not by the growth and preservation of civilization but by the vested interest in maintaining an established society.[14]

The performance principle

Domination (like alienation) has both an objective and a subjective aspect, referring to the external control over individual activity, and the concomitant internalisation of values and attitudes through which the pleasure principle is repressed, and indeed through which individuals repress themselves. '[It] can be exercised by men, by nature by things – it can also be internal, exercised by the individual on himself.'[15] Domination refers only to the element of unnecessary, surplus repression, not to the degree of repression necessary at any given stage of social development in order that individuals may survive and pursue their own ends. '[It] is in effect whenever the individual's goals and purposes and the means of striving for and attaining them are prescribed to him and performed by him as something prescribed.'[16]

Modes of domination vary according to the mode of production and in consequence give rise to different reality principles. The reality principle characteristic of advanced industrial society Marcuse calls the performance principle. This has some similarities with Weber's protestant ethic, or what is referred to in less religio-centrist terms as the work ethic, but Marcuse is concerned to stress that the interaction between the reality principle and the pleasure principle operates deep within the psyche so that what is at issue is the construction of a historically specific (and historically variable) human nature; we are not talking about a set of attitudes which are easily susceptible to change.

The first characteristic of the performance principle is that it keeps people working harder and longer than is reasonably necessary given the forces of production. But work in contemporary society involves alienated labour, and there is an irreconcilable conflict between alienated labour and Eros. Thus:

> For the vast majority of the population, the scope and mode of satisfaction are determined by their own labor; but their labor is work for an apparatus which they do not control, which operates as an independent power to which individuals must submit if they want to live. . . . While they work, they do not fulfil their own needs and faculties but work in *alienation*. Work has now become *general*, and so have the restrictions placed upon the libido: labor time, which is the largest part of the individual's life time, is painful time, for alienated labor is absence of gratification, negation of the pleasure principle.[17]

Secondly, therefore, through alienated labour, the performance principle involves the repression of Eros, the repression of sexuality in the broadest sense of 'deriving pleasure from the zones of the body'.[18] Sexuality is subject to both temporal and spatial restriction. Libidinal satisfaction is confined to free time, as well as limited by the conversion of general to genital and reproductive sexuality. (It is because of the latter restriction that Marcuse regards *some* 'perversions' as having a radical aspect, in that they represent a refusal to accept the dominance of the performance principle over Eros.) Nor does an apparent decrease in sexual repression necessarily indicate a genuine decrease in the dominance of the performance principle; it may constitute what Marcuse calls repressive desublimation – that is, an outlet for erotic energy in forms dictated and containable by the system of domination.

Thirdly, however, the performance principle not only means that 'body and mind are made into instruments of alienated labor' for the duration of the working day.[19] Precisely because the growth of productivity potentially reduces the length of the working day and thus threatens domination, control becomes more total. It penetrates both into the psyche through the creation of false wants and needs and into so-called leisure time, which is increasingly manipulated. False needs, and their satisfaction, are necessary to the maintenance of the system because the excessive amount of labour demanded by the performance principle serves not only wasteful and military production, but also the production of commodities which people think they want. It is not that there is anything wrong with a high standard of living *per se*, but its production under capitalist conditions entails internal and external domination:

> The high standard of living . . . is *restrictive* in a concrete
> sociological sense: the goods and services that the individuals
> buy control their needs and petrify their faculties. In exchange
> for the commodities that enrich their life, the individuals sell not
> only their labor but also their free time. The better living is
> offset by the all-pervasive control over living. People . . . have
> innumerable choices . . . which . . . keep them occupied and
> divert their attention from the real issue – which is the
> awareness that they could both work less and determine their
> own needs and satisfactions.[20]

Fourthly, the result of the increasing domination necessitated by the gap between actual and potential social conditions, the increasing degree of surplus repression, is the progressive destruction of the human subject. There is less and less space in which individuals can develop their own demands and decisions, although they may have the illusion of having an increasing amount of choice; mental processes are themselves increasingly subject to external control. The performance principle thus involves the abolition of thought.[21]

The forces of domination, especially as they operate in the third and fourth aspects of the performance principle, are stressed in *One Dimensional Man*, the very title of which reflects Marcuse's pessimism about the decreasing scope for human subjects to oppose and transform existing conditions. In a Weberian sense, this increasing domination involves increasing rationality; from a human point of view, however, it is irrational. Surplus repression is by definition unnecessary repression and it is unnecessary precisely because of the (partial) abolition of scarcity. The expansion of productive forces makes possible a radically different society, governed by a new reality principle, the aesthetic principle. Marcuse fluctuates between pessimism at the prospect of total domination and optimism about the potential for a new society which may emerge from the struggle between the pleasure principle and the performance principle. This oscillation illustrates precisely the point which Krishan Kumar makes in relation to writers of utopian and dystopian fiction, namely that the optimism of utopia and the pessimism of dystopia represent opposite sides of the same coin – the hope of what the future could be at best, the fear of what it may be at worst.[22]

Beyond scarcity

While Marcuse argues that 'the performance principle has become obsolete', and that the potential new reality principle presupposes a high degree of productivity, he does not suggest that abundance is unlimited. He argues that 'the reconciliation between pleasure and reality principle does not depend on the existence of abundance for all'; it depends on the abolition of surplus repression, rather than of repression itself, so that the question becomes 'whether a state of civilization can be reasonably envisaged in which human needs are fulfilled in such a manner and to such an extent that surplus-repression can be eliminated'. In material terms, a lower standard of living may result: 'many would have to give up manipulated comforts if all were to live a human life' – a life, that is, where social productivity is 'redirected toward the universal gratification of individual needs'.[23]

In terms of Davis's typology (see Chapter 7 below) Marcuse closes the scarcity gap, the gap between needs and satisfactions, not by a Cokagyne-type fantasy of effortless, idle abundance; he posits both increased productivity and an arcadian containment of wants. Yet Marcuse sees the issue as one of an *expansion* of needs and satis-factions, albeit an expansion which does not imply quantitative increases in material consumption. What is central to Marcuse's argument is a qualitative change in the character of needs and wants, such that material consumption by the currently affluent will decrease, while 'real' needs, wants and satisfactions increase for all. This qualitative shift reflects the character of the new reality principle. Whereas the characteristics of the performance principle are domi-nation and exploitation, the new reality principle would encapsulate 'receptivity, sensitivity, non-violence, tenderness'. These character-istics 'pertain to the domain of Eros . . . [and] . . . express the energy of the life instincts'.[24] The good society is predicated on sufficiency, not super-abundance.

Nevertheless, the possibility of sufficiency and the transformation of work both stem from technological advance and mechanisation.

Thus Marcuse's view is radically different from Morris's and he would not agree that 'the multiplication of machinery will just – multiply machinery'.[25] The emergence of the good society is not based on de-industrialisation or simplification; the possibility of transformation depends upon high productivity and near-total automation. It is not just that the realm of freedom increases and the realm of necessity decreases as automation decreases the length of the working day. Marcuse argues that this can precipitate a situation in which the realm of freedom breaks into the realm of necessity – that is, those human characteristics of 'thinking, knowing, experimenting, and playing' are brought into effect as automation eliminates the need for alienated labour subordinated to the dictates of the machine. In an almost Fourierist sense, work becomes play:

> It can be seen that precisely the most exaggerated, 'eschatological' conceptions of Marxian theory most adequately anticipate social tendencies: for instance the idea of the abolition of labor, which Marx later rejected. Behind all the inhuman aspects of automation as it is organized under capitalism, its real possibilities appear: the genesis of a technological world in which man can finally withdraw from, evacuate and oversee the apparatus of his labor – in order to experiment freely with it. . . . The apparatus becomes in a literal sense the subject; this is practically the definition of an automaton. And to the extent to which the apparatus itself becomes the subject, it casts off man as a serving and working being and sets him free as a thinking, knowing, experimenting and playing being. Freedom from the need for the intervention of human service and servitude – that is the law of technological rationality.[26]

The abolition of alienated labour does not imply the abolition of labour itself, which would be neither necessary nor desirable. Whereas under the performance principle, the need to work is 'the . . . introjected necessity to perform productively in order to earn a living',[27] under the new reality principle the (non-repressive) subli-mation of Eros would provide the incentive for work. Work would be cooperatively organised, and redirected towards the satisfaction of real needs, high among which is the creation of a better physical environ-ment which does not depend on the destructive exploitation of nature. Collective ownership and collective control of the means of production and distribution are necessary but not sufficient conditions for the new society. It is the transformation of goals and values, of human needs themselves, which underpins the qualitatively different way of being which Marcuse describes as the 'pacification of existence' – 'the development of man's struggle with man and with nature, under conditions where the competing needs, desires and aspirations are no longer organized by vested interests in domination and scarcity'.[28] The transformation of needs, the education of desire, is thus the lynch-pin of the good society.

It is perhaps significant that Marcuse (like both Bloch and Morris) uses the generic male throughout his writing. For despite the centrality of the transformation of labour in Marcuse's image of the good society, and despite his avowed 'feminism', there is virtually no mention of domestic labour or child-care. The role of automation in the home is not discussed nor, in his twin concerns with ecology and automation, are we offered the self-changing, bio-degradable, disposable nappy. The reduction and transformation of the working day to the extent that work becomes play is not applied to the home front. Indeed, Marcuse views women as relatively free from what Kellner describes as 'repression in the work sphere, brutality in the military sphere, and competition in the social-public sphere', and hence as a repository for the 'creative receptivity' which characterises Eros and will characterise the new sensibility and new reality principle.[29]

Although this accords to women a special role in the process of transformation, as in more recent arguments about the women's movement as a key part of the 'new social forces', it is both less accurate and less flattering than it looks. We can hardly avoid the inference that Marcuse not only grossly underestimates women's participation in (low) paid labour, but regards domestic labour and child-care as activities which are intrinsically satisfying and where the goals and means are not externally prescribed – a supposition at odds with the experience of most women. Shulamith Firestone's broader utopian vision of the liberating potential of technology emphasises the one-sidedness of Marcuse's approach, when she writes:

> The double curse that man should till the soil by the sweat of his brow and that woman should bear in pain and travail would be lifted through technology to make human living for the first time a possibility.[30]

(Indeed, the only male utopian writer to address these issues does so by the alteration of the biological characteristics of parents and children. In the hermaphrodite society described by Gabriel de Foigny in 1676:

> As soon as an Australian has conceived, he quits his apartment and is carried to the Heb, where he is received with testimonies of an extraordinary bounty, and is nourished without being

obliged to work. They have a certain high place, upon which they go to bring forth their child, which is received upon some balsanick leaves; after which the mother (or person that bore it) takes it and rubs it with these leaves, and gives suck, without any appearance of having suffered any pain. They make no use of swaddling clothes or cradles. The milk it receives from the mother gives it so good nourishment, that it suffices without any other food for two years; and the excrements it voids, are in so small a quantity, that it may almost be said, it makes none.[31])

If the underlying values of Marcuse's good society are clear enough, its details are absent. The reasons for this general abstraction and lack of specificity are both similar and diametrically opposed to those influencing Marx. Just as Marx argued that it was not possible to predict the needs that would arise in post-revolutionary society, Marcuse is hesitant to pre-empt the historical process: 'when all present subjective and objective potentialities of development have been unbound, the needs and wants themselves will change' and 'for the first time in our life, we shall be free to think about what we are going to do'.[32] And if the needs of the future cannot be predicted from within the objective and subjective limits imposed by domination, nor can its institutional form be worked out in advance:

> We are still confronted with the demand to state the 'concrete alternative'. The demand is meaningless if it asks for a blueprint of the specific institutions and relationships which would be those of the new society: they cannot be determined a priori; they will develop, in trial and error, as the new society develops.[33]

Marcuse puts a greater distance between present and future than either Marx or Bloch, both of whom see the conditions of future society emerging out of the present. Not only can the new society not 'be the object of theory, for it is to occur as the free creation of the liberated individuals'.[34] The leap into the future is too great to be made even in the imagination:

> If we could form a concrete concept of the alternative today, it would not be that of an alternative; the possibilities of the new society are sufficiently 'abstract,' i.e., removed from and incongruous with the established universe to defy any attempt to identify them in terms of this universe.[35]

However, despite his assertion of the unpredictability of what people might want in a liberated future, Marcuse addressed much more attention to the issue of the transformation of needs than did Marx. For Marcuse, new needs are not just a potential product of revolutionary change but a condition and an integral part of that process. Marcuse's emphasis on the new reality principle and the new complex of needs that it embodies is analogous to Bloch's *docta spes* and Thompson's 'education of desire'; so that whereas Marx and Engels were wary of images of potential futures as possibly counter-revolutionary, Marcuse has no such fears. Images and experiences which anticipate the future state, or indeed merely serve to negate the present, are essential to the possibility of transformation. The future is a realm of possibility – possible liberation, but also possible barbarism with or without nuclear destruction. Negative thinking (i.e. thinking which negates present reality) contains within itself the positive alternative, and guides the praxis which constitutes the transformation. Here Marcuse is closer to Bloch than to Marx, both in his view of the future as indeterminate and in his emphasis on the role of fantasy, imagination and art in sustaining and ultimately realising an alternative way of being.

Real and false needs

One of the defining characteristics of the performance principle is that it generates false needs, whose satisfaction then leads to excessive labour; both the labour and the needs themselves are products of domination. Marcuse is aware that the distinction between true and false needs is problematic. People may experience real satisfaction in the gratification of false needs. Indeed, for Marcuse one of the stabilising characteristics of capitalism is its ability to satisfy the false needs which it creates, although he greatly overestimated the extent to which capitalism does come up with the goods for the mass of the population. Marcuse simultaneously sees the high standard of living which he perceives as increasingly prevalent in the capitalist West as restrictive, presenting individuals with spurious choice, and as affording real benefits. Further, the main reason why the proletariat no longer constitutes a revolutionary class is that it has been bought off in a particularly profound way by becoming incorporated at the level of needs and satisfactions. Thus 'the narrowing of the consumption gap has rendered possible the mental and instinctual coordination of the laboring classes: the majority of organized labor shares the stabilizing, counterrevolutionary needs of the middle classes'.[36] In spite of the fact that people may derive pleasure from the satisfaction of really

143

experienced but nonetheless false needs, the process perpetuates a system which impedes real individual fulfilment. Happiness cannot therefore be used as a criterion of whether the needs being satisfied are true or false; Marcuse argues both that 'happiness is an objective condition which demands more than subjective feelings', and that what passes for happiness is for the most part 'euphoria in unhappiness'.[37]

In one sense, it is easy enough to define false needs. They are 'those which are superimposed upon the individual by particular social interests in his repression: the needs which perpetuate toil, aggressiveness, misery and injustice'.[38] Identifying them is more complex, because they are internalised and experienced as real needs. Marcuse is adamant that they remain false: 'No matter how much such needs may have become the individual's own, reproduced and fortified by the conditions of his existence; no matter how much he identifies with them and finds himself in their satisfaction, they continue to be what they were from the beginning – products of a society whose dominant interest demands repression'.[39] The distinction is historical rather than absolute, just as any complex of needs is itself historical rather than absolute, but it is nonetheless objective. Yet the problem remains: 'What tribunal can possibly claim the authority of decision?'.[40]

In the last analysis, says Marcuse, the decision must be taken by the individuals themselves: indeed, since the definition of false needs lies in their external prescription, this must be so. But only in the last analysis, for how can the choices made in conditions of unfreedom be regarded as free? The eradication of false needs can therefore only come about through praxis, in the process of social transformation:

> Insofar as unfreedom is already present in wants and not just in their gratification, they must be the first to be liberated – not through an act of education or of the moral renewal of man but through an economic and political process encompassing the disposal over the means of production by the community, the reorientation of the productive process towards the needs and wants of the whole society, the shortening of the working day, and the active participation of individuals in the administration as a whole. When all the present subjective and objective potentialities of development have been unbound, the needs and wants themselves will change.[41]

In conditions of freedom the distinction between true and false needs can be made in reality on the basis of reason, the ultimate arbiter.

Marcuse's distinction between true and false needs has been called into question by William Leiss in a general critique of distinctions between different types of needs and wants. Leiss argues that human needs are always and necessarily culturally mediated; capitalism is not alone in the social construction of needs and satifactions. Despite the surface appeal of a distinction between real and manipulated needs it is not clear on what grounds it can be made:

> The critical viewpoint has based its negative judgement of the high-consumption life-style on some form of the distinction between spontaneous vs. artificial or true vs. false needs. The sheer volume of advertising in modern capitalist societies appears to lend this thesis a plausible air. Why else would such an intensive effort at persuasion be necessary? Yet if the socialization process is so intense that the imperatives of the capitalist system market economy itself (the necessity in the productive system for continually expanding the realm of commodities) become internalized as deeply felt needs in the experience of individuals, as Marcuse has argued, are there reasonable grounds for describing them as false?[42]

Such a designation does not so much permit a distinction between different needs experienced within the system, but represents a rejection of the whole society and the needs constructed within it; an alternative society and a concomitant alternative set of 'true' needs exists only hypothetically:

> one may . . . argue that 'the whole is false', i.e., that the entire system of needs thwarts the development of autonomous, self-actualizing individuals who are capable of forming non-exploitative interpersonal relationships. So long as the society as a whole and the majority of persons in it continue to function effectively enough to perpetuate the 'false' system, however, any proposed alternative remains merely an abstract possibility. It may well be an inherently self-destructive system, but only its general collapse would verify the hypothesis.[43]

Leiss identifies two crucial difficulties with this sort of theory. The first is the attempt to deduce 'an objective standard for judging the relative authenticity of felt needs' from human nature, when that nature can only be observed as expressed in the oppressive conditions of the present; Marcuse has recourse to Freud to provide a model of human nature, but it remains contentious. The second is the problem of transition from one complex of needs to another and thus one society to another – in other words, the problem of the education of desire and the agency of social transformation. As Leiss puts it, 'the conundrum for the theory is the difficulty in depicting realistically the stages through which persons who have been conditioned by hetero-genous needs – the consumer demands which actually reflect the market economy's own requirements for continuous expansion – could proceed to the state of autonomy and freedom'.[44]

Before proceeding to a consideration of how Marcuse deals with this second problem it should be noted that Leiss shares much of Marcuse's antipathy to advanced capitalist society, and agrees that 'in our society individuals are encouraged to misinterpret the character of their needs'.[45] In any society, the system of needs that develops does so in interaction with the means potentially available for their satisfaction; as with Bloch's Not Yet, lack and the sense of what would fill it are intimately related. The 'high-intensity market setting' of advanced capitalism orients needs to the consumption of commodities. More-over, commodity production contains an inbuilt tendency towards the proliferation of products ('satisfactions') and thus the proliferation and fragmentation of needs. Even where money is not a problem (and it usually is), ever-expanding 'choice' places a burden of time and knowledge upon the individual struggling to match needs and satisfactions with accuracy. What ensues is not so much a set of false needs as a generally confused state of needing. The resulting high level of material consumption also has negative environmental conse-quences. Leiss thus identifies four negative aspects of the way in which capitalism constructs human needs: first, 'a fragmentation and "destabilization" of the categories of needing'; secondly, 'the difficulty of "matching" the qualities of needs with the characteristics of goods'; thirdly, 'a growing indifference to the qualities of needs or wants'; and fourthly, 'an increasing environmental risk for individuals and for society as a whole'.[46]

The implication is that the system is inherently unstable, not just in ecological terms but because there is a limit to how far such a system can provide satisfaction; Marcuse's assumption that the opposition can simply be bought off through the proliferation of material goods is thus called into question. Leiss agrees with Marcuse that transformation is necessary, the goal being a 'conserver society' entailing an ecological sensitivity which echoes Marcuse's pacification of existence, and a new structure of needs which, again, cannot be specified in advance. And again, the education of desire is central:

> Our essential task is to free the processes for the satisfaction of needs from their tendency to become exclusively oriented to the blandishments of the marketplace. The first priority of social change in the industrialized nations is to initiate this reinterpretation of needs and satisfaction, regardless of whether

the present economy sustains growth or eventually enters a
period of prolonged decline.[47]

The problem of agency

'Between "unfreedom" and emancipation', claimed Marcuse, 'lies not
only the revolution but also the radical transformation of needs'.[48]
Although Leiss's argument raises questions about the distinction
between true and false needs, it underlines rather than challenges the
point that a transformation of needs is entailed in the transition to
unalienated society; it simply means that the evaluation of one set of
needs and satisfactions as intrinsically better than another cannot be
legitimated by appeal to human nature, but entails specific value
judgements. A profound education of desire is involved, at an
ontological as well as a cognitive level, since Marcuse is not positing
the untrammelled expression of the pleasure principle in a Land of
Cokaygne of instant gratification; the new reality principle is still a
reality principle, requiring a certain degree of repression. The role of
the ego within the psyche is still to coordinate and control the impulses
of the id 'so as to minimize conflicts with the reality: to repress
impulses that are incompatible with the reality, to "reconcile" others
with the reality by changing their object, delaying or diverting their
gratification, transforming their mode of gratification . . . and so on'.[49]
Thus the ego at the individual level of the psyche, and reason at the
cognitive and collective level, mediate between the pleasure and
reality principles. A similar process of mutual adjustment between the
desired and the possible is posited by Bloch in the emergence of
concrete from abstract utopia. There are two problems. First, as Leiss
points out, although new needs will emerge in praxis they also have to
be there first, to counteract and override the stablising needs created
by the system. Secondly, there is no obvious agency of social
transformation, especially given Marcuse's assertion that it cannot be
the proletariat.

With respect to needs, Marcuse has two answers. The earlier
answer, dominant in *Eros and Civilisation*, is that Eros, as an aspect of
human nature, represents the pleasure principle and that this provides
the basis for the desire for something better from the world than that
which is offered by capitalism. In other words, there is an inbuilt
tendency for liberatory needs to make themselves felt even in the face
of considerable repression. Repression, however, does mean that the
sphere of expression of Eros is severely limited, and confined to

147

sexuality and to the sphere of imagination and art – and in his more pessimistic moments, domination may threaten to repress the liberatory potential of Eros altogether. In his later writings, notably in *Counterrevolution and Revolt*, Marcuse argued that capitalism was itself inadvertently creating precisely the new needs which could provide the basis for its overthrow. This argument is similar to views advanced from politically disparate positions in the 1970s, that capitalism was suffering from 'cultural contradictions' which were producing a 'legitimation crisis', and is more compatible with Leiss's position.[50] In spite of this shift of view, Marcuse continued to place great emphasis on the role of art in sustaining and cultivating Eros.

Marcuse's view of the role of art is very similar to Bloch's although they differ on the significance of artistic form and on the source of art. For Bloch, the source is the creative aspect of the unconscious; for Marcuse, who accepts Freud's view of the unconscious, art represents the return of the repressed. Nevertheless, both see art as an arena in which an alternative world can be expressed – not in a didactic, descriptive way as in traditional 'utopian' literature, but through the communication of an alternative experience. Art, as the socially sanctioned realm of fantasy, is simultaneously critical of existing reality and anticipatory in that it posits an alternative and thereby acts as a catalyst in transformation. It is a dream of a better world, 'but the dream must become a force of changing rather than dreaming the human condition: it must become a political force'.[51] And it does this through developing an alternative sensibility, an alternative structure of needing: 'Art cannot change the world, but it can contribute to changing the consciousness and drives of the men and women who could change the world'.[52]

Not all art unequivocally serves to negate the present and anticipate the possible future; it is a process dependent upon form, content and context. Even 'great' art can be reduced to decorative visual or aural wallpaper by mass communications and mass marketing and become incorporated into the commodity culture of capitalism, losing its ability to challenge. And art carries the limitations of the context of its production, so that bourgeois art both affirms and negates at the same time; like Bloch, Marcuse is anxious to stress the ambiguity of an art which is produced by bourgeois society but which nevertheless contains the awareness of the human condition which is now becoming possible:

> But bourgeois idealism is not merely ideology, for it expresses a correct objective content. It contains not only the justification of the established form of existence, but also the pain of its

establishment: not only quiescence about what is, but also remembrance of what could be. By making suffering and sorrow into eternal, universal forces, great bourgeois art has continually shattered in the hearts of men the facile resignation of everyday life. By painting in the luminous colors of this world the beauty of men and things and transmundane happiness, it has planted real longing alongside poor consolation and false consecration in the soil of bourgeois life. This art raised pain and sorrow, desperation and loneliness, to the level of metaphysical powers and set individuals against one another and the gods in the nakedness of physical immediacy, beyond all social mediations. This exaggeration contains the higher truth that such a world cannot be changed piecemeal, but only through its destruction. Classical bourgeois art put its ideal forms at such a distance from everyday occurrence that those whose suffering and hope reside in everyday life could only rediscover themselves through a leap into a totally other world.[53]

Marcuse similarly stresses the ambiguous character of religion, echoing Bloch's extended argument that religion is a crucial ground of anticipations of concrete utopia which must be repossessed. Marcuse argues that the idea of the freedom of the soul has been used to excuse, as fundamentally unimportant, material deprivation and suffering, while in reality 'it anticipates the higher truth that in this world a form of social existence is possible in which the economy does not pre-empt the entire life of individuals'.[54] Art expresses the goal of revolution – 'a world of tranquillity and freedom' – in a medium which is not overtly directed towards transforming the world but which encapsulates liberation. Like Bloch, Marcuse offers Beethoven as an example, citing Stravinsky's response:

> Thus Stravinsky heard the revolution in Beethoven's quartets: 'My further personal belief is that the quartets are a charter of human rights, and a perpetually seditious one. . . . A high concept of freedom *is* embodied in the quartets. . . . They are a measure of man . . . and part of the description of the quality of man, and their existence is a guarantee'.[55]

There are differences between the aesthetic theories of Bloch and Marcuse, but they need not detain us here. Both writers regard art as the expression of a wished-for world which has now become possible; both see this expression as essential to the process of transformation, because it offers both vision and experience of an alternative which can then be realised. Art operates therefore on both cognitive and ontological levels, and its role is indispensable.

Marcuse's argument is, however, always rooted in a more concrete analysis of the problems and possibilities of transformation. And since art cannot carry out the revolution by itself, but only through human agency, the question arises as to who the agents might be. Marcuse's problem is that he dismisses the proletariat as a revolutionary agent, because it is incorporated into capitalism through the spread of consumer goods and the cultivation of stabilising needs. The absence of any obvious alternative group to act as the bearer of revolution leads Marcuse to stress the importance of the 'Great Refusal', a general term for opposition which can be seen to be a 'protest against unnecessary repression, the struggle for the ultimate form of freedom – "to live without anxiety" '.[56] Marcuse saw the student movements of the late sixties as part of the refusal, but did not identify students as in any way a new proletariat, in spite of the way many people chose to mis-understand him at the time. For Marcuse, 'no particular class can be the subject of the universal emancipation'.[57] Art, too, forms part of the Great Refusal, even (or perhaps especially) when political action does not follow. It simultaneously negates the present and offers an alternative, just as Bloch argues that wishful thinking in its manifold forms carries the image of a better world in the most inauspicious circumstances. Again, what is distinctive about both writers is their insistence that this image is now an image of a *possible* better world. In spite of the difficulty of specifying the agents and processes of transition (a difficulty which may render them both 'utopian' in the pejorative sense in some people's eyes), both regard utopia (the good society) as no longer utopian (impossible) but as a possible real future within our grasp. And this future will have solved the problem of 'the reconciliation of human beings and nature, of non-alienated labour as creative activity, the creation of human relations freed from the struggle for existence'.[58]

Meanings of utopia

Marcuse, however, uses the concept of utopia quite differently from Bloch, at least until the very end of his life, when he seems to have grasped the usefulness of Bloch's terminology for coping with some of the ambiguities of his own. However, it was not until the mid-seventies that Marcuse used 'concrete utopia' as a positive term to signify the real possibility of utopia; until that point, his use of the term utopia is shifting and elusive. This derives both from his own ambivalence and, more importantly, from a deliberate use of ambiguity to encapsulate the concepts of critical theory; Marcuse sets out to 'subvert and reverse meanings' in order to reveal their ideological potential in customary usage and thus to rupture conventional views of the world.

Five different meanings of the term utopia can be found in Marcuse's work. First, it is used in the classic sense of a non-existent good place, probably one which is impossible, certainly one which is 'outside history'. When used in this sense, however, it is purely descriptive and lacks the sneer of the 'anti-utopian' theorist, Marxist or otherwise. Secondly, it is used to draw attention to the deliberate (ideological) invalidation of real or potential possibilities by their designation as utopian and thus by implication impossible. Thirdly, it is used to refer to a possible good society in the forseeable future – that is, in much the same sense in which Bloch uses the term 'concrete utopia'. Fourthly, Marcuse uses utopia in a sense which withdraws from evaluation, as 'projects for social change which are considered impossible', although this definition itself is accompanied by a distinction between the first and third meanings, i.e. between projects which really are impossible because they '[contradict] certain scientifically established laws' and those which are only provisionally so in that the conditions for their realisation do not immediately exist. This distinction is similar to that made by Mannheim between absolute and relative utopias, although Marcuse is rightly critical of Mannheim's criteria for practical distinction between the categories. It also parallels Bloch's distinction between abstract and concrete utopia – between uneducated but authentic desire which contains substantial elements of purely wishful thinking, and the potentially real possible future which could be grasped. Lastly, the term utopia is used in a slightly different sense in relation to art, especially in *The Aesthetic Dimension*.

The first two uses dominate Marcuse's earlier work. In *Eros and Civilization* the first meaning is most common: Marcuse opens his discussion with the assertion that 'the notion of a non-repressive civilization will be discussed not as abstract and utopian speculation'.[59] The contrast between the free society (possible) and utopia (impossible) is reiterated when he writes that 'utopias are susceptible to unrealistic blueprints; the conditions for a free society are not. They are a matter of reason', and when he refers critically to 'the relegation of human fulfilment' and of human freedom 'to a perpetual utopia'.[60] The inherent problems signalled in the second use are also noted: 'The relegation of real possibilities to the no-man's land of utopia is itself an essential element of the ideology of the performance principle', and the suggestion that utopia is indeed possible is made when Marcuse observes that 'the utopian claims of imagination have become saturated with historical reality'.[61]

Again, in *One Dimensional Man*, Marcuse shifts between using utopia to signal impossibility and both denying the impossibility and pointing to the ideological uses of the accusation. Thus 'the unrealistic sound of these propositions is indicative, not of their utopian character, but of the strength of the forces which prevent their realization'.[62] He explicates the point later:

> We know that destruction is the price of progress as death is the price of life, that renunciation and toil are the prerequisites for gratification and joy, that business must go on, and that the alternatives are Utopian. This ideology belongs to the established societal apparatus; it is a requisite for its continuous functioning and part of its rationality.[63]

Again, 'confronted with the omnipresent efficiency of the given system of life, its alternatives have always appeared utopian'. But then, in reversing the accusation, Marcuse reverts to the 'non-existent and impossible' meaning of the term:

> And insight into necessity, the consciousness of the evil state, will not suffice even at the stage where the accomplishments of science and the level of productivity have eliminated the utopian features of the alternatives – where the established reality rather than its opposite is utopian.[64]

This last quotation encapsulates the deliberately ambiguous use Marcuse makes of the concept of utopia – a use which, in the best tradition of critical theory, requires the reader to question which versions of the world are real, which possible, and whose interests are served by the answers. The same point can be found in *Negations*, where Marcuse also comments on the fact that 'utopian' possibilities which are disallowed in any effective sense may be allowed in art in forms which remove them into a separate sphere of the beautiful. Thus 'what counts as utopia, phantasy and rebellion in the world of fact is allowed in art' because what occurs in art in bourgeois society 'occurs without obligation'. Outside the realm of affirmative culture, the new order both appears as and is denounced as utopia.[65]

It is only in 'The End of Utopia' (1967) that Marcuse actually defines utopia; and his definition embodies the ambiguity already noted in his earlier usage. 'Utopia', says Marcuse, 'is a historical concept':

> It refers to projects for social change that are considered impossible. . . . In the usual discussion of utopia the impossibility of realizing the project of the new society exists

when the subjective and objective factors of a given social
situation stand in the way of the transformation – the so-called
immaturity of the social situation. . . . The project of a social
transformation, however can also be considered unfeasible
because it contradicts certain scientifically established laws. . . .
I believe we can now speak of a utopia only in this latter sense,
namely when a project for social change contradicts real laws of
nature. Only such a project is utopian in the strict sense, that is,
beyond history – but even this 'ahistoricity' has a historical
limit.[66]

Marcuse retains the classical meaning of utopia as an impossible
scheme while arguing that radical transformation necessarily rejected
by the dominant forces of existing society as utopian is in fact a real ·
possibility. As Kellner points out, *One Dimensional Man* presents the
spectre of the end of utopia in the sense that advanced industrial
society invalidates, represses and ultimately prevents the expression
of the need for an alternative order. Here, the end of utopia is hailed
because that which was utopian and is still rejected as such is now
possible: 'the so-called utopian possibilities are not utopian at all'.[67]
And (in *An Essay on Liberation*, in 1979) 'utopian possibilities are
inherent in the technical and technological forces of advanced capitalism and socialism'.[68] Marcuse is quite ready to assert that 'a society
without conflicts would be a utopian idea', clearly meaning that it is
unrealistic; what is attainable, and therefore not utopian, is a society in
which these conflicts 'can be resolved without oppression and
cruelty'.[69] And whereas his usage of the term in 1972 in *Counterrevolution and Revolt* stresses the ideological use of utopia as a means of
invalidation, in the same year he rejected the term, claiming that
'utopian means, if it has any meaning at all, something that can
nowhere be realized'.[70]

Some of this is a deliberate use of multiple meanings to stress the
essentially contested and political nature of the designation utopian.
Some of it, however, is sheer inconsistency. Kellner observes that
Marcuse later shifted to the use of Bloch's term 'concrete utopia' to
signify the 'realizability-in-principle of possibilities ideologically
defamed as "utopian"'.[71] He did this, indeed, in conjunction with the
use of the idea of the 'not yet', in a review of Bahro's *The Alternative in
Eastern Europe*, writing of:

> a socialism that does not yet actually exist. Does 'not yet' exist:
> thus the concrete utopia . . . becomes the guiding thread of the
> empirical analysis . . . [which] . . . reveals that the
> transcendence of utopia is an already existing, real possibility.[72]

The 'not yet' has a longer history in Marcuse's work, however. Not only is it present in *Counterrevolution and Revolt*, where Marcuse asks 'what faculty other than the imagination could invoke the sensuous presence of that which is *not* (yet)',[73] but it can be found as early as 1937 in 'Philosophy and Critical Theory': 'in order to retain what is not yet present as a goal in the present, phantasy is required'.[74] On one occasion at least Marcuse acknowledged Bloch's influence. Martin Jay makes reference to an occasion when 'Bloch . . . embraced Marcuse at a conference in Yugoslavia in 1968 and welcomed him back to the ranks of the utopian optimists'.[75] Both were in their seventies and in the process of becoming fêted as gurus of the student movements in their respective countries. Marcuse's public acknowledgement is instructive:

> I am happy and honoured to talk to you in the presence of Ernst Bloch today, whose work *Geist der Utopie*, published more than forty years ago has influenced at least my generation, and has shown how realistic utopian concepts can be, how close to action, how close to practice.[76]

What is striking is that Marcuse does not mention *The Principle of Hope*. A possible inference is that Marcuse did not read this until the early seventies, whereupon he adopted Bloch's concept of concrete utopia. It is a meaning of the term utopia which Marcuse had identified and used earlier; but he badly needed Bloch's formulation as a way out of the contradictions of his own usage. It is a need which is more acute in his later work where the optimism and claims that utopia is indeed a real possibility become more pronounced, and Marcuse must distinguish between the 'bad' and 'abstract' utopia of mere negation and the 'good' utopia of transcendence. In his last book, *The Aesthetic Dimension*, Marcuse claims that the role of art is to keep alive the possibility of 'an historical alternative – a utopia to be translated into reality'.[77] This, in the end, could provide the motive force for a revolution more profound than any previous revolution – one which would be more genuinely liberatory. Now, it seems, the contradiction of the reality principle is the province of art; and although Marcuse claims that 'the horizon of history is still open',[78] the agency of revolution is a heavy burden for art to carry.

Like most Marxists, Marcuse's orientation to the concept of utopia is to consider it in terms of its relation to the process of social change, since what runs consistently through all his work is a critique of the human consequences of capitalist society and the need for radical transformation. His emphasis therefore is on the function of utopia. But the classical position is one of seeing this function as negative; that is, inhibiting change by diverting energies from the real struggle. Bloch's position, in contrast, is to see the function as positive, in that concrete utopia is a necessary part of and motivation to change. Marcuse's usage both echoes Bloch and contradicts it. Utopia, in the sense of the vision of unalienated society, does indeed have the function of catalysing change and the problem in capitalist society is to keep this vision and the possibilities of change alive. As Geoghegan puts it, 'the faculty of imagination enables one to transcend the given by cognitively creating the future which will then serve as a spur to its practical realisation'.[79] A key part of this process of transformation is the transformation of needs, the education of desire. Abstract utopia does not have this transformative function. Thus far Marcuse substantially agrees with Bloch. But Marcuse makes a further point, made both by Bloch and by Mannheim but here given more emphasis, and that is the function of the designation 'utopian' as distinct from the function of utopia itself. For if the function of utopia is transformation, the function of the designation (which Marcuse's ambiguous usage actually feeds and encourages) is quite the opposite: not to change the world, but to control and subordinate those who seek liberation and reconstruction.

The prime consideration then is the function of utopia. Yet in posing the question of what is really utopian, both in the sense of whether it really poses a challenge to the existing order and in the sense of whether or not it is really impossible, Marcuse must have recourse, as we all must, to content. And the question of what is or is not a utopia, both in the sense of what may be desirable and what may be possible, remains a matter for political debate. Marcuse is quite clear that the desirable is now possible; one has only to overcome the institutional supports of surplus repression to enter the promised land.

7

A hundred flowers:
contemporary utopian studies

In this chapter we turn to the way in which the various issues and
problems already discussed are dealt with in contemporary utopian
studies. Although utopian studies has undergone a dramatic growth
in the last three decades, it remains a relatively new field of academic
study. Moreover, it is interdisciplinary in character, drawing on
literature (in many languages), history, philosophy, architecture,
sociology, politics and religion. In consequence there is a great
diversity of both subject-matter and approach. Such a situation may be
viewed as one of creative disorder or of debilitating confusion. In either
case, there is a problem of identifying the distinctive object of study or
distinctive theoretical approach which characterises the field; the
definition of utopia thus has important implications for its development. The range and diversity of utopian studies means that this
overview can only seek to map the main features of contemporary
scholarship and illustrate the way in which the concept of utopia itself
is defined and deployed.

   Outside academic circles the term utopia is used frequently, but
with very little rigour. Colloquial usage reiterates More's pun: the good
place is no place; utopia is a nice idea but totally unrealistic. Sometimes
the positive connotations are missing altogether and utopian becomes
synonymous with unrealistic. Sometimes utopia is viewed even more
negatively and equated with totalitarianism. Within utopian studies
one would expect both a more positive orientation to utopia and a
greater degree of reflection on the use of the term. Although utopists
are generally more sympathetic to their material than others are, they
often manifest considerable ambivalence to utopia. And although
some regard the question of definition as important, conceptual rigour

is the exception rather than the rule. Many scholars work with a taken-for-granted view of what constitutes utopia; the definition remains implicit. Despite assertions about the importance of the role of utopia in directing social progress – a view common to both Marxist and liberal–humanist approaches – this implicit definition is construed in terms of form and content and frequently identifies utopia with a literary genre.

In terms of approach as well as definition most current research is dominated by the historical orientation of the liberal–humanist tradition. Marxism does not have a high profile within utopian studies, any more than utopia has a high profile within Marxism. But there are some signs of a rapprochement. Marxism, at least within academia, has undergone a partial re-ordering away from economism and is more sympathetic to the importance of ideas (and thus utopia) in the process of social change. The influence of Marxism, often through the Frankfurt School but also through the work of Raymond Williams, has led to a more analytical approach to literary criticism. Some recent work, notably Tom Moylan's *Demand the Impossible*, draws on both traditions in exploring the relationships between literary form, content and function. The availability of English translations of Bloch's work is also likely to encourage this process.

Definition in terms of form also governs the subject-matter of utopian studies. Most work falls into one of two empirical areas, communal societies and utopian literature. This is related to the fact that interest in utopianism has been particularly strong in the USA and in Israel. The US has a strong communitarian tradition; it was and is home to an enormous number of attempts to create 'utopian' communities and the history and analysis of these has provided a rich source of material for scholars. The counter-culture of the late sixties fed an interest in contemporary communes and in the history and theory of communal living, while the expansion of higher education created greater space for reflection on the place of utopia in history and in the modern world. In Israel, the kibbutzim provide similarly extensive material for analysis. The study of utopian literature has also benefited from academic expansion, as well as from the expansion of its primary data. Utopian novels themselves enjoyed something of a resurgence in the 1970s, stimulated particularly by the growth of feminism. However, it also became apparent that there are far more utopian novels in existence than had hitherto been realised; the view of utopian tradition that emerged in earlier decades had barely skimmed the surface. Moreover, as if to emphasise that traditions are always constructs reflecting present concerns projected back into the past, the recovered material includes substantial numbers of utopian novels

157

written by women, some of which are explicitly feminist.

These two areas represent the original concerns of the utopian 'tradition', corresponding to the rough definitions in terms of form and content that are typical of the liberal–humanist approach: utopianism is the attempt to describe in fiction or construct in fact an ideal society. Where attempts to implement utopia are concerned, the focus tends to be on relatively small-scale examples of community building; beyond this lies the world not of utopia but of politics. This is not a necessary feature of the study of utopia, and there are exceptions. Nevertheless, just as contemporary utopias themselves tend to withdraw into the interstices of a seemingly irredeemable actually existing society rather than confidently heralding its transformation, perhaps utopian studies too exhibits a tendency to prefer the study of the small and friendly, rather than the large, unwieldy and ambiguous.

The point is not that utopists are unconcerned with social change or with the function of utopia in bringing this about. But these are not the dominant concerns, and particularly not those which serve to define the concept of utopia or the subject-matter of utopian studies. In many ways, while the field has expanded and has become more analytical, it has done so within the confines of an implicit and habitual definition. In this chapter, therefore, we will look first at what happens when utopia is left undefined. We can then examine the problems that arise from some recent attempts to work with definitions in terms of form, in terms of function and in terms of the relationship between these, in each case considering the implications for the specification of the utopian object.

The absent definition

One of the most recent attempts to provide an encyclopaedic compendium of utopias is the Manuels' *Utopian Thought in the Western World*. This is a hugely ambitious project which covers an enormous range of material, organised into a series of 'constellations' largely on the basis of historical periods and thus similarities of context. The aim is 'to identify historical constellations of utopias with reasonably well marked time–space perimeters and common elements that are striking enough to permit framing generalisations'.[1] Utopia 'proper' begins with Thomas More, although Renaissance utopias also include the Italian designers of ideal cities and the millennial expectations of the Anabaptists and Thomas Münzer. This section is preceded by an account of the 'sources', which includes Judaeo–Christian images of paradise and the classical utopias but not the Celtic myths which Morton argues feed into popular utopias such as the Land of Cokaygne. Renaissance utopias are superseded by the next constellation, which embraces both the pansophist belief in the emergence of a perfect world through knowledge and science (which receives most of the attention given to the seventeenth century) and the ideological turmoil of the English Civil War. The chapters which follow deal mainly with the utopian elements in eighteenth-century French social thought and the system builders of the early nineteenth century. From this point, in the sections on Owenism, Marx and 'Utopia Victoriana' (which includes Morris, who is subsumed under the generalisation that 'no blood was shed in the storybook transition from anarchic industrialism to the agreeable planned society' and 'the Victorian family was preserved intact'), the treatment is much less thorough; brevity is justified on the grounds that 'over the centuries the English utopian tradition has largely gone its own parochial way'.[2]

Although the book is a mine of information, especially on material to which the authors are sympathetic (which does not include Marx or Morris), there are a number of problems in its approach. The book is marred by an underlying psychoanalytic approach derived from Jung, so that there are repeated references to the collective unconscious. We are told that 'creating a utopian world . . . is psychologically a regressive phenomenon for an individual', an attempt to return to the womb.[3] Such an approach to the origins of the utopian impulse leads to a significant amount of space being devoted to the childhood experiences of utopian writers, such as the information that when Robert Owen was a small child 'he stuck his finger into a keyhole and had to cry for help to extricate it' (the implications of which are, mercifully, left to the reader's imagination).[4] It also releases them from the more onerous task of tracing connections between the content and context of utopia. Occasionally we are given a choice of explanation between the psychoanalytic and the material:

> The marked preponderance of oral over sexual pleasures is characteristic of Greek as well as Jewish popular fantasies of utopia, which may either throw light upon their infantile character or bear witness that bread and wine have always been the heaven of the poor and hungry.[5]

A more serious problem in the present context is the failure of the authors to define what they mean by utopia. Without such a definition, what is included, and what is given the most attention, can only be a matter of habit, tradition or personal preference. There is a vagueness of definition about the arrangement into constellations; Davis argues that they are quite arbitrary, and that it is possible to 'rearrange the constellations, querying omissions and redistributing individual works almost at will', so that the book ends up 'by dissolving the history of utopia in a fine mist of blurred categories, tenuous relationships and imprecisely conceived movements'.[6] The origin of this problem is the complete absence of a definition of the utopian object. The Manuels claim the existence of a utopian propensity in 'man', but decline to define their terms more precisely:

Utopia acquires plural meanings in the course of our study, in which we presuppose the existence of a utopian propensity in man. . . . We aim to communicate the diversity of experiences in which this propensity has manifested itself in Western society . . . The utopian propensity is no more equally distributed among men in all times and places than the religious propensity, though it is doubtful if any one is totally devoid of it. There may even be a utopian vocation.[7]

Utopia may be a literary genre, a perfect constitution, a state of mind or 'the religious or scientific foundations of a universal republic'; on the other hand there are references to 'proper' utopias, although these have been so mixed with 'discussions of utopian thought' and 'portrayals of utopian consciousness' that 'the perimeters of the concept of utopia have to be left hazy'.[8] In justifying the inclusion of Hobbes they abandon even these hazy perimeters and say 'in the present work we declare writers to be utopians by sovereign fiat' – a subjective choice influenced largely by reference to form and content, which refuses even to address the obvious problems of such an approach.[9]

Encyclopaedic compendia such as this face particular difficulties beyond the specific and sometimes avoidable weaknesses of any particular examples. The vast expansion of scholarship on individual utopian writers, thinkers and movements means that the wide-ranging knowledge and powers of synthesis required for such projects are increasing. Besides the problem of selectivity which is exacerbated by laxity of definition, any such work is bound to be uneven. For example, both Bloch and the Manuels are quite appalling in their treatment of William Morris, concentrating almost exclusively on *News from Nowhere* and making no reference to available secondary sources; but they deal much better with some other sections of the field. In consequence, few scholars now risk attempting comprehensive coverage in this way but confine themselves to individual studies or to compendia which address a limited field selected on the basis of particular themes, although the 'limited' field may still be very large. Such compendia may be roughly divided into four groups, although there is some overlap between the categories. First, there are studies of the communitarian tradition, which may set geographical or historical boundaries upon their subject-matter and may approach it either descriptively or analytically. Secondly, there are studies of literary utopias, grouped on the basis of country of origin, or date, or some other theme. Thus there are studies of women's utopias, 'critical' utopias, the relationship between utopia and dystopia. In all these cases the inclusion or exclusion of material is decided primarily on the basis of form and content. Thirdly, writers may select an area of political thought such as utopian socialism, early modern utopianism or post- industrialism. Again, the selection of utopian material tends to be conventional, even where the analysis is incisive or where, as in the case of J. C. Davis, there is an explicit attempt to define utopia in a new way.[10] Fourthly, writers may set out to explore the utopian possibilities in contemporary culture (or deplore their absence), either directly or through the critical analysis of other commentators. Elements of this approach of course enter into the other three categories; but it is only with this question that the issue of the function of utopia is foregrounded to the point where it becomes part of the defining characteristic of utopia.

Utopia as form

One of the most interesting attempts at a definition in terms of form occurs in Davis's *Utopia and the Ideal Society*, in which he attempts both a classification of ideal societies and a simultaneous definition of utopia as a category within this. His material is drawn from English utopianism in the sixteenth and seventeenth centuries, thus including More, Bacon, Winstanley and Harrington, among others. Davis differentiates ideal societies in terms of how they deal with the 'scarcity gap', that is the gap between wants and satisfactions which, he contends, all societies, real or imaginary, have to bridge. Thus 'all ideal societies must solve the problem of relating the existing and changing supply of satisfactions, some of which are by nature limited in supply to the wants of a heterogenial [sic] group, the desires of which will be, in some respects, unlimited'.[11] All ideal societies must address this 'collective problem', the 'paucity of satisfactions weakly coordinated with the desires and aspirations of a community of individuals' and the fundamental conflicts and tensions which arise from this mismatch. Davis locates four types of ideal society besides that which he designates as utopia, the fifth and most important type.

The first of these is Cockaygne. This refers, of course, to the medieval folk-poem *The Land of Cokaygne*, which Morton translates into modern English at the end of *The English Utopia*. This poem contains many motifs which are common in earthly paradise myths throughout the world, notably abundant food and water, clement weather, absence of conflict, fountains of youth and difficulty of access. It takes the form of a fantasy, with reference to geese that 'fly roasted on the spit' and 'larks that. . . fly right down into man's mouth, smothered in stew', but also incorporates satirical references to monastic corruption and debauchery (possibly a later addition), as well as including elements from both Christian myths of Eden and Celtic myths of a western paradise.[12] The result is plainly a male utopia in which women are constantly sexually available; Davis rightly, though unwittingly, observes that Cockaygne is characterised by the 'fullest. . . satisfaction of men's appetites',[13] and while Adam's labour is abolished, Eve's is unmentioned. Davis's category of Cockaygne builds on a particular feature of this tradition, namely its provision of unlimited satis-factions. This form of ideal society deals with the scarcity gap by abolishing the shortage of satisfactions and providing enough 'to satiate the grossest appetite'.[14]

Davis's second category of ideal society is Arcadia. Here too we see natural abundance and a temperate climate, but the abundance is a moderate one. Wants do not outstrip satisfactions, not because satisfactions are limitless, but because wants are reduced to a 'natural' level. Arcadia implicitly involves a distinction between true and false needs and abolishes the scarcity gap by limiting true needs to believably available satisfactions. Although Morton describes *News from Nowhere* as a latter-day Cokaygne, in terms of Davis's typology it is plainly arcadian; when we cease to be alienated from our true wants, we will find that there are more than enough satisfactions to go round. Even Marcuse, who, of all the Marxist utopians, comes closest to the Cockaygne model, uses the arcadian device of true needs being materially limited to deal with the problem of scarcity. If Cockaygne deals with the problem by denying the limited supply of satisfactions, arcadia deals with it by denying the unlimited demands made by human wants.

Davis plainly finds both these approaches unsatisfactory, not just intellectually but morally: Cockaygne is grossly indulgent, while arcadia is escapist. Early modern Europeans invented two further forms of ideal society, the perfect moral commonwealth and the millennium. In the perfect moral commonwealth the problem is dealt with by the moral reformation of individuals, so that while existing social and political institutions remained untouched and the scarcity gap persisted, it ceased to be a problem, since no individual would attempt to take more than the system permitted them: 'the collective problem was solved, not by increasing the range or quantity of satisfactions available, but by a personal limitation of appetite to what existed for every group and individual'.[15]

The fourth category is Millennium, which Davis concedes is rather different, since what defines the millenarian approach is not so much the type of society which will ensue (and hence the means of dealing with the scarcity gap), but rather the means of transition to the new society. Peter Worsley uses the term millenarian 'to describe those movements in which there is an expectation of, and preparation for, the coming period of supernatural bliss'. Divine intervention is anticipated but in some cases human activity is also necessary to the change, and this is particularly true of those movements expecting imminent salvation.[16] Davis argues (in my view, wrongly) that the concern of the millenarian is not secular, and the nature of the new society is consigned, along with the process of transition, into the hands of a *deus ex machina*. He adds (rightly) that where images of the good society are spelt out at all in the millenarian vision, they must use at least one of the previous three means of addressing the collective problem. He argues that 'where . . . visualisation of the new society is undertaken by millenarian writers, it tends to assume changes in nature and man which lead to arcadian or perfect moral common-wealth images or a combination of both' – although one might add that there are definite echoes of Cockaygne in some millenarian move-ments, notably Cargo Cults.[17]

None of these constitutes utopia proper. For Davis, none of these approaches is acceptable, since all are unrealistic. 'The utopian is more "realistic" or tough-minded in that he accepts the basic problem as it is: limited satisfactions exposed to unlimited wants', and thus seeks to design a set of political and social institutions to contain the conflicts of interest and potential social disorder which may result from the collective problem.[18] In other words, the scarcity gap is taken as given and utopia becomes merely 'a holding operation' to contain its ill-effects, not a means of abolishing it; it is above all a social and political solution to an intrinsic problem of the human condition. To sum up:

> Arcadia and Cockaygne idealise nature. The perfect moral commonwealth idealises man. The millennium envisages an external power capable of transforming man and nature. The utopian idealises not man nor nature but organisation.[19]

Utopia here is defined principally, but not solely, in terms of form, and additionally in terms of content. Davis is quite explicit that although utopias are sometimes given the form of literary fictions, this is not always so; indeed, in the period on which he concentrates the model constitution was a common form. Nevertheless, they are always descriptions of an ideal society 'conceived as total schemes' and projecting 'a total social environment'.[20] Totality, order and perfection become defining characteristics of the form and content of the utopian object. Utopia is 'distinguished by its approach to the collective problem and its vision of a total, perfect, ordered, environment'.[21]

One might perhaps argue that while the function of such a utopia is ostensibly transformative, its challenge to the present is very limited, and its acceptance of the scarcity gap may have conservative implications. Such a gap cannot simply be taken as given, since needs and wants themselves are socially constructed and, as Leiss has argued, are so constructed in interaction with available means of satisfactions. In any real society the relationship between wants and satisfaction is a dialectical one, not one of an a priori, intrinsically unbridgeable, gap. Marx, Morris, Bloch and Marcuse, it is true, fail to resolve the (perhaps unresolvable) 'tension between seeing needs as historically determined, and at the same time posing the goal of socialism as the creation and satisfaction of *true* needs'.[22] Nevertheless, the recognition of the problem makes it difficult to dismiss as necessarily unrealistic approaches to the ideal society which insist on the radical transformation of needs, of satisfactions, and the relationship between them. To be convincing as a political programme, to be sure, such visions must think through 'the processes of transformation of conditions and needs',[23] but utopias are generally not convincing as political programmes, nor are they necessarily intended to be; the transition to the good society is frequently not addressed, because utopia is the expression of desire, and desire may outstrip hope while not necessarily outstripping possibility.

If Davis's exclusion of Arcadia and Cockaygne from the category of utopia is thus arbitrary and ill-founded, he does nevertheless raise an issue which is very helpful in exploring and comparing utopias. For all must address the scarcity gap – and we should widen the question from how the collective problem of the scarcity gap is dealt with to include how it is conceived in the first place. As a classification of utopias Davis's scheme then has some – if limited – usefulness; as a definition of utopia it is both overly restrictive and profoundly anti-utopian.

A literary genre?

Besides his insistence *contra* the Manuels that definition of utopia is necessary both for the demarcation of the field and for its analysis, Davis justifies his use of the concept with reference to More. It would be quite possible, he argues, to use the term utopia for the whole field of ideal societies; but we would then have to find a new label for the kind of ideal society that accepts the collective problem and seeks to deal with it by political means. But, says Davis, More had already done that; and since 'we have to treat his work as a defining *locus classicus* for the genre',[24] the limited definition of utopia stands. However, there seems little reason to select that aspect of More's *Utopia* as its defining characteristic. Indeed, its assertion of the moderate wants of people in a society based upon community of property fits Davis's category of arcadia. Nor is it clear that we must define utopia with reference to any aspect of More's work, rather than in terms which meet contemporary needs. However, Davis is not alone in using More's name to legitimate a definition of utopia in terms of form. Similar authority is invoked more recently by Krishan Kumar, in *Utopia and Anti-Utopia in Modern Times*.

The central core of Kumar's book is a compellingly argued thesis about the relationship between utopian and dystopian writing in the first half of the twentieth century; these forms are not fundamentally opposed but mutually dependent. Dystopia (or anti-utopia) represents the fear of what the future may hold if we do not act to avert catastrophe, whereas utopia encapsulates the hope of what might be. This relationship is explored with great erudition through the work of Edward Bellamy, H.G. Wells, Aldous Huxley, George Orwell and B. F. Skinner. Kumar notes that there is a perennial problem of distinguishing between utopia and dystopia, illustrated by the reception by some of Huxley's *Brave New World* as utopian and Skinner's *Walden Two* as dystopian, in both cases in opposition to the author's intention. At the beginning of the book, Kumar discusses the definition of utopia and the history of utopia up to the end of the nineteenth century; at the end he addresses the period from 1950–87, and the 'decline' in both utopian and dystopian genres.

Kumar argues that although anti-utopia is the dominant form in the first half of the twentieth century, utopia has undergone a revival. It is however a revival in which both the form of the utopian novel and its intended constituencies are less cohesive and more fragmented than previously. On the one hand, the technological optimism which underpins theories of 'post-industrialism' produced a new wave of utopianism predicated on abundance (and Marcuse, at least at his more optimistic, would fall into this category). On the other hand prophecies of disaster, including ecological and nuclear catastrophe, made optimistic speculation about the future difficult and also influenced the content of these more recent utopias towards 'ecotopia'. Kumar identifies Ursula Le Guin's *The Dispossessed* as the best example of this, although many critics regard Marge Piercy's *Woman on the Edge of Time* as a more significant book. Ecotopia merges with socialism in the work of such writers as Rudolf Bahro, André Gorz and Raymond Williams.[25] In Kumar's view the new novels do not reverse the decline of utopia since, following the pattern of the novel in general, they have retreated into private worlds, concerning themselves with inner space rather than the transformation of the outer public world. They are therefore unable to carry out the utopian function of social transformation.

Kumar defines utopia as a literary genre: 'the utopia is closer to the novel than to any other literary genre; *is* in fact a novel'.[26] Furthermore, and here Kumar echoes Davis, it is a literary genre which was 'invented, more or less single handedly', by More.[27] This is an unequivocal definition in terms of form. Although utopias are primarily interesting for their social and political content rather than their narrative qualities, they differ from model constitutions. Utopia is essentially a novel which shows a society in operation. Form in the sense of literary form, however, is less important than content; since 'the didactic purpose overwhelms any literary aspiration' (which is a polite way of saying that many utopian novels are both badly constructed and badly written!), 'the literary form of utopia is not an important concern of this study, nor perhaps should it be in any serious treatment of utopia'.[28]

Like Davis, Kumar regards utopia as a modern phenomenon. Classical traditions of the golden age and arcadia, ideal cities, Cokaygne, Christian images of paradise and hopes of the millennium are all excluded from utopia 'proper' and are regarded as pre-figurations of it. But Kumar does not, like Davis, hang the definition of utopia either upon the problem of scarcity or the means of its solution; there are utopias of abundance as well as those of scarcity. Nor would he wish to apply the definition rigidly: 'a strict definition of utopia would serve no useful purpose', and 'for some purposes . . . it makes perfectly good sense to discuss as utopias works which are not formally so but are, as it were, in the "utopian mode", products of the utopian imagination or temperament'.[29] Implicity, Kumar accepts that there are limits to the usefulness of definition in terms of form, since function too is important, and this too can be traced back to More:

Thomas More did not just invent the word 'utopia', in a typical witty conflation of two Greek words (*eutopos* = 'good place', *outopos* = 'no place'): he invented the *thing*. Part of that new thing was a new literary form or genre; the other, more important, part was a novel and far-reaching conception of the possibilities of human and social transformation.[30]

If More can be credited with the creation of a literary genre, it is patently absurd to credit any individual with anything as profound, diverse and diffuse as this second element of the utopian 'thing'. Nevertheless, Kumar's broadening of the category is important, and underlines his main thesis: utopia is about hoping for a transformed future, which we may simultaneously hope for while fearing the worst. (Or, to paraphrase Gramsci, if utopia is the optimism of the will, anti-utopia is the pessimism of the intellect.) And Kumar must address the function of utopia to arrive at his conclusion that 'utopia as a form of the social imagination has clearly weakened – whether fatally we cannot say', and to end with the gloomy quotation which concludes Mannheim's *Ideology and Utopia*: 'with the relinquishment of utopias, man would lose his will to shape history and therewith his ability to understand it'.[31]

The definition of utopia as primarily a literary genre and the simultaneous recognition of the inadequacy of this is shared by the field's main bibliographer, Lyman Sargent. For Sargent, utopia is 'a non-existent society described in considerable detail'.[32] This general category can be divided into three, on the basis of the author's intentions. Thus eutopia and dystopia are descriptions meant to be read by a 'contemporaneous reader' as better or worse than their own, while utopian satires are primarily intended as criticisms of contemporary societies. Dystopia, rather than anti-utopia, is used for negative images; Sargent argues that the term anti-utopia 'should be reserved for that large class of works, both fictional and expository, which are directed against Utopia and utopian thought'.[33]

Sargent notes a number of problems, including the possibility of readers misconstruing the author's intentions and the difficulty of deciding what constitutes sufficient detail. Utopia is not limited to the fictional form but where non-fiction is concerned, stricter application is made of the criterion of detail. He makes a further distinction, however, between utopia, which is a text, and ' "utopianism" or "utopian thought" that falls outside the boundaries of the utopia as described above'. Thus he argues:

> We must recognise that in no time period were all the social
> aspirations of a people expressed in a form that fits within the
> boundaries of a literary genre no matter how elastic those

boundaries are to be made. . . . Therefore, if we are to fully understand the utopian vision of a people we must step beyond [texts] . . . to other forms of expression such as religion, architecture and music . . . the social dreaming that we call utopianism exists in every form of human expression.[34]

There is some element in utopia that may be expressed in the form of a text but cannot be confined to this form, and which can be found, as Bloch argued, throughout culture. A definition of utopia not confined to texts would have to address itself to the nature of this common element. For bibliographical purposes, however, the focus on texts is unavoidable and the practical problems concern the differentiation between utopian and non-utopian texts; Sargent's reasons for viewing utopia as a literary genre are more pragmatic than theoretical.

Utopia as function

Kumar's pessimism about the role of utopia in the modern world rests not just on the nature of the contemporary utopian novel (to which we will return), but on a broader consideration of utopian possibilities in contemporary culture. This inevitably shifts the focus from the form to the function of utopia. Among his arguments is the claim that socialism might have functioned as a utopia but fails to do so for two reasons. First, it could do so in so far as it became a religion, but then the decline of religion in the modern world undermines the possibility of utopia. Secondly, and this is the dominant element in Kumar's argument, socialism is doomed as utopia because of the experience of Stalinism, the nature of actually existing socialism and the 'increasing evidence of cynicism and disbelief in Marxism among the intelligentsia of Eastern Europe'.[35] This argument is a familiar one; 'it used to be possible to believe in socialism, but now, when we see what it is really like, it is impossible to do so'.

A similar argument, and a similar pessimism about the prognosis for utopia, can be found in Bauman's *Socialism: The Active Utopia*, published twelve years before *Utopia and Anti-Utopia in Modern Times*. Bauman argues that socialism is *the* utopia of the modern world, and has been so since the early nineteenth century. However, since utopias lose their creative powers once they are realised, socialism is no longer able to fill this space: 'the two centuries of modern socialism's history extend from its majestic advent in the attire of utopia to the incapacitation arising from its alleged realisation'.[36]

However, for Bauman it is not so much the realisation of socialism which is the problem, but the fact that actually existing socialism has failed to measure up to the ideal, and that in many ways it does not fundamentally challenge bourgeois values and institutions:

What . . . took place in the Soviet Union was a modernising revolution, complete with industrialisation and urbanisation, nation-building, construction of a modern state towering over vast domains of public life, ruled by a narrow minority, with the masses engaged in their habitual everyday routine and rarely transcending the confines of common sense.[37]

Indeed, Bauman's critique of a utopia drawn from the reality of the Soviet system reads much like Morris's critique of Bellamy's *Looking Backward*. Bauman writes:

It is no longer a utopia situated on the other side of the industrialisation process. . . . It is now a utopia of industrialisation as such; a capitalist utopia with no room for capitalists, a bourgeois utopia in which the private tycoons of entrepreneurship have been replaced by the smart grey conformity of the bureaucratic octopus, and risky initiative by secure discipline. On the other hand, the morality . . . is bourgeois through and through. It extols, as if following to the letter the Protestant recipe, the virtues of hard work, austerity and thrift; it calls for an enthusiastic self-abandonment in work which bears no resemblance to the liberated, self-propelled creativity painted in bright humanistic colours by people as different as Marx and Weitling.[38]

The effect of this deformation of the socialist utopia has been two-fold. To begin with, it reduces the support for socialism in the West. More than this, though; for, by reinforcing bourgeois values such as progress, work discipline, puritan morality, it cooperates in 'denouncing the aim of dis-alienation and the popular demand for control, which had constituted the uniqueness of the socialist utopia'.[39] Changes in capitalist society have also made socialism a less apposite and powerful counter-cultural critique. For example, Bauman argues, 'it has become an indelible mark of the hegemonic culture to view blatant inequality as injustice, human misery as society's fault'.[40] What is needed then is a new utopia to take the place of socialism, which is directed at both capitalist and socialist realities. Bauman is pessimistic about such a development, fearing that utopia-producers have run out of ideas, and also arguing that the ascendancy over common sense which has been gained by the combined forces of capitalist and socialist bourgeois culture means that, even given the ideas, utopia faces unprecedentedly difficult obstacles.

There are many observations which can be made on Bauman's thesis. The first is that it is not so much the reality of actually existing socialism which undermines the prospects for the socialist utopia in the West, but the ideological representation of it; most people's images are derived from media representation, not reality. That reality is in any case now in such a state of flux that it is unclear whether the eventual outcome will serve to further discredit socialism (as Western governments clearly hope), or whether it will reinforce socialism's utopian potential. Secondly, the argument that capitalist society has been so transformed as to reduce the relevance of socialism sounds less convincing in 1989 after ten years of Thatcherism than it did in 1976 when we could still perceive ourselves as being in an era of consensus politics, even if the consensus was always more limited than is sometimes claimed. Thirdly, the extent to which socialism used to attract mass support can be seriously overstated. Fourthly, the prospects for a utopian counter-culture do not look totally bleak.

What Bauman sought was a utopia which would challenge both capitalism and actually existing socialism and which would have the potential to mobilise popular support. It is interesting to observe that socialist utopias continue to emerge from both actually existing socialism and from capitalism, alongside feminist and green visions of a better future. One can also identify a convergence of themes which might be seen as heralding the new counter-culture which Bauman hopes for. It is characterised by an emphasis on self-management, unalienated labour, ecological responsibility, distributive justice, sexual equality.[41] Nevertheless, Bauman, like Kumar, fears that contemporary utopias do not have the power to enter popular consciousness and mobilise people politically. Increasing political support for the Green movement in Western Europe may be a hopeful sign, although it is already clear that ecological concerns are subject to co-option by the status quo. However, it is plain that for both writers the question of the death of utopia is not just one of whether utopias exist or not, but whether they can carry out the function of transformation. And it is this function which, for Bauman, is central to the definition of utopia.

Bauman argues that utopias have a 'crucial and constructive role in the historical process', a role which can be represented in terms of four functions. First, 'utopias relativise the present', that is they undermine the sense that the way things are is inevitable and immutable by presenting alternative versions of human society. Secondly, 'utopias are those aspects of culture . . . in which the possible extrapolations of the present are explored'. Bauman refers back to Bloch, in observing that utopias ask the question 'what may I hope?' Thirdly, utopias relativise not only the present but the future, by dividing it into a set of competing and class-committed projects and fourthly, utopia does influence action.[42] Bauman is more cautious than some, in qualifying his definition with the words 'in the sense in which it will be used in this study', but describes it as follows. Utopia is:

an image of a future and better world which is:
(1) felt as still unfulfilled and requiring an additional effort to be brought about;
(2) perceived as desirable, as a world not so much bound to come as one which should come;
(3) critical of the existing society; in fact a system of ideas remains utopian and thus able to boost human activity only in so far as it is perceived as representing a system essentially different from, if not antithetical to, the existing one;
(4) involving a measure of hazard; for an image of the future to possess the qualities of utopia, it must be ascertained that it will not come to pass unless fostered by a deliberate collective action.[43]

This definition recalls Mannheim's. Utopia is not to be defined in terms of form but in terms of function. But where Mannheim defined utopia in terms of the idea which, on passing into action, transforms the world, and thus required utopia to be successful, Bauman, like Ricoeur, drops this criterion. Utopia is desired and fought for, but it does not have to be won to be utopia. He also partially abandons the distinction between ideology and utopia, which we have already seen is practically unworkable, and adopts the view which is implicit in Mannheim's own typology of utopias, namely that utopian futures may be pursued by all social classes, since the future becomes the locus of competing class-based projects. The distinction does not disappear entirely, however, since Bauman reiterates the point that to call something utopian it must at least be perceived as radically different from the status quo. This begs the question, as does Mannheim's original distinction, of how great this difference must be.

Kumar defines utopia in terms of form but also addresses himself to the question of the utopian function, suggesting that the form and content of the contemporary utopian novel does not lead to an optimistic view of its political potency. Bauman, perhaps more consistently, and to a substantial extent following Mannheim, regards the function(s) of utopia as the prime concern and thus as the defining characteristic of what is utopian. He too is pessimistic about the survival or reconstitution of utopia as an effective political force, addressing himself to the broader field of contemporary political culture rather than the characteristics of the utopian novel.

Critical utopias

A less pessimistic assessment of the current supply of utopias and their potential to change the world can be found in Tom Moylan's *Demand the Impossible*. Moylan concentrates on utopian novels by four authors: Joanna Russ, Ursula Le Guin, Marge Piercy and Samuel Delaney. Although the focus is on the revival of the literary utopia in the 1970s and thus implicitly identifies utopia with a literary genre and defines it in terms of form, Moylan is mainly concerned with form in a different sense, the literary form of the novel. He claims that these books represent a new genre which he terms the 'critical utopia', which differs in important ways from the 'traditional' literary utopia; and he goes on to argue that there are connections to be traced between the characteristics of the genre and its potential for catalysing social change. Although it is again form which defines utopia, it is function which lends it significance.

According to Moylan the 'critical utopia' differs from its predecessors in both content and literary form. It presents in much greater detail the society of which the utopia constitutes a critique. Utopia itself is presented ambiguously as imperfect, subject to difficulties, inconsistencies, faults, change. And utopia is not a necessary outcome of the present but a possible future, which may or may not be achieved. Indeed, recent novels frequently contain alternative dystopian futures as well as eutopian ones, as warnings of what may come about if appropriate action is not taken. (Thus these utopias in fact combine the key features of both utopian and dystopian genres as indentified by Kumar, underlining Kumar's thesis.) The critical utopia brings into question both whether and how the good society may emerge, as well as the possibility of any society achieving perfection. In novels such as Bellamy's the visitor to the new world is merely an observer, a cipher through whom the new society and the old can be contrasted in a static way. In the critical utopia, the traveller is both more developed as a character and more central to the action of the novel; the active human subject is emphasised both in the structure of the novel and in the processes of transformations from old society to new, and both worlds are backgrounds to the development of character and plot. Thus 'the alternative society and indeed the original society fall back as settings for the foregrounded political quest of the protagonist'. The agency of transformation is collective action, but 'in the critical utopia the . . . heroes of social transformation are presented off-center and usually as characters who are not dominant, white, heterosexual, chauvinist males but female, gay, non-white, and generally operating collectively'.[44] Critical utopias also depart from the unified and representational narrative form typical of Bellamy, Wells and indeed, Morris. They shift backwards and forwards in time, deny its unilinear nature and thus the unidirectional nature of change and causality, and offer alternative futures. They present male and female versions of the same character, and divide characters into multiple parts.

Moylan's central thesis is that these changes in the utopian form are crucial to the survival of the utopian function. The ambiguity of the critical utopia renders it both more exploratory and less open to charges of totalitarianism. Not only does the focus on action make it less static and less boring than the traditional form, but it is less easily negated by dystopia and less easily co-opted to the service of the status quo. In concentrating on action rather than system, it is more capable of performing the consciousness-raising function of representing and stimulating the will to transformation which is a key function of utopia. The critical utopia is thus a transforming force:

> Oppositional cultural practices such as the critical utopias can be understood as part of a broader, ongoing cultural revolution as the dominant mode of production is challenged by the possibility of one that can redirect post-industrial reality towards the goal of human fulfillment.[45]

Bauman views such 'oppositional cultural practices' with more scepticism. He sees 'largely intellectual' cultural criticism as the result of the retreat of socialism from the field of political struggle, and representing a 'divorce between cultural challenge and socialist politics'.[46] Bauman shares Kumar's pessimism, addressing the question of why the utopia of socialism no longer has political potency, and doubting the likely emergence of a new utopia which will mobilise people behind its implementation. Similarly Kumar argues that contemporary utopias fail to capture the imagination of significant numbers of people, whereas substantial social movements were catalysed by Bellamy's *Looking Backward* and the utopian socialists. The connection between cultural and political opposition which is embedded in these different positions is crucial to the question of the function of utopia.

Moylan's enthusiasm about the political potency of oppositional cultural forms in general and the critical utopia in particular depends upon identifying the cultural sphere as the key arena for political struggle and makes no distinction between oppositional and alternative forms. Moylan reiterates an alarming if increasingly common misconception of Gramsci, claiming that Gramsci identified 'the terrain of ideology and culture as *the* [rather than a] major site for contesting the dominant power', and contending that 'under late capitalist conditions economic struggles no longer retain their subversive content'.[47] The issue of how dissatisfaction and even articulate criticism are converted into oppositional and transformative action is, as Bauman recognises, far from simple. However, Moylan assumes a connection, since many of the writers of critical utopias are actively involved in politics, mainly in those movements which would be identified as part of the 'new social forces', and particularly the women's movement. Utopian writers have often written from positions of engagement: Bellamy, Morris and Gilman all did so. But the issue is the effect of the text upon the reader, not the relationship between the text and the author. (This also calls into question whether it should be authorial intent, as Sargent suggests, which is used to categorise literary utopias, or whether the social meaning is of greater consequence.) The emphasis on the importance of utopia as a consciousness-raising device resembles the theme that runs through Bloch, Abensour, Thompson and Marcuse, of the function of utopia as the education of desire. But even if the text operates effectively in terms of the education of desire, this will not automatically be read off into political action. Desire must be transformed into hope, the wish for change into the will for change and the belief that there is an agency available to execute it.

It is the inability to identify any such agency which leads to much of the prevalent pessimism about the possibility of utopia – a problem which Marcuse addressed, once having written off the proletariat, but did not solve. It is, as Boris Frankel points out in his analysis of post-industrial utopians, an area of weakness in contemporary utopian thought; it is also an area of weakness in contemporary socialist thought. Yet if Moylan's failure to address the problem of agency, and his too easy assumption that the raising of consciousness will necessarily lead to political action, render him over-optimistic about the prospects for the realisation of utopia, his argument remains important. Rather than confining his argument to the form or the function of literary utopias, he brings these issues together. The specific question that is highlighted is the relationship between the utopian function of social transformation and the literary form of the contemporary utopian novel. This points us in the direction of a broader question, still insufficiently considered: what is the relationship between utopian form and utopian function?

Possible worlds

Questions of the definition of utopia in terms of both form and function are addressed in more general terms in *The Politics of Utopia*, by Barbara Goodwin and Keith Taylor. This book is not typical of utopian studies as it has recently developed in Britain and the United States, being both more theoretical and less concerned with utopian literature. The authors seek to establish the importance of utopia in relation to both political theory and political practice, that practice ranging from the activities of the nineteenth-century utopian socialists (on whom both authors have written extensively), to the macro-political application in actually existing socialism (utopia writ large) and the micro-political application in the utopian community (utopia writ small). The end of the book also addresses utopian features of contemporary political culture, including feminism and the green movement.

In terms of the issues addressed here the first part of the book, written by Barbara Goodwin, is the most important. She argues that utopia should be regarded as a particular kind of political theory, adopting a form which enables it to perform a specific function. Here again, we have an argument that form and function are connected. The primary function of utopia is to distance us from the present. This view is shared by Bauman, who refers to relativising the present. It is also emphasised as an experiential as well as intellectual process by Moylan who, following Darko Suvin, refers to estrangement as a function of utopia. Suvin defines utopia as 'the verbal construction of a particular quasi-human community where sociopolitical institutions, norms and individual relationships are organized according to a more perfect principle than in the author's community, this construction being based on estrangement arising out of an alternative historical hypothesis'.[48]

In Goodwin's formulation a conceptual break from here and now is made for the purposes of comparison. However, she argues that there are at least six ways in which such a contrast with the present may operate, only one of which is utopian. First, it may involve an idealisation of the past as a criticism of the present, as in the representation of a Golden Age, which has largely conservative implications. Secondly, the present may be justified by reference to a hypothetical past – a feature of contemporary conservatism – or, thirdly, by reference to a hypothetical present, this being the effect of writers as different as John Rawls and Robert Nozick. Fourthly, the present may be inverted for critical purposes, as in Butler's *Erewhon* (or, more recently, Gerd Brantenberg's *The Daughters of Egalia*). Such satires may provide a stimulus towards change but provide no blueprint for it, unlike the fifth category of utopia which carries out a 'constructive criticism of the present via an ideal alternative (future or present)'.[49] In the sixth category we have dystopias such as *Brave New World, 1984* and *We*, and Hayek's *The Road to Serfdom* which, Goodwin argues, justify the present by reference to a worse future.[50]

Criticisms can be levelled at the detail of this typology. In particular, the last category treats dystopias in the same way that Morton does in *The English Utopia*, as apologetics for the status quo rather than as expressions of the fear which, for Kumar, is intimately connected with the utopian impulse itself and which may be deeply critical of the present. What is important for our purposes is that utopia is defined primarily in terms of its function. This function is social criticism, but utopia is differentiated from golden ages and from satire (which also have a critical function) in terms of the form which this criticism takes. This form also involves a second function. Utopia entails criticism through the construction of an alternative and points towards change: 'the defining characteristic of utopianism is that it is a political theory specifically directed towards the creation of human happiness'.[51] The relation between critical and constructive modes underpins much ambivalence towards utopia: we may, she suggests, find it relatively easy to agree on the criticisms of the present (although this depends who 'we' are), but we are almost certain to disagree on the appropriate remedies. This was certainly true of the response of Marx and Engels to the utopian socialists – praise for their critique of capitalism was accompanied by dismissal of their political strategies.

Goodwin's definition of utopia in terms of its form is less clear. Utopia is not identified with a literary genre but with the rather wider category of the social fiction. Historical changes in the content and form of utopia make definition difficult, and mean that it cannot be confined to 'the traditional utopian form' of 'a voyage to a lost island or into the future'.[52] She suggests 'an account of an ideal society' as a preliminary filter, despite finding the phrase 'anodyne and empty'.[53] The condition of such accounts being regarded as utopian is that they constitute 'social criticism through the depiction of an ideal society'. Alternatively, utopia, 'denotes an elaborate vision of "the good life" in a perfect society which is viewed as an integrated totality'.[54] (Moylan and Abensour, for different reasons, question whether recent utopias are intended to represent perfection; Sargent suggests that few utopias are, the goal being simply a very much better society.) The requirements of form are relaxed, however, with the idea of extending the utopianism to include utopian 'elements'. Such elements, if they relate to form, may be merely glimpses of the good life in the good society, rather than an elaboration of it; if they relate to function, they might include any critical elements. The boundaries of utopia have once again dissolved.

The insistence on the critical role of utopia serves to exclude some fictions which might fit in terms of form, including some science fiction and millennial beliefs. Goodwin sees utopias as exercises in speculative theory whose counterfactual nature enables us to criticise and ultimately perhaps to change society. They must therefore be *possible* worlds: 'any proposal must be subject to reasoned justification which draws on our experience of man and society'.[55] A similar point was made by Riesman, when he argued that utopia 'must not violate what we know of nature, including human nature'.[56] However, the degree of possibility assumed by the builders of these worlds varies and is not always clear: they may be intended as intellectual experiments, explorations of possibilities or realisable objectives. Goodwin's aim is to justify the study of utopia as a crucial aspect of social and political theory and thus to counter the objection that utopias are a waste of time because they cannot be realised. (H. G. Wells similarly argued that the creation of utopias and their exhaustive criticism is the proper and distinctive method of sociology.) For the purposes of social criticism only theoretical possibility and internal coherence are necessary, not practical possibility. We are returned to Mannheim's distinction between the relative utopia (which may not be immediately achieveable, but is not intrinsically impossible) and the absolute utopia (which can never be achieved), a distinction echoed by both Bloch and Marcuse.

The issue of practical possibility is less of a problem for Goodwin than for some other commentators because both her defence and her definition of utopia rest upon its function as social criticism. Realisability is therefore unnecessary, although the power of criticism depends on a degree of credibility. However, if the function of utopia is to bring about change, then the question of practical possibility and the problem of transition are real ones. Goodwin's argument about the value of utopias applies here too, and is illustrated by Frankel's *The Post-Industrial Utopians*, a critique of the work of Rudolf Bahro, André Gorz, Alvin Toffler and Barry Jones.[57] Frankel sees utopias as having a range of functions, as suggested by Bauman, but follows Goodwin in arguing that these functions are performed through the specific form of the presentation of political goals as part of an integrated picture of an alternative way of life. However, in so far as utopias are political goals, they must be judged in terms of both their theoretical and their practical possibility, their actual attainability from the here and now. Frankel finds the post-industrialists lamentably lacking both in terms of internal coherence and in terms of the identification of potential agencies of transformation, but the criticism calls for better utopias, not a rejection of the utopian mode. Like Goodwin's, Frankel's definition of utopia draws upon both form and function.

The persisting problem

It is clear that there is no consensus within utopian studies about the meaning of the term utopia and therefore no agreement about the object of analysis. Many writers do not address the issue at all, but even among the most considered explorations of the problem there are wide variations of approach. In 1979, Lyman Sargent wrote that 'some basic agreement on terms would seem to be needed and is not there'; this has not changed in the last decade.[58] It remains the case that most people operate with a loose and implicit definition in terms of form, in which utopia is simply the description of an ideal society, and the inclusion or exclusion of particular cases based on habit, tradition or hunch. Many writers, however, are also concerned with the question 'what is utopia for?' – and 'what will we do without it?', and thus address the question of function while not necessarily seeing this as a defining characteristic. Where an explicit definition is offered it may be in terms of form or function or both, and it depends very much on the particular purposes of the author. Thus Sargent concentrates on the issues of discrimination which confront a bibliographer, while Goodwin focuses on the place of utopia within the academic discipline of political theory. We have a range of definitions, related to a range of different questions, all of which are problematic as general definitions of utopia. In the following chapter, we shall consider whether there is any way forward out of this confusion.

8

Future perfect:
retheorising utopia

The definitions of utopia discussed in this book, and those current in contemporary utopian studies, refer to form, function or content, or some combination of these; thus they may have descriptive, analytic and normative elements. They may lead to broad views of what is utopian, as in the case of the Manuels, or (even more so) Bloch, or to narrow demarcations as in the case of Mannheim or Davis. Further, the broad/narrow distinction cuts across that of defining utopia in terms of form or function; Davis (and to some extent the Manuels) use a definition in terms of form, Bloch and Mannheim concentrate on function. In this final chapter it will be argued that narrow definitions in terms of content or form or function are all undesirable; that any definition must be able to incorporate a wide range of forms, functions and contents; and that therefore a broad definition is essential. This will necessarily leave the boundaries of utopia vague but while this may be problematic, it is greatly less so than the problems which arise from more restrictive definitions.

Any general definition needs to accommodate the fact that utopian scholarship does encompass a wide variety of approaches and questions, and this multi-dimensional approach is itself fruitful. One of the reasons why people work with different definitions of utopia is because they are asking different questions; Davis's desire to understand the institutional means by which seventeenth-century utopians contained the scarcity gap is different from Bauman's interest in what, if anything, will provide a transforming counter-culture in the late twentieth century. Yet although they are totally different questions they are also clearly related; their inclusion within the general field of utopian studies is appropriate because they are both concerned with

179

the imagination of alternative worlds intended to represent a better way of being for the human beings in them. We should be encouraging the pursuit of more and different questions relating to this process of imagining, not attempting to impose orthodoxy; and any attempt at a rigid and narrow definition will have the effect of defining some questions as not properly part of utopian studies. The present absence of consensus, however, results not simply in the peaceful coexistence of different definitions but in competing claims for primacy: less a hundred flowers blooming than a number of weeds seeking to colonise the same habitat. An agreed definition should be sought, but it must be an inclusive one.

Such a definition cannot be cast in terms of content, form or function, because all of these vary considerably. Changes in content are taken for granted, although there is still a temptation to introduce normative elements into definitions of utopia. Several scholars have remarked on the difficulty of tracing the history of utopia or defining it across any substantial timespan precisely because the form is variable. Kumar quotes Nietzsche: 'only that which has no history can be defined'.[1] This is an obstacle to definition in terms of form. It does not present the same problem to those seeking a definition in terms of function who, of course, can accommodate the fact that the form changes; Bloch draws attention to the fact that the form of utopian reaching beyond the present is something which is culturally determined and thus historically and culturally variable. However, definitions in terms of function are not therefore necessarily to be preferred, for they have their own parallel problem, namely that the function of utopia may also vary. The main functions identified are compensation, criticism and change. Compensation is a feature of abstract, 'bad' utopia for Bloch, of all utopia for Marx and Engels and of ideology for Mannheim. Criticism is the main element in Goodwin's definition. Change is crucial for Mannheim, Bauman and Bloch. Utopia may also function as the expression or education of desire, as for Bloch, Morton and Thompson, or to produce estrangement, as for Moylan and Suvin. If we define utopia in terms of one of these functions we can neither describe nor explain the variation.

The definition of utopia in terms of content, form or function not only limits the field of study, but leads to mistaken judgements. The repeated fear that utopia is in decline results from the application of specific narrow views of what constitutes utopia. It also leads us to miss questions which could fruitfully be asked. If both the form and the function of utopia vary with the social and cultural context, what are the conditions which prescribe particular forms and functions for utopia? When does utopia become pure compensation and why? How and when does it become the catalyst of change? And what is the relationship between form and function? We need, then, a definition which will enable us to include utopias taking different forms and performing different functions, and to continue asking different questions about them. The problem still remains, however: what is the thing we call utopia? How far can we identify its boundaries? First, though, we must address the question of why utopias arise.

The utopian impulse?

The essence of utopia seems to be desire – the desire for a different, better way of being. The fact that this is so widespread yet so various in form and content has led several writers to suggest that there exists a utopian propensity in human beings. The Manuels suggest that utopian motifs may be part of a collective unconscious;[2] Bloch explicitly claims that the unconscious is a source of utopian thinking, a claim that this is in some sense an aspect of human nature. It is implicit that the scarcity gap, the gap between needs and satisfactions, is given. Marcuse, too, looks to Eros as a fundamental drive towards utopia. Bloch seems to share with Marcuse the supposition that scarcity in this sense, and thus repression and dissatisfaction, have historically been actually and necessarily present, even if both of them see this situation as now potentially subject to change. According to Geoghegan:

we can speak of a utopian disposition, a utopian impulse or mentality, of which the classic utopia is but one manifestation. This impulse is grounded in the human capacity, and need, for fantasy; the perpetual conscious and unconscious rearranging of reality and one's place in it. It is the attempt to create an environment in which one is truly at ease . . . fantasy would seem to be a constant in any conceivable society.[3]

The idea of a utopian impulse is, however, both unnecessary and unverifiable. The idea of an innate impulse to utopianising is intimately bound up with essentialist definitions of human needs and human nature, which are themselves deeply problematic. Such definitions point towards the existence, if only we could discover it, of some ultimate, universal utopia, and thus the evaluation of actual utopias in terms of how far they measure up to this – that is, in terms of content. However, utopia is a social construct which arises not from a 'natural' impulse subject to social mediation, but as a socially constructed response to an *equally* socially constructed gap between the needs and wants generated by a particular society and the satisfactions available to and distributed by it. *All* aspects of the scarcity gap are social constructs, including the propensity to imagine it away by some means or other.

It is possible to sustain this position without asserting that there is no such thing as human nature and thus actually or apparently denying the fact that human beings are biological organisms with clear and identifiable survival needs, or setting up natural and cultural explanations as antagonists. The suggestion that there is no such thing as human nature is in one sense patently absurd. As Marvin Harris puts it:

> In principle there can be no disagreement that *Homo sapiens* has a nature. . . . A culture-bearing species whose physiology was based on silicon rather than carbon and that had three sexes instead of two, weighed a thousand pounds a specimen, and preferred to eat sand rather than meat would acquire certain habits unlikely to be encountered in any *Homo sapiens* society.[4]

(It would also produce very different utopias.) In another sense, as Leiss argues, the identification of survival needs is not a definition of human nature, even if it is possible to identify these as 'a minimum nutrient intake, proper conditions for retaining or dissipating bodily heat, and socialization experiences to maintain group cohesion in social animals such as man'.[5] These needs are common to many species and are not exclusively human. More importantly, they are expressed at a level of abstraction which obscures the fact that this is not the way in which needs are actually experienced. Needs (whether one's own or those of others) are always experienced as needs for specific concrete objects or processes – objects and processes which not only meet material needs but are given social and symbolic meanings. Thus:

> there is no aspect of our physiological requirements (the famous basic needs for food, shelter, and so forth) that has not always been firmly embedded in a rich tapestry of symbolic mediations. Likewise what are called the higher needs – love, esteem, the pursuit of knowledge and spiritual perfection – also arise within a holistic interpretation of needs and are not separated from the material aspects of existence.[6]

Leiss's point is that the distinction between nature and culture is inappropriate; culture is not something which is added on to human nature, but something which is intrinsically embedded in it. The same point is implicit in Raymond Williams's observation that 'We cannot abstract desire. It is always desire for something specific, in specifically impelling circumstances'.[7] The point is also integral to Leiss's rejection of the distinction between true and false needs: all needs, once concretely expressed, are in a sense artificial in that they are socially constructed, but they remain real needs.

Utopianism, then, has as a precondition a disparity between socially constructed experienced need and socially prescribed and actually available means of satisfaction. To posit a utopian impulse, however, suggests both that it is part of human nature and that therefore it is only the form in which it is expressed which will be historically variable (which is the implication of Bloch's approach). There is no reason to suppose that this is the case – indeed, there is every reason to expect that societies will differ both in the extent to which a gap between needs and available or potential satisfactions is experienced, and in the extent to which there are cultural hypotheses about the potential closure of this gap, as well as in the nature of these hypotheses. If we dispense with the idea of a utopian impulse, we cannot discount the frequently expressed fears of utopia's demise, but we can explore the extent to which this demise is real or an illusion produced by a restrictive definition of utopia combined with a historical shift in the form of its expression.

Utopia versus ideology

The perceived decline in utopia is bound up with a supposition that utopia is intrinsically both oppositional and transformative. This involves assumptions about the function of utopia (to which we will return). It also involves an implicit definition in terms of content. Intuitively, most people are unwilling to include in the category of utopia prognoses or plans as morally offensive as Nazism, although we would no doubt draw the line in different places. There is a normative element in many definitions which excludes evil utopias and regards them as a contradiction in terms. Conversely, such a normative element implies that some utopias are objectively better than others. While such judgements are politically and morally necessary, they are not properly part of a definition of utopia as an analytic category and indeed produce misleading conclusions. The difficulty lies in trying to represent evaluative judgements as objective ones: is the good society more than a matter of personal preference?

Goodwin attempts to provide a solution to this problem by providing an evaluative criterion which does not involve passing judgement on the actual content of the proposed society. The minimal requirement for calling something a utopia is that it should 'have universal scope and offer benefits to all within this frame of reference'. We might then apply a test derived from Rawls, namely whether it is a society in which we would be willing to live irrespective of our position in it. This would exclude any society which subjugated some for the benefit of others.[8] She does not remark on the fact that almost all existing 'utopias' would be excluded, even if this criterion were limited to subjugation on the basis of ascribed characteristics, since most utopias conceived by men, including More's, subjugate women. This illustrates the strength and weakness of Goodwin's proposal. She is undoubtedly correct that if we are to use a criterion of content in the definition of utopia it can only be at a level of abstraction removed from the details of particular social institutions, or we shall be back in the problem that utopia is a matter of taste. In practice, however, in assessing whether any particular utopia meets those abstract criteria, we are in precisely that position, as it is the concrete social arrangements that must be judged against them. The problem is similar to that identified by Leiss in relation to human needs: we can define them in the abstract, perhaps, but they can only be experienced and evaluated in terms of their concrete manifestations; and the shift of level from abstract to concrete alters the nature of the problem.

Our earlier argument that needs, nature and utopia are all equally subject to social construction leads to a similar conclusion. There can be no universal utopia, not just because needs are differently perceived by different observers but because needs actually do vary between societies. If needs are socially constructed, the project of trying to read off the good society from a definition of human nature and human needs is doomed to failure. In one sense this is obvious. But it is notable that most utopians do, in fact, make implicit or explicit claims about human nature; it is difficult to see how a utopia could be constructed otherwise. In theory, the propensity to invent utopias could be eliminated by the removal of the scarcity gap which they seek to bridge. In reality this is a trivial problem, since any complex system of needs is likely to contain contradictory elements both for and between individuals; but the theoretical possibility underpins both the quest for utopia and the anti-utopian objection to utopia on the grounds of totalitarianism. We might argue that to achieve such a fit between needs and satisfactions is the attainment of utopia. Yet this is unsatisfactory; both the anti-utopian and the utopian are driven back to the concept of true needs in the evaluation of actual and imagined societies. Utopias are seen by their opponents as totalitarian because they visibly shape needs and match them with available satisfactions, thus moulding the individual to the system. Against this, some notion of true needs or real human nature is waiting in the wings – often in the form of innate desire as the expression of individual freedom. Desire in the guise of sexual desire is the irrepressible reality which challenges the totalitarian state in all three of the great dystopias, *We, Brave New World* and *Nineteen Eighty-Four*, as well as the outcome of Marcuse's *Eros*. For the utopian, this challenge can only be met by the assertion that the needs constructed in a particular society are indeed the true needs which correspond to 'real' human nature. It is a claim made even by those who clearly and explicitly recognise the historical nature of human needs. The tension between this recognition and the claim that *this* utopia is indeed the good society, what people really need, is particularly acute for Marxist utopians such as Marcuse.

Most utopias are portrayed as universal utopias. This portrayal entails that they necessarily make claims about human nature as a means of legitimising the particular social arrangements prescribed. Indeed, without the criterion of human needs and human nature we have no objective measure for distinguishing the good society from the bad, except the degree of fit between needs and satisfactions; and this does not distinguish happiness in unfreedom, the happiness of the cheerful robot, from 'real' happiness. The appeal to needs is made, in fact, to provide precisely such a (pseudo)-objective criterion, rather than make explicit the values involved in particular constructions of individuals and societies, and present this as what it is – a matter of moral choice. Contemporary literary utopias are, as has been observed by Moylan and by Abensour, more inclined to make the evaluative element in utopia central and explicit; the effect of this is to render such utopias ambiguous. The utopian claim to universality, however, cannot be accepted; and this makes any definition of utopia in terms of content problematic.

But once we abandon the supposition that utopia is both nice and oppositional (not that these are coincident), there is much less reason to suppose that it is in decline. The 'weakening' that is observed is always related to the counter-cultural aspect of utopia, not least because some connection between socialism and utopia is frequently assumed by those for whom the catalysing function of utopia is paramount. Even on the basis of such assumptions the rise of the Green movement in Europe suggests that the decline is overstated (although green issues are subject to co-option by all parts of the political spectrum). However, once we move away from attempts to define utopia in terms of content and abandon Mannheim's distinction between ideology and utopia, we have to recognise that utopias are not the monopoly of the Left. Indeed, even while preserving the definition in terms of function both Mannheim, in his second formulation of the problem, and Bauman see utopias as class-committed projects and thus include utopias of the dominant classes in society. The complaint that the utopian imagination has weakened may simply be a reflection of the fact that the dominant utopias are not recognised as such because utopists find them uncongenial. The rise of the New Right throughout the industrialised West can itself be seen as embodying a utopian project, in which utopia still functions as a catalyst of change. In Britain this has been the politically dominant project for the last ten years, although the rise of the New Right can be dated back to the mid-seventies. The New Right amalgamates two strands of thought in a synthesis which combines liberalism and conservatism. It thus contains two utopias, new versions of the liberal and conservative utopias noted by Mannheim. Although philo-sophically contradictory, with one emphasising the virtues of the free market and nominally espousing minimal state intervention, and the other focusing on a strong state and a unified nation, in practice these are connected at the level of policy through the mutual interdepend-ence of the free market and the strong state. The free market requires state power to prevent incursions by (especially) organised labour and to contain political unrest arising from the operations of the market (viz. the 1984/5 miners' strike); the strong state uses the operations of the free market as a mechanism of social discipline.

As utopias, though, the ideas merit further exploration. It is arguable that such right-wing utopias are not properly to be con-sidered utopias; Ricoeur might argue that they are not oppositional since they do not seek to implement change, whereas Mannheim would see them as sustaining the status quo and thus as ideologies. Quite apart from theoretical objections to these grounds for exclusion, it is empirically incorrect to see such utopias as not seeking or effecting change: they do, even if it is in the direction of increasing the power of already powerful groups and further subordinating the powerless. In any case, this is not how the neo-liberal New Right understands itself. In the mid-seventies its populist appeal was demonstrated by a plethora of groups representing ratepayers and small businesses seeking to reduce taxation and bureaucracy, to get the state off their backs. In the eighties, much has been made of reducing the power of professional groups in education, in medicine, in law, by reference to the notion of 'producer capture', the process whereby (especially) public sector organisations are said to be run in the interests of those who work in them rather than 'consumers'.

In political terms, the neo-liberal New Right sees itself as under-mining the power of entrenched interests and handing power back to 'the people'. In economic terms, too, it encapsulates an image of a good society. The assumption is that a free market is economically the most efficient mode of organising production and consumption, that in the long run it maximises economic growth and that consequently everyone will, in absolute terms, be better off. The poorest members of society also see an increase in their real standard of living, even though inequality may increase so that they are relatively poorer. But neo-liberalism does not recognise the concept of relative poverty, nor is equality of outcome any part of the content of its utopia. The picture is of individuals employed in a free market in which they and the (small) firms which they work for compete and therefore maximise productivity.

Of course capitalism does not work quite like that. Monopolies manipulate markets. The pursuit of profit results both in the pollution and destruction of the environment and in the absolute as well as relative impoverishment of those less able to compete in the labour market. However, the fact that some may judge this as a situation which fails to maximise human happiness does not mean that it is not a utopia. First, its proponents would probably argue that, according to the Rawlsian criterion suggested by Goodwin, it is the best possible system; even those starving in shanty towns in the underdeveloped world are argued to be better off, on the grounds that were it not for capitalism they would not even be alive. Secondly, having already rejected content as a criterion for declaring something utopian or otherwise on the grounds that it is unnecessarily evaluative, we can only say that this is someone else's utopia. We can criticise it in terms of internal coherence, particularly by reference to what it does not address in terms of the more vulnerable members of society. We can even extrapolate it and portray it as dystopia, as does Pete Davies in *The Last Election* or Bill Jordan in *The Common Good*.[9] But utopia it is; and as Mannheim observed of the liberal utopia, one of its tasks is to invalidate the socialist utopia, which it has been doing effectively through the central concepts of efficiency, accountability and freedom.

The neo-conservative utopia is different. It emphasises not the individual and freedom but nation, authority, tradition and loyalty. Again, the neo-conservative utopia has characteristics very like those identified by Mannheim. In particular, he argued that while both liberal and socialist utopias were future-oriented the conservative utopia is oriented to the past. Institutions and practices are value-laden in so far as they represent the past as immanent in the present; their merit is in their persistence. The conservative utopia depends, in Max Weber's terms, on traditional legitimations, while both liberal and socialist utopias depend (most of the time) on legal–rational ones. The meaning of conservatism, as explicated by the Salisbury Group and particularly by Roger Scruton, corresponds closely to Mannheim's description. It arose in opposition to the liberal utopia, as this became increasingly influential in the Conservative Party under Thatcher's leadership; *Conservative Essays* was written expressly to counter the increasingly prevalent view that conservatism was about freedom rather than authority.[10] Scruton himself even exemplifies Mannheim's point that the ideologues of conservatism who articulate their utopias attach themselves to the class interests it serves rather than arising from within the class itself.

The utopian character of the conservative stress on tradition has been elucidated with great elegance by Patrick Wright in *On Living in an Old Country*. Wright discusses at length, in a series of linked essays, how the definition and representation of 'heritage' is used to delineate 'us', the members of the nation, in a way which reinforces old hierarchies and excludes and subordinates some citizens, particularly in terms of race. He also makes the point that this involves the presentation of a utopia:

> In its historical repertoire National heritage borrows many of the trappings of the English utopia . . . but it stages utopia not as a vision of possibilities which reside in the real – nor even as a prophetic if counterfactual perspective on the real – but as a dichotomous realm existing alongside the every day. . . . what much utopianism has alluded to or postulated as the challenge of history – something that needs to be brought about – ends up behind us already accomplished and ready for exhibition as the past.[11]

Utopia refers not simply to a past state, but to the past as immanent in the present. Conservatism is future-oriented only in the sense of preservation and restoration: its purpose is 'to maintain existing inequalities and restore lost ones', and its means 'to command and coerce those who would otherwise reform or destroy'.[12] Again, as with the neo-liberal utopia, some may find this offensive but there is no doubt that there is an image of a desired society here, one where there is unquestioned loyalty to the state (and where trade union activity is seen as a form of subversion), where there is hierarchy, deference, order, centralised power – and, incidentally, where the patriarchal family is the fundamental unit of society and where sexuality outside of this has been eliminated or at least effectively suppressed. It supports the idea of a strong state, particularly in terms of defence and policing, and the issues of national security and the prevention of subversion are paramount.

Both utopias have shown themselves to be much more politically potent in terms of actually effecting change than the oppositional utopias of socialism, ecology or feminism in recent years. The free market utopia is also having a profound impact upon the societies of Eastern Europe. By defining these as utopias rather than ideologies we can ask whether there really has been a decline in the role of utopia in politics or whether, in the struggle between class-committed projects, the utopias of subordinated groups have themselves been sub-ordinated. Mannheim is not alone, however, in seeking to make a distinction between the oppositional views of subordinated groups (utopias, supposing those groups to be rising) and ideologies (the situationally transcendent views by which the ruling classes maintain their domination). One cannot, of course, assume that the rising classes are those who are currently subordinate; in a capitalist society whose level of technological development decreases its need for labour, the rising class may be that which is already in power, with existing power differentials simply increasing. But in any case, one can only reiterate that Mannheim's distinction is untenable. If utopia is the expression of aspirations for a desired way of being, or a future state of society, by an individual or group, then these are clearly utopias. Furthermore they are, like many other utopias, legitimated with reference to claims about human nature.

There may perhaps be those who would exclude these on the grounds that they are not genuinely believed in by those who propagate the views – that the ideas of the New Right represent a cynical manipulation of politics. But one of the features of ideologies (including utopias) is that their proponents genuinely do believe that the social arrangements which are in their interests are also in the interests of the rest of humanity. This is not to deny that utopian images may be used for manipulative purposes. Much advertising uses images of the good life (the idyllic island, the sophisticated life of leisure and consumption, the cosy nuclear family) to sell products. Advertisements work, though, because they key into utopian images which are already present among the audience, reflecting their desires, their lack. Even at this level, the utopias current in a society tell us much about the experience of living in it, because they tell us in a way that we cannot directly ascertain where the felt absences are in people's lives – the spaces, that is, that utopia offers to fill, whether in fantasy or reality.

Hope and desire

If we are seeking a broad definition which permits the consideration of different forms and functions for utopia and which is non-evaluative as to content, the idea of the 'possible world' would seem to be the best option on offer so far. Even this, however, may be too limiting. It is possible for an imagined world to carry out any of the functions of compensation, criticism or change without being possible – even if, in the manner of the Sorelian myth, the results are not always those intended; neither of the New Right utopias are actually possible worlds. To function as criticism or compensation, utopia does not even need to be believed to be possible. Thus while the questions of whether alternative worlds are theoretically or practically possible, and whether they are believed to be so by those who produce, peruse or pursue them, are important questions to ask, again, they cannot be definitive ones. The problem of limiting utopia to the 'possible world' is that it conflates the categories of hope and desire. It limits utopia to the question 'what may I hope?', and refuses the question 'what may I dream?'. It implies also that the function of utopia is necessarily that of change; and indeed, for Bloch, hope was just that – a means of grasping and effecting the hoped-for future.

But if we examine a utopia such as *The Land of Cokaygne*, the question of possibility seems beside the point. There are rivers of oil, milk, honey and wine, as well as healing springs and springs of wine. The garlic-dressed geese that fly roasted on the spit and the cinnamon-flavoured larks flying into the mouth do indeed, in Riesman's terms, 'violate what we know of nature'.[13] So too does the much later song 'The Big Rock Candy Mountains' with its little streams of alcohol, its lakes of stew and whisky, where 'The jails are made of tin, And you can bust right out again As soon as they put you in'.[14] Not only are these fantasies both theoretically and practically impossible – in other words, they are not possible worlds – but we have every reason to suppose that audiences knew this to be the case. Medieval peasants did not believe that larks could fly when cooked. American hobos did not believe in alcoholic lakes or totally ineffective jails. Yet both these examples are expressions of desire – desire for the effortless gratification of need and the absence of restrictive sanctions; they are not expressions of hope. Not all utopias of the Cokaygne type are self-conscious fantasies: Cargo Cults expect 'cargo' (material wealth) to be brought to them, it having (typically) been intercepted by white colonists.[15] An expectation of plenty is predicated on a millennial transformation, the beliefs arising from an amalgam of indigenous and Christian myths. Again, the beliefs of Cargo Cults would have to be

190

said to violate what *we* 'know' of nature, though not what their followers 'know'; but in this case, they express both desire and hope. The distinction between hope and desire reflects too on the location of utopia. Some writers see utopia as necessarily located in the future – mainly because this is the appropriate location when the function of utopia is to catalyse change. But early utopias – and this includes Thomas More's – were more commonly located elsewhere in space, on remote islands or, in some cases, on the peaks of high mountains, or in mountain valleys, such as Shangri-La. Cokaygne was 'out to sea, far west of Spain', sharing its location with the Celtic paradise. On the medieval Mappa Mundi in Hereford Cathedral, Eden is depicted as an island in the East. If utopia is hoped for, then it must indeed be set in the future; but if it is merely the expression of desire, or a criticism of existing conditions, then this is not necessary.

When utopia is compensatory or expressive then the issue of possibility is beside the point. If its function is critical, then theoretical possibility and internal coherence may have some relevance. This is much more true, however, in the context in which Goodwin is defending the merits of utopia, that is within the discipline of political science, where utopia is an intellectual device. In a broader context, consistency may be less crucial: given the lack of consistency of most people's beliefs, it is not clear that estrangement, the education of desire or political criticism require this characteristic of an alternative world. At most, they require that the inconsistencies are not made too obvious. When the function of utopia is to catalyse change, then of course the issue of practical possibility becomes salient. But even here, utopia does not need to *be* practically possible; it merely needs to be believed to be so to mobilise people to political action. The idea of the possible world, besides presenting enormous problems of defining what is possible, is restrictive as to the form and content of utopia; and these problems arise from treating utopia primarily as an intellectual model.

The issue of perceived possibility is important, though, since it is this that differentiates between desire and hope. Utopia expresses and explores what is desired; under certain conditions it also contains the hope that these desires may be met in reality, rather than merely in fantasy. The essential element in utopia is not hope, but desire – the desire for a better way of being. It involves the imagining of a state of being in which the problems which actually confront us are removed or resolved, often, but not necessarily, through the imagining of a state of the world in which the scarcity gap is closed or the 'collective problem' solved. This definition goes beyond that of an alternative world, possible or otherwise. It does so for two reasons. First, the pursuit of a better way of being does not always involve the alteration of external conditions, but may mean the pursuance of spiritual or psychological states; and again, the question of what governs such changes is an interesting one. The pursuit of individual psychological and physical 'fitness' in contemporary society can be seen as one aspect of a withdrawal of utopia from the social to the personal. Secondly, the definition is intended to be analytic rather than descriptive, and thus to include the utopian aspects of a wide range of cultural forms and behaviours. In other words, the subject-matter is not defined in terms of form, but neither is utopia limited to a specific function. Using such a broad definition makes it possible to address questions which are otherwise closed off. It allows us to explore the ways in which form, function and content interact and are conditioned by the social context of utopia. An illustration of some of these relationships also casts further doubt on the proposition that utopia is in decline.

Utopian transformations

In situations where there is no hope of changing the social and material circumstances, the function of utopia is purely compensatory. It may take the form of a myth of a golden age or an other-worldly or remote this-worldly paradise. Such myths are common and occur in many cultures, but they are not universal, and thus not evidence of a 'natural' utopian impulse. They also have common themes – of good weather, abundant food and water, magical springs or fruits with healing properties or which give everlasting life. It is not necessary to refer to some misty notion of a collective unconscious to explain these similarities; the concerns of survival, as well as the issues of ageing, pain and death are material circumstances which confront most human societies, albeit always in socially mediated forms. The problem of death is the least soluble of these, which is why both Bloch and Adorno refer to it as the ultimate problem for utopia.[16] The location of these happy lands is always remote – on distant islands, on high mountains, under the hills – in order to explain why everyone is not there, or inaccessibility is achieved by locating them beyond death or in the past.

Goodwin is right to observe that such utopian images, while they may be critical of the present, are typically conservative in implication.[17] And it is for this reason that Mannheim excludes them from the category of utopia and consigns them to that of ideology. They may nevertheless serve as images of the good life, illustrating the kind of society perceived by a particular culture as good; thus these utopias may tell us about the desires current in a particular situation while, through the location, also telling us that this desire was not simultaneously a hope. We also need to recognise that such utopias are often imposed from above and that the different utopias current in a society may be an arena of struggle for definition of the situation, even where they do not, as Bauman claims, turn the future into a set of class-committed projects. Thus Morton's discussion of Cokaygne is enlightening. Both its location in the West and its resolution of the scarcity gap by the expansion of needs may be seen as oppositional to the Christian Eden, located in the East and arcadian in nature.[18] Indeed, one might go further than Morton and suggest that the fact that most earthly paradise myths are arcadian, in that they close the scarcity gap through the assertion that true needs are limited, shows that in terms of content as well as location, they may operate as a means of social control, through the function which utopias have of 'educating desire' or defining needs.

Even where this is not the case – and this is what makes the Cokaygne myth different – the mere fact that these are expressions of desire, or what desire is supposed to be, and not versions of a possible future, liberates the content from the constraint of plausibility. To reiterate, compensatory utopias do not need to be possible or plausible precisely because there is no perceived possibility of attaining this or any other improved situation. For this reason, also, they are unlikely to be located in the future. In one sense, this frees the imagination. If utopias are, as Bauman says, 'shaped . . . under the double pressure of the galvanising feeling of deprivation and the . . . chastening squeeze of . . . stubborn realities',[19] these pressures do not have the same force in all situations. Where utopia is not expected to be realised, one is constrained only by what it is possible to imagine, not by what it is possible to imagine as possible.

Goodwin sees the primary function of utopia as the constructive criticism of the present by reference to a hypothetical future. She also points out that there are prerequisites for the existence of this kind of reconstructive political theory. First, the notion that society is an artefact subject to change by human agency; secondly, that progress is possible; and thirdly, an absence of fatalism.[20] Plainly, without these conditions there is limited scope for oppositional utopias. It is not, however, impossible for such utopias to exist. For utopia to be located in the future at all, then some notion of change, and an agency capable of effecting this, is necessary. But that agency need not be human. And this is the point of the millennialist utopia. Human agency may not be capable of implementing the good society, but a literal *deus ex machina* may be invoked to do so. Davis follows Mannheim in arguing that chiliastic movements seek an experience of perfect time, the state of ecstasy, rather the perfect society.[21] Worsley points out however that even where this appears to be the case (as with the 'Vailala madness'), the behaviour can be interpreted as oppositional.[22] In this case, with the Cargo Cults, it occurs as part of a system of beliefs which is quite definitely oppositional and which does embody images of a utopian future. Millennial beliefs are known to occur most frequently among powerless groups – i.e. groups which perceive themselves, often correctly, as unable to exert control over the course of history without divine intervention. The millennial transition, then, enables utopia to be located in the future as an expression of desire, and frequently also permits action which is at least expressive of opposition in symbolic form, if not instrumental in implementing the desired transition. Chiliasm moves the utopia of desire into the future; but because divine agency is involved, along with a radical break from the present, the content is still relatively free from the constraints of plausibility – and of course plausibility is culturally relative.

Both of Goodwin's first two criteria – the idea that society is a human artefact, and the idea of progress – emerged in the seventeenth century. Davis is quite right that this produced a different kind of utopia, even if it is unhelpful to say that this is the only kind of ideal society worthy of the name. It is from this point that utopias are temporally rather than spatially located, at least in real time. Thus the idea that a new society could be implemented by political means through an ideal constitution emerges only when Goodwin's criteria are met. The transition is not, at first, necessarily a smooth one. Winstanley's *Law of Freedom* was to be imposed from above by Cromwell, while his earlier beliefs were millennial. The all-powerful ruler rather than God may be the redeemer of society (and More's *Utopia* was set up by the benevolent despot, King Utopos), but a radical break is still required. The idea of progress, and thus utopia as the end point of evolutionary change (as in Bellamy's *Looking Backward*) itself occurred more gradually and reached its high point in the nineteenth century. Nevertheless, both belief in human capacity to control society and belief in progress have always been unevenly distributed through society and for many groups, particularly the less powerful, the idea of a radical break before utopia could be implemented remains crucial.

Utopias located in the future and intended as goals, as real projects for the future, are bound by the criterion of perceived possibility in a way that compensatory and millennial utopias are not. This possibility refers to both internal coherence and the possibility of implementation. Again, Bauman is right that socialism, as the dominant oppositional utopia of the nineteenth and early twentieth centuries, depended upon the belief that the utopia of non-alienation could be produced through the collective action of the working class. He is also right that this aspect of the socialist utopia has been weakened. This does not mean that the content of the socialist utopia no longer has power as an expression of desire, rather that contemporary oppositional utopias have undergone yet another transformation as a result of the weakening of the belief in progress and in the extent of human control over society, and a corresponding increase in fatalism. This has particular consequences for socialist utopias, but it has broader implications for the utopian element in contemporary culture in general.

Evolutionary images of time and social change used to be regarded as synonymous with progress. Images of decline, however, are now much more prevalent – both the idea of a gradual slide into a worsening situation and the fear of dramatic and radical collapse caused by social breakdown, nuclear catastrophe or ecological disaster. It is a climate conducive to dystopia, the warning of what will happen if . . . – and there is often little conviction that averting action can be assured. Dystopias are not necessarily fictional in form; neither predictions of the nuclear winter nor fears of the consequences of the destruction of the rain forests, the holes in the ozone layer, the greenhouse effect and the potential melting of the polar ice caps are primarily the material of fiction, although they have given rise to some compelling literary representations, such as Mordecai Roshwald's *Level 7*.[23] Nor were the predictions of ecological disaster that began with *Silent Spring* and continued through the 1960s written as fiction.[24] A sense of decline is not in itself an obstacle to utopianism but it does require that any utopia involves the reversal of this decline and thus a radical break from the present system. This means that, again, the discontinuity between now and utopia has a certain freeing effect on utopia's content. But it is no longer obvious how the utopia is supposed to be arrived at from where we are.

However, it is not the sense of decline that has the most dramatic effect on utopia; many of the most potent oppositional utopias of the past utopias have required a radical break, most obviously in the form of revolution. It is hardly a weakness in *News from Nowhere* that such a break is assumed; indeed, it increases its credibility in comparison with Bellamy's utopia, besides giving greater scope for an image of a qualitatively transformed life. Rather, it is fatalism that is the key issue. Where it is no longer assumed that social organisation is inherently controllable by human agents, or where it is no longer believed that the agents who are in control can themselves be made accountable to the rest of us, much of the motive for the construction of utopias as goals is lost. They cease to be images of a hoped-for future and become again expressions of desire. The role of fantasy increases and utopia is less and less intended as a literal goal, and less bound by constraints of literal plausibility. Sally Miller Gearhart's *The Wanderground* does not rely for its effect upon the reader's belief in the actual possibility of telepathy between human beings and other animals or even trees.[25] Utopia may be critical of present reality, but the transformative element is no longer primary.

The function of utopia thus reverts from that of goal and catalyst of change to one of criticism, and the education of desire, without any necessary move forward into action. It is perhaps this which Bauman identifies as a shift of the locus of opposition into the realm of culture. It is, as we saw in the discussion of Marcuse, something of a last resort to require artistic production to be *the* source of transformative energy in society. Whereas Moylan sees the critical utopia, with its fragmentary structure and ambiguous content, as a positive development in terms of utopia's transformative potential, the reality is otherwise. The ambiguity of utopia is not merely exploratory and open, it is also disillusioned and unconfident (in a way which is not true of the equally exploratory, heuristic utopias of Morris and Gilman). The presentation of alternative futures, multiple possibilities and fragmented images of time reflects a lack of confidence about whether and how a better world can be reached. The representation of the 'heroes of social transformation' as 'female, gay, non-white' rather than 'dominant, white, heterosexual, chauvinist males' makes a political point, but does not satisfactorily address the issue of the transition.[26]

Indeed, this crucial problem of agency which afflicts the contemporary socialist, ecological or feminist utopia is connected to the issue of fatalism. And it is a problem which lies not in the utopian genre, although it has effects there, but in political culture in general. The belief that society is out of control may actually be less prevalent than it was ten years ago. The problem now, at least for the disciples of counter-cultural and oppositional utopias, is that those in control are out of control. There is no sense of who is going to effect change, or how, although such change is seen as imminently necessary, if unfortunately not necessarily imminent. It is predictions of ecological crisis and collapse which provide the sense of urgency. But ever since the abandonment of the assumption that the proletariat would be the agents of revolution, the problem of agency has been acute. We have seen how, once he decided it was not-the-proletariat, Marcuse was unable to substitute convincingly any group or element which would form the basis of opposition. The problem is present in all the post-industrial utopians, reaching its most absurd in Gorz's claim that the revolutionary agent would be a non-class of non-workers.[27] The appeal to a rainbow alliance of groups other than the industrial working class rightly points to the way in which that class, as traditionally constituted and conceived, excludes women, blacks, gays. But the supposition that it therefore would replace the working class as the saviour of us all was always naïve. As Stuart Hall put it (having himself been one of the most influential voices stressing the importance of the 'new social forces'):

> The multiplication of new points of antagonism, which is . . . characteristic of our emerging 'post-industrial' societies, while making available new potential sites of intervention, further fragments the political field, dispersing rather than unifying the different social constituencies.[28]

The problem of agency does not arise because the desire for an alternative has weakened, but because hope depends on the transition appearing to be practically possible. What weakens then is the capacity of utopia to perform a transformative function. And yet, unless one assumes that this is the only function of utopia, there is no reason to infer from this a general weakening of the utopian genre. Politically, this may be symptomatic of serious problems, but those problems are not caused by a dearth of utopias. Rather, there has been another shift in the social role of utopia. The move from compensation to criticism to change has become a move from change to criticism. And this has benefits as well as costs. For the fact that utopia is no longer constrained by the need to appear immediately possible allows a freer exploration of desire. Utopia can be a much deeper exploration of the implications of alternative values than when it must be seen as realistically attainable from the here and now. And most utopias now present the transition as (i) merely possible, rather than inevitable; (ii) involving some kind of radical break from the present, necessary because it is not possible to identify trends in the present which seem likely to lead to utopia; (iii) a very vaguely defined event. The transition does not form a central issue. If it is true, as Kumar observes, that utopias do not have as potent an effect in terms of inspiring people to political action, the problem does not lie in the utopias themselves but in the field where that action should take place.

The edge of utopia

The merits of a broad analytic definition of utopia should by now be clear. In avoiding the normative element in definitions in terms of content, it enables us to see that utopia is not necessarily oppositional. In avoiding the descriptive aspect of definition in terms of form, it enables us to explore the changes in the form of utopia over time and potentially to explore the effect of different forms upon the content and function of utopia. In casting the analytic definition of utopia in terms of the desire for a better way of being rather than in terms of the function of utopia, we can explore both historical changes in the dominant function of utopia and the relationships between content, form, function and indeed the location of utopia, demonstrating that the fear that utopia is dead is unfounded. An inclusive view of what constitutes utopia shows the disappearance of utopia to be an illusion, while simultaneously illuminating the real changes which have taken place. In contrast, more restrictive definitions are always repressive: cast in terms of form, they obscure questions about changes in form; cast in terms of function, questions about changes in function are effectively eliminated; in both cases, questions about the relationship between form and function are not merely unanswerable, but unaskable. In terms of the consequences for the developing field of utopian studies our broad definition allows the inclusion within this domain of wide variety of material and approaches; yet it provides a basis for understanding the common theme of this work, and for identifying utopian elements expressed in different ways across the whole of human culture.

There are however problems which such a definition does not solve, the most important of which is that of the boundaries of the field. Embedded in the conflict between descriptive and analytic definitions is a disagreement about whether utopian studies is to be defined in terms of particular empirical subject-matter or in terms of a particular approach to that subject-matter. The problem of boundaries is greatest in the first case. If utopia is defined descriptively in terms of an empirical object, this intrinsically involves the specification of limits (although in practice the boundaries often dissolve, as for Sargent and Goodwin). Analytic definitions not only do not imply the existence and necessity of boundaries, they suggest their irrelevance. The principle of addressing the utopian aspects of different cultural phenomena implies that there are no limits to the material that can be looked at from this point of view. A consequence of adopting an analytic definition is that the issue of boundaries ceases to be a theoretical problem.

The question of boundaries may nevertheless remain as a practical, rather than a theoretical, issue. It is, for example, impossible to compile a bibliography of utopian texts without criteria which distinguish these from other, 'non-utopian' texts. More generally, since all studies involve a selection of material, without clear criteria there is always the danger that this will be done on the basis of the subjective judgements, prejudices and idiosyncrasies of individual commentators, or on the basis of tradition or collective habit. It is precisely this which led to the neglect for so many years of women's utopian writing. Although narrow definitions, particularly descriptive ones, may seem to be preferable in that they provide more explicit criteria on the basis of which material can be included or excluded they have, as we have seen, serious disadvantages. The solution cannot be to pursue agreement on a narrow definition of utopia. Such agreement will not be achieved, since it cannot encompass the range of questions that are already being asked; and if it were to be achieved, the result would be a thoroughly undesirable repressive orthodoxy. The only solution to these problems lies not in a descriptive definition of utopia, but in greater explicitness about the principles governing the choice of empirical material in particular studies. The definition of utopia as the desire for a better way of being can work only in conjunction with a generally greater degree of conceptual rigour in the identification of different kinds of utopia relevant to the different questions which, it is to be hoped, scholars will continue to ask. Conceptual clarity is not only a more attainable goal than conceptual convergence, it is also a more appropriate one. Of course distinctions can and should still be made between different kinds of utopias on the basis of form, function, location and content. The study of utopia should, however, in-corporate all of these. And if utopia is the repository of desire, we should be wary of suggesting that one mode of its expression is better or more properly utopian than another.

The temptation to make such judgements arises from the difficulty of separating the study of utopia from the quest for utopia, the pursuit of a better world to which many practitioners in the field of utopian studies are also committed. But this is a political question, and the political question is different. Here judgements about the content of utopias, both in terms of their merit and their possibility, are entirely appropriate and concern with utopia's potential role in social trans-formation is central. If utopia arises from desire, the transformation of reality and the realisation of utopia depend upon hope, upon not only wishful thinking but will-full action. The presence of hope affects the nature of utopian expression; but while utopia may keep alive the sense that the here and now is unsatisfactory, and can contribute to the belief that it might be otherwise, it is not the source of hope. If utopia is not to remain 'draped in black', that hope must be recovered – the hope that we may collectively build a world of peace, justice, cooperation and equality in which human creativity can find its full expression. The dream becomes vision only when hope is invested in an agency capable of transformation. The political problem remains the search for that agency and the possibility of hope; and only if we find it will we see our dreams come true.

Notes

Introduction

1. Edward Fitzgerald (1859), *The Rubáiyát of Omar Khayyám*, 1st edn, quatrain 73 (Collins: London, 1953) p. 81.
2. E. M. Kirkpatrick (ed.) (1983), *Chambers Twentieth Century Dictionary* (Chambers: Edinburgh) p. 1433.
3. C. T. Onions (ed.) (1983), *Shorter Oxford English Dictionary* (Book Club Associates and Oxford University Press: Oxford), vol. II, p. 2444.
4. Karl Popper (1961), *The Open Society and its Enemies* (Routledge & Kegan Paul: London) (first published 1945); Friedrich Hayek (1944) *The Road to Serfdom* (Routledge & Kegan Paul: London).
5. George Kateb (1972), *Utopia and its Enemies* (Schocken Books: New York) (first published 1963).
6. Oscar Wilde (1891), 'The Soul of Man under Socialism', in *Selected Essays and Poems* (Penguin: London, 1954) p. 34.

Chapter 1

1. J. C. Davis (1984), 'The History of Utopia: The Chronology of Nowhere', in P. Alexander and R. Gill (eds), *Utopias* (Duckworth: London) p. 2.
2. Moritz Kaufmann (1879), *Utopias* (Kegan Paul: London) p.v.
3. *ibid.*, p. 114.
4. *ibid.*, p. 1.
5. *loc. cit.*
6. *ibid.*, p. 122.
7. *ibid.*, p. 87.
8. *ibid.*, p. 139.
9. *ibid.*, p. 2.
10. *ibid.*, p. 264.
11. *ibid.*, p. 263.

12. Lewis Mumford (1923), *The Story of Utopias: Ideal Commonwealths and Social Myths* (Harrap: London), p. 108.
13. *ibid.*, p. 310.
14. *ibid.*, p. 123.
15. *ibid.*, p. 124.
16. *ibid.*, p. 18.
17. *ibid.*, p. 20.
18. *ibid.*, p. 22.
19. *loc. cit.*
20. *ibid.*, p. 309.
21. *ibid.*, p. 23.
22. *ibid.*, p. 194.
23. *ibid.*, p. 267.
24. *ibid.*, p. 11.
25. *ibid.*, p. 13.
26. *ibid.*, p. 24.
27. *ibid.*, p. 22.
28. Joyce Oramel Hertzler (1922), *The History of Utopian Thought* (Allen & Unwin: London), p. 269.
29. *ibid.*, pp. 64–5.
30. *ibid.*, pp. 1–2.
31. *ibid.*, p. 2.
32. *ibid.*, pp. 2–3.
33. *ibid.*, p. 268.
34. *ibid.*, p. 197.
35. *ibid.*, p. 138.
36. *ibid.*, pp. 83–4.
37. *ibid.*, p. 227.
38. *ibid.*, p. 254.
39. G. Negley and J. M. Patrick (1971), *The Quest for Utopia* (McGrath: Maryland) (first published 1952), p. 8.
40. Harry Ross (1938), *Utopias Old and New* (Nicholas & Watson: London), p. 128.
41. *ibid.*, p. 175.
42. *ibid.*, p. 153.
43. *ibid.*, p. 215.
44. *ibid.*, p. 12.
45. *ibid.*, p. 25.
46. *ibid.*, p. 200.
47. *ibid.*, p. 13.
48. *ibid.*, p. 13.
49. *ibid.*, p. 47.
50. *ibid.*, p. 101.
51. *ibid.*, p. 102.
52. *ibid.*, p. 101.
53. *Timewatch*, BBC 2, 9 August 1989.
54. Marie Louise Berneri (1971), *Journey through Utopia* (Schocken Books: New York) (first published 1950), p. xi.
55. *ibid.*, p. 9.
56. *ibid.*, p. 137.
57. *ibid.*, p. 57.
58. *ibid.*, p. 218.

59. *ibid.*, p. 218.
60. *ibid.*, p. 207.
61. *loc. cit.*
62. *loc. cit.*
63. *ibid.*, p. 209.
64. *ibid.*, p. 219.
65. *ibid.*, p. 309.
66. *ibid.*, p. 317.
67. Negley and Patrick, *op. cit.*, Preface.
68. *loc. cit.*
69. *loc. cit.*
70. *ibid.*, p. 3.
71. *loc. cit.*
72. *ibid.*, p. 5.
73. *ibid.*, p. 2.
74. *ibid.*, p. 3.
75. *ibid.*, p. 252.
76. *ibid.*, p. 257.
77. *loc. cit.*
78. *ibid.*, p. 4.
79. *loc. cit.*
80. A. L. Morton (1969), *The English Utopia* (Lawrence & Wishart: London), (first published 1952), p. 221.
81. *ibid.*, p. 12.
82. *ibid.*, pp. 11, 13.
83. *ibid.*, p. 15.
84. *ibid.*, p. 275.
85. *ibid.*, p. 262.
86. *loc. cit.*
87. *ibid.*, pp. 274–5.
88. William Morris (1924), *A Dream of John Ball* (Longmans, Green: London), pp. 39–40.
89. Morton, *op. cit.*, p. 103.

Chapter 2

The abbreviation MECW is used for the *Collected Works of Marx and Engels* (Lawrence & Wishart: London), 1975 onwards.

1. Martin Buber (1949), *Paths in Utopia* (Routledge & Kegan Paul: London), p. 6.
2. T. Bottomore *et al.* (eds) (1983), *A Dictionary of Marxist Thought* (Basil Blackwell: Oxford).
3. This outline is of necessity very brief. Useful secondary sources on the utopian socialists include B. Goodwin (1978), *Social Science and Utopia* (Harvester: Sussex); K. Taylor (1982), *The Political Ideas of the Utopian Socialists* (Cass: London); B. Goodwin and K. Taylor (1982), *The Politics of Utopia* (Hutchinson: London); F. E. Manuel (1963), *The New World of Saint-Simon* (University of Notre Dame: Paris); M. C. Spencer (1981), *Charles Fourier* (Twayne: Boston); J. F. C. Harrison (1969), *Robert Owen and*

Notes

the *Owenites in Britain and America* (Routledge & Kegan Paul: London); B. Taylor (1983), *Eve and the New Jerusalem* (Virago: London).

4. Cited in Buber, *op. cit.*, p. 17. It is interesting to note that this division of society into producers and parasites, using exactly that terminology, has recently become current among the New Right, where it corresponds to a distinction between the private and public sectors of employment. See D. Edgar, 'The Free and the Good' in R. Levitas (ed.) (1986), *The Ideology of the New Right* (Polity: Cambridge). See also various articles in the *Spectator* by Richard West and others commenting on the support for the National Union of Mineworkers during the 1984/5 strike.

5. Cited in Goodwin, *op. cit.*, p. 41.
6. Cited in Vincent Geoghegan (1987), *Utopianism and Marxism* (Methuen: London), p. 17.
7. *ibid.*, p. 12.
8. B. Ollman (1977), 'Marx's vision of communism', *Critique*, 8, pp. 4–41.
9. See chapter 5.
10. K. Marx, *Economic and Philosophical Manuscripts*, MECW, Vol. 3, p. 296.
11. K. Marx and F. Engels, *The German Ideology*, MECW, Vol. 5, pp. 47, 394.
12. Engels, *Anti-Dühring*, MECW, Vol. 25, p. 278.
13. Marx and Engels, *The German Ideology*, MECW, Vol. 5, p. 76.
14. Cited in Ollman, *op. cit.*, p. 8.
15. Marx, *Grundrisse*, MECW, Vol. 28, p. 530; MECW, Vol. 29, p. 97; A. Schmidt (1971), *The Concept of Nature in Marx* (NLB: London).
16. Marx, *Critique of the Gotha Programme*, MECW, Vol. 24, p. 87.
17. Marx and Engels, *The German Ideology*, MECW, Vol. 5, p. 49.
18. Marx, *Critique of the Gotha Programme*, MECW, Vol. 24, p. 95.
19. Marx and Engels, *Manifesto of the Communist Party*, MECW, Vol. 6, pp. 504–5.
20. Marx (1976), *Capital* (Penguin: Harmondsworth), Vol. 1, p. 614.
21. Marx, *Critique of the Gotha Programme*, MECW, Vol. 24, p. 87.
22. Buber, *op. cit.*, pp. 14, 13.
23. *ibid.*, Foreword, p. 80.
24. *ibid.*, p. 132.
25. *ibid.*, p. 13.
26. The development of Engels's political thought during this period is outlined in Gregory Claeys (1985), 'The Political Ideas of the Young Engels, 1842–1845: Owenism, Chartism and the question of violent revolution in the transition from "Utopian" to "Scientific" Socialism', *History of Political Thought*, Vol. VI, 3, pp. 455–78.
27. Engels, 'Letters from London', MECW, Vol. 3, pp. 385–7.
28. Engels, 'Progress of Social Reform on the Continent', MECW, Vol. 3, p. 407.
29. Engels, 'Description of recently founded communist colonies still in existence', MECW, Vol. 4, pp. 214, 227.
30. *ibid.*, p. 226.
31. Engels, 'Speeches in Elberfeld', MECW, Vol. 4, p. 252.
32. *ibid.*, p. 253.
33. *loc. cit.*
34. Marx, *Economic and Philosophical Manuscripts*, MECW, Vol. 3, pp. 296, 306.
35. *ibid.*, p. 349.
36. K. Marx and F. Engels, *The Holy Family*, MECW, Vol. 4, p. 84.
37. Engels, *The Condition of the Working Class in England*, MECW, Vol. 4, p. 525.

38. *ibid.*, pp. 581–3.
39. Engels to Marx, 17 March 1845, *MECW*, Vol. 38, p. 27.
40. *ibid.*, p. 26.
41. Engels, 'A fragment of Fourier on trade, *MECW*, Vol. 4, pp. 642–3, 613–14.
42. Marx and Engels, *The German Ideology*, *MECW*, Vol. 5, p. 461.
43. Marx, *The Poverty of Philosophy*, *MECW*, Vol. 6, pp. 209–10.
44. Engels to Marx, 19 August 1846, *MECW*, Vol. 38, p. 55.
45. Marx and Engels, *Manifesto of the Communist Party*, *MECW*, Vol. 6, pp. 515–16.
46. *ibid.*, p. 517.
47. *ibid.*, p. 515.
48. Claeys makes a simlar point, see *op. cit.*, p. 472.
49. Marx and Engels, *Manifesto of the Communist Party*, *MECW*, Vol. 6, pp. 515–16.
50. Engels to Marx, 23 September 1852, *MECW*, Vol. 39, p. 192.
51. Marx, *The Eighteenth Brumaire of Louis Bonaparte*, *MECW*, Vol. 11, pp. 110–11.
52. *MECW*, Vol. 11, pp. 573–91 (2 articles written in collaboration with Ernest Jones).
53. Marx to F. A. Sorge, 19 October 1877, in Saul K. Padover (1979), *The Letters of Karl Marx* (Prentice Hall: New Jersey), pp. 319–20.
54. Engels, *Anti-Dühring*, *MECW*, Vol. 25, pp. 186, 253, 279.
55. *ibid.*, pp. 20–21.
56. Engels, added to *Socialism: Utopian and Scientific*, *MECW*, Vol. 25, p. 634.
57. *Anti-Dühring*, *MECW*, Vol. 25, p. 246.
58. *loc. cit.*
59. *ibid.*, pp. 247, 248, 251.
60. Geoghegan, *op. cit.*, p. 27.
61. *ibid.*, p. 54.
62. V. I. Lenin (1975), *What is to be Done?* (Foreign Languages Press: Peking), p. 211.
63. Marx, *MECW*, Vol. 17, p. 79.
64. *Critique of the Gotha Programme*, *MECW*, Vol. 24, p. 93.

Chapter 3

1. J. R. Jennings (1985), *Georges Sorel* (Macmillan: London), p. 158.
2. Richard Vernon (1978), *Commitment and Change: Georges Sorel and the Idea of Revolution* (University of Toronto Press: Toronto), p. 61.
3. See Jennings, *op. cit.*, and Steve Fenton (1984), *Durkheim and Modern Sociology* (Cambridge University Press: Cambridge).
4. John L. Stanley (ed.) (1976), *From Georges Sorel* (Oxford University Press: Oxford), p. 90.
5. Jennings, *op. cit.*, pp. 112–18.
6. Vernon, *op. cit.*, p. 91.
7. *ibid.*, p. 117.
8. *From Georges Sorel*, pp. 90–91.
9. *ibid*, pp. 91, 95.
10. Georges Sorel (1925), *Reflections on Violence*, tr. T. E. Hulme (Allen & Unwin: London), p. 164.
11. *ibid.*, p. 161.

Notes

12. *From Georges Sorel*, pp. 130ff, p. 235.
13. *ibid.*, p. 138.
14. *ibid.*, p. 134–5.
15. Sorel, 'The Decomposition of Marxism', in Irving Louis Horowitz (1961), *Radicalism and the Revolt against Reason: the social theories of Georges Sorel* (Routledge: London), p. 201.
16. Sorel, *Reflections on Violence*, p. 203.
17. *From Georges Sorel*, p. 135.
18. *ibid.*, p. 73.
19. Sorel, *Reflections on Violence*, p. 133.
20. *ibid.*, p. 22.
21. *ibid.*, p. 137.
22. *ibid.*, p. 33.
23. *ibid.*, p. 34.
24. *From Georges Sorel*, p. 147.
25. *ibid.*, p. 75.
26. *ibid.*, pp. 203–4. This quotation is from *Reflections on Violence*, but I have used the translation given in *From Georges Sorel* at this point because the earlier translation of the Bergson quotation makes little sense.
27. *ibid.*, p. 221.
28. Jennings, *op. cit.*, p. 1.
29. Sorel, *Reflections on Violence*, p. 244.
30. Lagardelle, cited in Horowitz, *op. cit.*, p. 201.
31. Karl Mannheim (1979), *Ideology and Utopia* (Routledge & Kegan Paul: London) (first published in English in 1936), p. 173.
32. *ibid.*, p. 176.
33. *ibid.*, p. 185.
34. *ibid.*, p. 184.
35. *ibid.*, p. 175.
36. *ibid.*, p. 177.
37. *ibid.*, p. 184.
38. *ibid.*, pp. 191, 192, 195.
39. *ibid.*, p. 193.
40. *ibid.*, p. 198.
41. *ibid.*, p. 204.
42. Engels, *The Peasant War in Germany*, MECW, Vol. 10, pp. 409, 422, 426.
43. Mannheim, *op, cit.*, p. 200.
44. *ibid.*, p. 205.
45. See Levitas (ed.), *op. cit.*
46. Mannheim, *op. cit.*, pp. 206, 207.
47. *ibid.*, pp. 220, 221.
48. *ibid.*, pp. 223, 222.
49. *ibid.*, p. 236.
50. *ibid.*, p. 175.
51. *ibid.*, p. 185.
52. *ibid.*, p. xxiii.
53. Paul Ricoeur (1986), *Lectures on Ideology and Utopia* (Columbia University Press: New York), pp. 17, 310, *passim*.
54. Mannheim, *op. cit.*, p. 174.
55. Raymond Williams (1980), 'Base and Superstructure in Marxist Cultural Theory', in *Problems in Materialism and Culture* (Verso: London), p. 38.
56. *ibid.*, p. 40.

57. *ibid.*, p. 36.
58. *loc. cit.*
59. *ibid.*, p. 3.
60. Theodor Adorno (1983), *Prisms* (MIT Press: Cambridge, Massachusetts), p. 48.
61. Mannheim, *op. cit.*, p. 141.
62. *ibid.*, pp. 143–4.
63. David Kettler, Volker Meja and Nico Stehr (1984), *Karl Mannheim* (Tavistock: London), esp. pp. 111–113.

Chapter 4

1. Bloch (1986), *The Principle of Hope* (Basil Blackwell: Oxford), p. 15.
2. *ibid.*, p. 33.
3. Stanley Cohen and Laurie Taylor (1978), *Escape Attempts: the theory and practice of resistance to everyday life* (Penguin: London), which also discusses daydreams and fantasies as means of getting through the day.
4. Bloch, *op. cit.*, p. 11.
5. *loc. cit.*
6. *ibid.*, p. 5.
7. *ibid.*, p. 119.
8. *ibid.*, p. 197.
9. *ibid.*, p. 249.
10. *ibid.*, p. 12.
11. W. Hudson (1986), *The Marxist Philosophy of Ernst Bloch* (Macmillan: London), pp. 18–19.
12. Bloch, *op. cit.*, p. 157.
13. *ibid.*, p. 12.
14. *ibid.*, p. 157.
15. *ibid.*, p. 158.
16. Cited in J. Bentley (1982), *Between Marx and Christ* (Verso: London), p. 87.
17. Bloch, *op, cit.*, p. 154.
18. *ibid.*, p. 156.
19. *loc. cit.*
20. Bloch (1987), *Natural Law and Human Dignity* (MIT Press: Cambridge, Massachusetts), p. 220.
21. Bloch, *The Principle of Hope*, p. 1103.
22. *ibid.*, p. 1101.
23. *ibid.*, pp. 1375, 18.
24. *ibid.*, p. 197.
25. *ibid.*, p. 209.
26. *loc. cit.*
27. *loc. cit.*
28. *ibid.*, pp. 155–6.
29. *ibid.*, p. 76.
30. *ibid.*, pp. 9–10.
31. Bloch (1988), *The Utopian Function of Art and Literature* (MIT Press: Cambridge, Massachusetts), p. 42.
32. Bloch, *The Principle of Hope*, p. 1376.
33. See Chapter 2, p. 40 above.

34. Bloch (1970), *The Philosophy of the Future* (Herder & Herder: New York), p. 91.
35. *The Principle of Hope*, p. 17.
36. *loc. cit.*
37. *Natural Law and Human Dignity*, pp. 163, 144.
38. *ibid.*, pp. 164–5.
39. *ibid.*, pp. 167, 168.
40. *ibid.*, p. 156.
41. *ibid.*, p. 203.
42. *ibid.*, p. 222.
43. *ibid.*, pp. 203–4.
44. *ibid.*, p. 280.
45. *The Principle of Hope*, p. 515.
46. M. Solomon (1972), 'Marx and Bloch: Reflections on Utopia and Art', *Telos*, **13**, p. 79.
47. Bloch, *The Principle of Hope*, p. 515.
48. *ibid.*, p. 1288.
49. Hudson, *op. cit.*, p. 51.
50. Z. Bauman (1976), *Socialism: The Active Utopia* (Allen & Unwin: London).
51. Bloch, *The Principle of Hope*, p. 12.
52. *ibid.*, p. 18.
53. Cited in David Drew's introduction to E. Bloch (1985), *Essays in the Philosophy of Music* (Cambridge University Press: Cambridge), p. xl.
54. P. Tillich, 'Critique and Justification of Utopia', in F. E. Manuel (ed.) (1973), *Utopias and Utopian Thought* (Souvenir Press: London), p. 296.
55. *ibid.*, p. 298.
56. Bloch, *Natural Law and Human Dignity*, p. 192.
57. Bentley, *op. cit.*, p. 89.
58. *ibid.*, p. 90.
59. *ibid.*, p. 96.
60. *ibid.*, p. 88.
61. See, for example, J. G. Merquior (1986), *Western Marxism* (Paladin: London).

Chapter 5

1. W. Morris (1905), *News from Nowhere* (Longmans, Green: London), p. 83.
2. *ibid.*, p. 238.
3. Morris, 'Looking Backward', in A. L. Morton (1984), *Political Writings of William Morris* (Lawrence & Wishart: London), pp. 252–3.
4. *loc. cit.*
5. Morris (1907), *A Dream of John Ball* (Longmans, Green: London), p. 39.
6. *ibid.*, p. 41.
7. Bloch, *The Utopian Function of Art and Literature*, p. 71. This section is in fact an excerpt from *The Principle of Hope*, but is one of the points at which the Zipes translation seems preferable.
8. E. P. Thompson (1977), *William Morris: Romantic to Revolutionary* (Merlin Press: London), p. 658.
9. Morris, 'Art under Plutocracy', cited in Thompson, *op, cit.*, p. 642.
10. *ibid.*, p. 647.

Notes

11. Morris, 'The Lesser Arts', in G. D. H. Cole (ed.) (1934), *William Morris: Selected Writings* (Nonesuch Press: London) pp. 514–5.
12. Morris (with E. Belfort Bax) (1893), *Socialism: Its Growth and Outcome* (Swan Sonnenschein: London), p. 278.
13. Cited in Thompson, *op. cit.*, p. 656.
14. Morris, 'The Lesser Arts of Life' and 'The Deeper Meaning of the Struggle', cited in Thompson, *op. cit.*, p. 657.
15. *loc. cit.*
16. Bloch, *The Utopian Function of Art and Literature*, p. 14.
17. Morris, 'How I became a Socialist', cited in Thompson, *op. cit.*, p. 665.
18. R. P. Arnot (1934), *William Morris: A Vindication* (Martin Lawrence: London). More accessible is the same author's *William Morris: The Man and The Myth* (1964) (Lawrence & Wishart: London).
19. Bloch, *The Principle of Hope*, p. 614.
20. *loc. cit.*
21. Morton, *The English Utopia*, p. 282.
22. *ibid.*, p. 20.
23. *ibid.*, p. 221.
24. *ibid.*, p. 213; Thompson, *op. cit.*, pp. 695, 697; P. Anderson (1980), *Arguments Within English Marxism* (Verso: London), p. 158.
25. Thompson, *op. cit.*, p. 785.
26. J. Ruskin, *On the Nature of the Gothic*, quoted in R. Williams (1958), *Culture and Society* (Chatto & Windus: London), p. 147. (All page references are to the 1963 Penguin edition.)
27. Williams, *op. cit.*, pp. 161, 153.
28. *ibid.*, p. 258.
29. *ibid.*, p. 165.
30. See Williams (1979), *Politics and Letters* (Verso: London), pp. 128–9; also *Towards 2000* (1983) (Chatto & Windus: London).
31. Williams, *Culture and Society*, p. 159.
32. Thompson, *op. cit.*, pp. 778–9.
33. *ibid.*, p. 779.
34. *ibid.*, p. 802.
35. P. Meier (1978), *William Morris: The Marxist Dreamer* (Harvester: Sussex), p. 244.
36. *ibid.*, p. 53.
37. *ibid.*, pp. 244, 250, 282–3.
38. *ibid.*, p. 164.
39. *ibid.*, pp. xi, xii, xiii–xiv.
40. *ibid.*, p. 76.
41. *ibid.*, p. 578.
42. J. Goode, 'William Morris and the Dream of Revolution', in J. Lucas (ed.) (1971), *Literature and Politics in the Nineteenth Century* (Methuen: London), pp. 269–70.
43. Morris, *A Dream of John Ball*, p. 3.
44. Goode, *op. cit.*, p. 257.
45. Bloch, *The Principle of Hope*, p. 79.
46. Goode, *op. cit.*, pp. 274, 273.
47. *ibid.*, p. 275.
48. *ibid.*, p. 278.
49. Cited in Jack Zipes's introduction to Bloch, *The Utopian Function of Art and Literature*, p. xxxiii.

50. Goode, *op. cit.*, p. 277.
51. *ibid.*, p. 278.
52. The account of Abensour's work given here is taken from Thompson's discussion: Abensour's discussion of Morris is not available in English.
53. Thompson, *op. cit.*, p. 790.
54. *ibid.*, pp. 790–91.
55. *ibid.*, p. 792.
56. Bloch, *The Utopian Function of Art and Literature*, p. 41.
57. Thompson, *op. cit.*, p. 791.
58. *ibid.*, p. 806.
59. *ibid.*, p. 807.
60. *loc. cit.*
61. Roger Scruton, 'Socialist Enemies of the Earth', *The Times*, 27 March 1984. Scruton was devoting his column to the very excellent exhibition, then at the Institute of Contemporary Arts, on the contemporary relevance of Morris – an exhibition which Scruton describes as a 'rag-bag'.
62. Meier, *op. cit.*, p. 56.
63. Thompson, *op. cit.*, pp. 798–9.
64. Williams (1980), 'Utopia and Science Fiction', in *Problems in Materialism and Culture* (Verso: London).
65. *ibid.*, p. 203.
67. Williams, 'Beyond Actually Existing Socialism', in *Problems in Materialism and Culture*, p. 261.
68. Anderson, *op. cit.*, p. 175.
69. Morris and Bax, *op. cit.*, p. 279.
70. *ibid.*, pp. 17–18.
71. Morris, 'Looking Backward', p. 248.
72. Anderson, *op. cit.*, p. 160.
73. *ibid.*, p. 167.
74. *ibid.*, p. 168.
75. *ibid.*, p. 171.
76. *ibid.*, p. 174.
77. *ibid.*, p. 161.
78. K. Gibran (1964), *The Prophet* (Heinemann: London), p. 60.
79. M. Löwy (1987), 'The Romantic and the Marxist critique of modern civilization', *Theory and Society*, **16**, p. 900.

Chapter 6

1. D. Kellner (1984), *Herbert Marcuse and the Crisis of Marxism* (Macmillan: London), pp. 93, 115.
2. *ibid.*, p. 272.
3. H. Marcuse (1968), 'Philosophy and Critical Theory', in *Negations* (Allen Lane: London), p. 145.
4. *ibid*, p. 135.
5. Kellner, *op. cit.*, pp. 84, 194. Kellner sees this as a crucial problem in Marcuse's approach, preferring Bloch's formulation.
6. Nancy Chodorow, cited in C. Fred Alford (1987), 'Eros and Civilization after thirty years', in *Theory and Society*, **16**, p. 871.
7. K. Marx, *Theses on Feuerbach* (no. 6), *MECW*, Vol. 5, p. 4.
8. Marcuse (1970), *Five Lectures* (Allen Lane: London), p. 8.

Notes

9. *ibid.*, pp. 8–9.
10. *ibid.*, p. 8.
11. Marcuse (1955), *Eros and Civilization* (Vintage Books: New York), p. 84.
12. *ibid.*, p. 33.
13. *ibid.*, p. 34.
14. *Negations*, p. 251.
15. *Five Lectures*, pp. 1–2.
16. *loc. cit.*
17. *Eros and Civilization*, p. 41.
18. *Five Lectures*, p. 8.
19. *Eros and Civilization*, p. 42.
20. *ibid.*, pp. 90–1.
21. See *Five Lectures*, p. 14; *Negations*, pp. xii/xiii; *One Dimensional Man, passim*; Kellner, *op. cit.*, p. 235.
22. Krishan Kumar (1987), *Utopia and Anti-Utopia in Modern Times* (Basil Blackwell: Oxford), *passim*.
23. *Eros and Civilization*, p. 137.
24. 'Marxism and Feminism', cited in Kellner, *op. cit.*, p. 173.
25. Morris, 'Looking Backward', p. 252.
26. Marcuse, *Negations*, p. xix.
27. *An Essay on Liberation* (1970) (Allen Lane: London), p. 91.
28. *One Dimensional Man* (1968) (Sphere Books: London), p. 30.
29. Kellner, *op. cit.*, p. 340.
30. Cited in S. Lefanu (1988), *In the Chinks of the World Machine: Feminism and Science Fiction* (The Women's Press: London), p. 59.
31. Gabriel de Foigny (1676), *Les Aventures de Jacques Sadeur dans la Découverte de la terre Australe*, translated into English as *A New Discovery of Terra Incognita Australis* (1693); cited in Berneri, *op. cit.*, p. 194.
32. Marcuse, *Negations*, p. 193; *An Essay on Liberation*, p. 91.
33. *An Essay on Liberation*, p. 86.
34. 'Philosophy and Critical Theory', *Negations*, p. 135.
35. *An Essay on Liberation*, p. 86.
36. *ibid.*, p. 15.
37. *ibid.*, p. 14; *One Dimensional Man*, p. 22.
38. *One Dimensional Man*, p. 21.
39. *ibid.*, p. 22.
40. *loc. cit.*
41. Marcuse, *Negations*, p. 193.
42. W. Leiss (1978), *The Limits to Satisfaction: on needs and commodities* (Marion Boyars: London), p. 69.
43. *loc. cit.*
44. *ibid.*, pp. 69–70.
45. *ibid.*, p. 7.
46. *ibid.*, p. 98.
47. *ibid.*, p. 136.
48. Marcuse, 'Protosocialism and Late Capitalism: Towards a Theoretical Synthesis Based on Bahro's Analysis', in U. Wolter (ed.) (1980), *Rudolf Bahro: Critical Responses* (M. E. Sharpe: White Plains, New York), p. 28.
49. *Eros and Civilization*, p. 28.
50. D. Bell (1976), *The Cultural Contradictions of Capitalism* (Heinemann: London); J. Habermas (1976), *Legitimation Crisis* (Heinemann: London).
51. Marcuse (1972), *Counterrevolution and Revolt* (Allen Lane: London), p. 102.

52. *The Aesthetic Dimension* (1979) (Macmillan: London), p. 32.
53. *Negations*, pp. 98–9; see also *Counterrevolution and Revolt*, pp. 92–3.
54. *Negations*, p. 109.
55. *Counterrevolution and Revolt*, p. 104.
56. *Eros and Civilization*, p. 136.
57. 'Protosocialism . . .', p. 33.
58. *loc. cit.*
59. *Eros and Civilization*, p. 5.
60. *ibid.*, pp. 206, 214, 211–12.
61. *ibid.*, pp. 136, 141.
62. *One Dimensional Man*, p. 21.
63. *ibid.*, p. 121.
64. *ibid.*, p. 198–9.
65. *Negations*, pp. 114, 143.
66. 'The End of Utopia', *Five Lectures*, p. 63.
67. *ibid.*, p. 69.
68. *An Essay on Liberation*, p. 4.
69. 'The End of Utopia', p. 79.
70. Kellner, *op. cit.*, pp. 324, 470.
71. *loc. cit.*
72. Marcuse, 'Protosocialism . . .', p. 26.
73. *Counterrevolution and Revolt*, p. 96.
74. *Negations*, p. 154.
75. M. Jay (1970), 'The Metapolitics of Utopianism', *Dissent*, xvii, 4, p. 346.
76. Kellner, *op. cit.*, p. 429.
77. Marcuse, *The Aesthetic Dimension*, p. 57.
78. *ibid.*, p. 73.
79. Geoghegan (1981), *Reason and Eros: The Social Theory of Herbert Marcuse* (Pluto Press: London), p. 28.

Chapter 7

1. Frank E. Manuel and Fritzie P. Manuel (1979), *Utopian Thought in the Western World* (Basil Blackwell: Oxford), p. 13.
2. *ibid.*, pp. 760, 693. The section on Morris is grossly misleading and very inaccurate. Of six quotations from *News from Nowhere*, three are inaccurate and all six references are wrong. There is no discussion of the revolutionary transition, and no reference to Thompson's study.
3. *ibid.*, p. 27.
4. *ibid.*, p. 677.
5. *ibid.*, p. 81.
6. J. C. Davis, 'The Chronology of Nowhere', in Peter Alexander and Roger Gill (eds) (1984), *Utopias* (Duckworth: London), pp. 6–7.
7. Manuel and Manuel, *op. cit.*, p. 5.
8. *ibid.*, pp. 4–5.
9. *ibid.*, p. 336.
10. J. C. Davis (1981), *Utopia and the Ideal Society* (Cambridge University Press: Cambridge).
11. *ibid.*, p. 19.
12. Cited in Morton, *op. cit.*, p. 282. See also H. R. Patch (1950), *The Other*

Notes

World according to descriptions in Medieval Literature (Cambridge: Massachusetts). Various spellings of Cokaygne can be found in the literature. I have adopted Morton's use, except where referring specifically to Davis's typology.
13. Davis, *op. cit.*, p. 21.
14. *loc. cit.*
15. *ibid.*, p. 31.
16. Peter Worsley (1968), *The Trumpet Shall Sound* (MacGibbon & Kee: London), p. 12.
17. Davis, *op. cit.*, p. 36.
18. *ibid.*, p. 37.
19. 'The Chronology of Nowhere', p. 9.
20. *Utopia and The Ideal Society*, p. 38.
21. *ibid.*, p. 39.
22. Martin Barker (1983), 'Marxism and the Problem of Needs' (review of Kate Soper (1981), *On Human Needs* (Harvester: Brighton)), in *Radical Philosophy*, **30**, p. 31.
23. Williams, 'Beyond Actually Existing Socialism', p. 261.
24. Davis, 'The Chronology of Nowhere', p. 11.
25. See especially: Rudolf Bahro (1978), *The Alternative in Eastern Europe* (Verso: London); André Gorz, *Farewell to the Working Class* (1982) and *Paths to Paradise* (1985) (Pluto: London); Raymond Williams (1983), *Towards 2000* (Chatto & Windus: London).
26. Kumar, *Utopia and Anti-Utopia in Modern Times*, p. 25.
27. *loc. cit.*
28. *loc. cit.*
29. *ibid.*, pp. 32, 26.
30. *ibid.*, pp. 23–4.
31. *ibid.*, p. 423–4.
32. L. T. Sargent (1988), *British and American Utopian Literature 1516–1985* (Garland Publishing: New York & London), p. xii.
33. Sargent (1975), 'Utopia – The Problem of Definition', *Extrapolation*, **16**, 2, p. 138.
34. Sargent, *British and American Utopian Literature*, p. xiii.
35. Kumar, *op. cit.*, p. 421.
36. Bauman (1976), *Socialism: The Active Utopia* (Allen & Unwin: London), p. 36.
37. *ibid.*, p. 90.
38. *ibid.*, p. 91.
39. *ibid.*, p. 100.
40. *ibid.*, p. 104.
41. See Ruth Levitas (1985), 'Socialism and Utopia', *Sociological Review*, **33**, 3.
42. Bauman, *op. cit.*, pp. 13–16.
43. *ibid.*, p. 17.
44. T. Moylan (1986), *Demand the Impossible* (Methuen: London), p. 45.
45. *ibid.*, p. 51.
46. Bauman, *op. cit.*, p. 104.
47. Moylan, *op. cit.*, p. 208.
48. *ibid.*, p. 33.
49. Barbara Goodwin and Keith Taylor (1982), *The Politics of Utopia* (Hutchinson: London), p. 25.
50. *ibid.*, pp. 22–8.

51. *ibid.*, p. 207.
52. *ibid.*, p. 15.
53. *ibid.*, p. 16.
54. *ibid.*, p. 16.
55. *ibid.*, p. 29.
56. David Riesman (1964), 'Some observations of community plans and utopia' (1954), in *Individualism Reconsidered* (The Free Press: New York), p. 72.
57. Boris Frankel (1987), *The Post-Industrial Utopians* (Polity Press: Cambridge).
58. L. T. Sargent (1982), 'Is There Only One Utopian Tradition?', *Journal of the History of Ideas*, October, p. 689.

Chapter 8

1. Kumar, *op. cit.*, p. 32.
2. Manuel and Manuel, *op. cit.*, p. 14.
3. Geoghegan, *Utopianism and Marxism*, p. 2.
4. Marvin Harris, 'Sociobiology and biological reductionism', in A. Montagu (ed.) (1980), *Sociobiology Examined* (Oxford University Press: Oxford).
5. William Leiss (1978), *The Limits to Satisfaction* (Marion Boyars: London), p. 72.
6. *ibid.*, p. 75.
7. Williams, *Problems in Materialism and Culture*, p. 200.
8. Goodwin and Taylor, *op. cit.*, pp. 18–19.
9. Pete Davies (1986), *The Last Election* (André Deutsch: London); Bill Jordan (1989), *The Common Good* (Basil Blackwell: Oxford). For a fuller discussion of New Right utopias see R. Levitas (1985), 'New Right Utopias', *Radical Philosophy*, **39** or 'Competition and Compliance: the utopias of the New Right' in R. Levitas (ed.), *The Ideology of the New Right*.
10. Maurice Cowling (ed.) (1978), *Conservative Essays* (Cassell: London).
11. Patrick Wright (1985), *On Living in an Old Country* (Verso: London), p. 78.
12. Cowling, *op. cit.*, p. 9; Roger Scruton (1980), *The Meaning of Conservatism* (Penguin: London), p. 25.
13. Riesman, *op. cit.*, p. 72.
14. A version of this is reprinted at the end of Berneri, *op. cit.*
15. See Worsley, *op. cit.*
16. See the discussion between Bloch and Adorno, in Bloch, *The Utopian Function of Art and Literature*. A summary of Bloch's attempt to deal with the problem of death is given in F. Jameson (1971), *Marxism and Form* (Princeton University Press: New Jersey), pp. 135, 143–4.
17. Goodwin and Taylor, *op. cit.*, p. 23.
18. Morton, *op. cit.*, p. 18.
19. Bauman, *op. cit.*, p. 14.
20. Goodwin and Taylor, *op. cit.*, pp. 23–4.
21. Davis, *op. cit.*, p. 31.
22. Worsley, *op. cit.*, ch. 4.
23. Mordecai Roshwald (1981), *Level 7* (Allison & Busby: London) (first published 1959).
24. Rachel Carson (1965), *Silent Spring* (Penguin: London).

25. Sally Miller Gearhart (1985), *The Wanderground* (The Women's Press: London).
26. Moylan, *op. cit.*, p. 45.
27. Gorz, *Farewell to the Working Class, passim.*
28. Stuart Hall (1988), 'Thatcher's Lessons', *Marxism Today*, March, p. 27.

Select bibliography

Adorno, T. (1983), *Prisms* (MIT Press: Cambridge, Mass.).

Albinski, N. B. (1988), *Women's Utopias in British and American Fiction* (Routledge: London and New York).

Alexander, P. and Gill, R. (eds) (1984), *Utopias* (Duckworth: London).

Anderson, P. (1980), *Arguments Within English Marxism* (Verso: London).

Arnot, R. P. (1964), *William Morris: the Man and the Myth* (Lawrence & Wishart: London).

Bahro, R. (1978), *The Alternative in Eastern Europe* (Verso: London).

Bauman, Z. (1976), *Socialism: The Active Utopia* (Allen and Unwin: London).

Beecher, J. and Bienvenu, R. (1983), *The Utopian Vision of Charles Fourier* (University of Missouri Press: Columbia).

Bellamy, E. (1888), *Looking Backward* (Ticknor: Boston).

Bentley, J. (1982), *Between Marx and Christ* (Verso: London).

Berneri, M. (1971), *Journey Through Utopia* (Schocken Books: New York), (first published 1950).

Bloch, E. (1970), *The Philosophy of the Future* (Herder and Herder: New York).

Bloch, E. (1985), *Essays in the Philosophy of Music* (Cambridge University Press: Cambridge).

Bloch, E. (1986), *The Principle of Hope* (Basil Blackwell: Oxford).

Bloch, E. (1987), *Natural Law and Human Dignity* (MIT Press: Cambridge, Mass.).

Bloch, E. (1988), *The Utopian Function of Art and Literature* (MIT Press: Cambridge, Mass.).

Brantenberg, G. (1985), *The Daughters of Egalia* (Journeyman Press: London).

Buber, M. (1949), *Paths in Utopia* (Routledge & Kegan Paul: London).

Claeys, G. (1985), 'The Political Ideas of the Young Engels, 1842–1845: Owenism, Chartism and the question of violent revolution in the transition from 'Utopian' to 'Scientific' Socialism', *History of Political Thought*, Vol. VI, **3**, pp. 455 – 78.

Davis, J. C. (1981), *Utopia and the Ideal Society* (Cambridge University Press: Cambridge).

Bibliography

Firestone, S. (1970), *The Dialectic of Sex* (Bantam Books: New York).
Frankel, B. (1987), *The Post-Industrial Utopians* (Polity Press: Cambridge).
Geoghegan, V. (1981), *Reason and Eros: The Social Theory of Herbert Marcuse* (Pluto Press: London).
Geoghegan, V. (1987), *Utopianism and Marxism* (Methuen: London).
Gilman, C. P. (1979), *Herland* (The Women's Press: London) (first published in serial form, 1915).
Goode, J. (1971), 'William Morris and the Dream of Revolution', in J. Lucas (ed.), *Literature and Politics in the Nineteenth Century* (Methuen: London).
Goodwin, B. (1978), *Social Science and Utopia* (Harvester: Brighton).
Goodwin, B. and Taylor, K. (1982), *The Politics of Utopia* (Hutchinson: London).
Gorz, A. (1982), *Farewell to the Working Class* (Pluto: London).
Gorz, A. (1985), *Paths to Paradise* (Pluto, London).
Harrison, J. F. C. (1969), *Robert Owen and the Owenites in Britain and America* (Routledge & Kegan Paul: London).
Heller, A. (1976), *The Theory of Need in Marx* (Allison and Busby: London).
Hertzler, J. O. (1922), *The History of Utopian Thought* (Allen and Unwin: London).
Hill, C. (1972), *The World Turned Upside Down* (Temple Smith: London).
Hill, C. (1973), *Winstanley: The Law of Freedom and Other Writings* (Penguin: Harmondsworth).
Horowitz, I. L. (1961), *Radicalism and the Revolt against Reason: the social theories of Georges Sorel* (Routledge: London).
Hudson, W. (1986), *The Marxist Philosophy of Ernst Bloch* (Macmillan: London).
Huxley, A. (1955), *Brave New World* (Penguin: Harmondsworth) (first published 1932).
Jameson, F. (1971), *Marxism and Form* (Princeton University Press: Princeton NJ).
Jay, M. (1970), 'The Metapolitics of Utopianism', *Dissent*, xvii, **4**.
Jennings, J. R. (1985), *Georges Sorel* (Macmillan: London).
Kateb, G. (1972), *Utopia and its Enemies* (Schocken Books: New York).
Kaufmann, M. (1879), *Utopias* (Kegan Paul: London).
Kellner, D. (1984), *Herbert Marcuse and the Crisis of Marxism* (Macmillan: London).
Kessler, C. F. (ed.) (1984), *Daring to Dream: Utopian Stories by United States Women 1836–1919* (Pandora: London).
Kettler, D., Meja, V. and Stehr, N. (1984), *Karl Mannheim* (Tavistock: London).
Kumar, K. (1987), *Utopia and Anti-Utopia in Modern Times* (Basil Blackwell: Oxford).
Lasky, M. (1976), *Utopia and Revolution* (Macmillan: London).
Le Guin, U. K. (1975), *The Dispossessed* (Panther: London).
Le Guin, U. K. (1986), *Always Coming Home* (Gollancz: London).
Le Guin, U. K. (1989), *Dancing at the Edge of the World: Thoughts on Words, Women Places* (Grove Press: New York).
Lefanu, S. (1988), *In the Chinks of the World Machine: Feminism and Science Fiction* (The Women's Press: London).
Leiss, W. (1978), *The Limits to Satisfaction: on needs and commodities* (Marion Boyars: London).
Levitas, R. (1979), 'Sociology and Utopia', *Sociology*, **13**, No. 1.
Levitas, R. (1985), 'New Right Utopias', *Radical Philosophy*, **39**.
Levitas, R. (ed.) (1986), *The Ideology of the New Right* (Polity Press: Cambridge).
Löwy, M. (1987), 'The Romantic and the Marxist Critique of Modern Civilization', *Theory and Society*, **16**.

Bibliography

Mannheim, K. (1979), *Ideology and Utopia* (Routledge and Kegan Paul: London) (first published in English in 1939).

Manuel, F. E. (ed.) (1973), *Utopias and Utopian Thought* (Souvenir Press: London).

Manuel, F. E. and F. P. (1979), *Utopian Thought in the Western World* (Basil Blackwell: Oxford).

Marcuse, H. (1955), *Eros and Civilization* (Vintage Books: New York).

Marcuse, H. (1968), *One Dimensional Man* (Sphere Books: London).

Marcuse, H. (1968), *Negations* (Allen Lane: London).

Marcuse, H. (1970), *Five Lectures* (Allen Lane: London).

Marcuse, H. (1970), *An Essay on Liberation* (Allen Lane: London).

Marcuse, H. (1972), *Counterrevolution and Revolt* (Allen Lane: London).

Marcuse, H. (1979), *The Aesthetic Dimension* (Macmillan: London).

Marx, K. and Engels, F. (1975–), *Collected Works* (Lawrence & Wishart: London).

Meier, P. (1978), *William Morris: The Marxist Dreamer* (Harvester: Brighton).

Moltmann, J. (1967), *Theology of Hope* (SCM Press: London).

Morley, H. (1885), *Ideal Commonwealths* (Routledge: London).

Morris, W. (1924), *A Dream of John Ball* (Longmans, Green: London) (first published 1887).

Morris, W. (with E. Belfort Bax) (1893), *Socialism: Its Growth and Outcome* (Swann Sonnenschein: London).

Morris, W. (1905), *News From Nowhere* (Longmans, Green: London) (first published 1890).

Morris, W. (1934), *William Morris: Selected Writings*, ed. G. D. H. Cole (Nonesuch Press: London).

Morris, W. (1984), *Political Writings of William Morris*, ed. A. L. Morton (Lawrence & Wishart: London).

Morton, A. L. (1946), *A People's History of England* (Lawrence & Wishart: London).

Morton, A. L. (1969), *The English Utopia* (Lawrence & Wishart: London) (first published 1952).

Moylan, T. (1986), *Demand the Impossible* (Methuen: London).

Mumford, L. (1923), *The Story of Utopias: Ideal Commonwealths and Social Myths* (Harrap: London).

Negley, G. and Patrick, J. M. (1971), *The Quest for Utopia* (McGrath: Maryland) (first published 1952).

Nozick, R. (1974), *Anarchy, State and Utopia* (Basil Blackwell: London).

Ollman, B. (1977), 'Marx's Vision of Communism', *Critique*, **8**.

Orwell, G. (1954), *Nineteen Eighty-Four* (Penguin: Harmondsworth) (first published 1949).

Piercy, M. (1979), *Woman On the Edge of Time* (The Womens Press, London).

Rawls, J. (1971), *A Theory of Justice* (Harvard University Press: Cambridge, Mass.).

Ricoeur, P. (1986), *Lectures on Ideology and Utopia* (Columbia University Press: New York).

Ross, H. (1938), *Utopias Old and New* (Nicholas and Watson: London).

Russ, J. (1981), 'Recent Feminist Utopias' in *Future Females: A Critical Anthology*, ed. M. S. Barr (Bowling Green University Popular Press: Ohio).

Sargent, L. T. (1975), 'Utopia – The Problem of Definition', *Extrapolation*, **16**, No. 2.

Bibliography

Sargent, L. T. (1988), *British and American Utopian Literature 1516–1985*. (Garland Publishing: New York and London).

Solomon, M. (ed.) (1979), *Marxism and Art* (Harvester: Brighton).

Solomon, M. 'Marx and Bloch: Reflections on Utopia and Art', *Telos*, no. 13, Fall 1972.

Soper, K. (1981), *On Human Needs* (Harvester: Sussex).

Sorel, G. (1925), *Reflections on Violence* (Allen and Unwin: London).

Stanley, J. L. (ed.) (1976), *From Georges Sorel* (Oxford University Press: Oxford).

Taylor, B. (1983), *Eve and the New Jerusalem* (Virago: London).

Taylor, K. (1982), *The Political Ideas of the Utopian Socialists* (Cass: London).

Thompson, E. P. (1977), *William Morris: Romantic to Revolutionary* (Merlin Press: London).

Thompson E. P. (1978), *The Poverty of Theory and Other Essays* (Merlin Press: London).

Vernon, R. (1978), *Commitment and Change: Georges Sorel and the Idea of Revolution* (University of Toronto Press: Toronto).

Williams, R. (1958), *Culture and Society* (Chatto & Windus: London).

Williams, R. (1979), *Politics and Letters* (Verso: London).

Williams, R. (1980), *Problems in Materialism and Culture* (Verso: London).

Williams, R. (1983), *Towards 2000* (Chatto & Windus: London).

Wright, P. (1985), *On Living in an Old Country* (Verso: London).

Zamyatin, Y. (1970), *We* (Penguin: Harmondsworth) (first published in English 1924).

Index

220

Index

Carlyle, Thomas   114
Chernyshevsky, Nicolai   56
Chesterton, G. K.   29
children   22, 41, 44, 62, 107, 109, 141–2
chiliasm   24, 70–2, 74, 91, 129, 163, 194
Christian–Marxist dialogue   102–5
Cobbett, William   15, 39
Cockaygne, Davis's category of   139, 162–4
Cokaygne, Land of   28–30, 33, 113, 124, 139, 147, 159, 162, 166, 190–1, 193, 213n
communism   22–3, 36, 40–56, 65, 70, 72–4, 84, 93, 95–6, 99, 104, 106, 109, 110, 114, 123, 128
concrete utopia   7, 88–94, 96, 100–1, 104, 122, 125, 127, 131, 147, 149–51, 153–5
conservatism   70, 73–4, 81, 123, 175, 186–9, 192
critical theory   132–3, 151, 152, 154
critical utopias   161, 172–4, 196
Cromwell, Oliver   194

Davies, Pete   187
Davis, J. C.   9, 10, 139, 159, 161–6, 179, 194
death   1, 2, 99, 104, 152, 192, 214n
definition in terms of content   4, 5, 7, 12, 22, 25, 57, 95–6, 100-3, 125, 155, 157–8, 160, 163–4, 179, 180, 183–9, 198
definition in terms of form   4–7, 10–12, 17, 19, 22, 25, 27–9, 33, 34, 57, 123, 157–8, 160–4, 166, 171, 172, 175, 178–80, 192, 198
definition in terms of function   4–7, 29, 31, 57–9, 68, 74, 83, 87, 100–3, 106, 124–5, 154–5, 158, 170–1, 175–7, 178–80, 192, 198
Defoe, Daniel   21, 29
descriptive definitions   5, 87, 179, 192, 198–9
desire   7, 8, 15, 30, 106, 122–30, 151, 164, 174, 181, 183, 185, 190–9
desire, education of   6, 7, 106, 122, 124–9, 131, 141, 143, 145–7, 155, 174, 180, 191, 196
Diderot, Denis   23, 24
division of labour   36, 41, 42, 108
division of labour, sexual   39, 41, 48, 109, 114, 141–2, 170
domination, Marcuse's concept of   136–9, 141–3, 148

dreams, dreaming   1, 27, 55–6, 84–6, 94–5, 106, 118–21, 124–7, 132, 148, 168, 190, 200
Dreyfus, Alfred   60
Dühring, Karl Eugen   53–5
Durkheim, Emile   17, 60, 62
dystopia   11, 22, 23, 32, 139, 161, 165, 167, 172–3, 176, 187, 195

ecology   107, 112, 140–1, 146, 166, 170, 175, 185, 189, 195–6
Eden, Garden of   28, 33, 162, 166, 193
Engels, Friedrich   6, 12, 24, 25, 35–58, 71–2, 78, 89, 95, 99, 100, 117, 118, 121, 127, 143, 176, 180
Eros   134–5, 137, 139–40, 147, 148, 181
eutopia   2, 17, 167

fantasy   4, 19, 27, 28, 56, 85, 113, 119, 134, 143, 148, 152, 154, 181, 189–91, 196
fascism   21, 22, 23, 56, 60, 71, 82, 87, 129
feminism   39, 85, 141, 157, 158, 170, 174–5, 189, 196–7
Firestone, Shulamith   141
Foigny, Gabriel de   23, 24, 141
Forster, E. M.   29
Fourier, Charles   12, 15, 18, 21, 36–9, 41, 42, 45, 46, 49–55, 63, 140
Fourierism   38, 39, 51, 52
France, Anatole   17, 25
Frankel, Boris   174, 177–8
Frankfurt School   102–3, 132, 157
Freud, Sigmund   86, 131–6, 145, 148
Fromm, Erich   84, 102
fulfilled moment   90–2, 98, 104, 110, 122, 129

Geoghegan, Vincent   55, 155, 181
Gearhart, Sally Miller   196
Gilman, Charlotte Perkins   32, 109, 174, 196
golden ages   1, 28, 55, 166, 175–6, 192
Goodwin, Barbara   175–8, 180, 183–4, 187, 191–4, 198
Godwin, William   29, 50
Goode, John   118–22, 129
Gorz André   166, 177, 197
Gott, Samuel   29
Gramsci, Antonio   77, 104, 116, 127, 167, 174
Great Refusal   150

Index

Index

Morris, William 6, 15, 21, 23, 24, 26, 29, 31, 33, 40, 83, 85, 106–30, 133, 140, 141, 159, 160, 164, 169, 173, 174, 196

Morton, A. L. 10, 29–34, 56, 113–14, 118, 124, 128, 159, 162, 176, 180, 193

Moylan, Tom 157, 172–4, 175, 180, 185, 196

Mumford, Lewis 10, 15–18, 22, 34

Münzer, Thomas 54, 70–2, 84, 99, 158

music 85, 86, 90–1, 98–9, 149, 168

Mussolini, Benito 60

myth 15, 29, 32, 69, 86, 159, 162, 190, 192–3

myth, Sorelian 6, 16, 59, 60, 62–7, 75, 79, 82

Nazism 23, 68, 131–2, 183

needs 43, 45, 124–5, 131, 135–48, 150, 155, 161–4, 181–5, 193

Negley, Glenn 10, 20, 26–8, 32, 33

New Right 73, 123, 186–90, 204

Nietzsche, Friedrich Wilhelm 180

Not Yet 84, 86–8, 92–4, 101, 104, 132, 153–4

Nozick, Robert 175

Ollman, Bertell 40–2

Orwell, George 29, 30, 33, 165

Owen, Robert 12, 18, 21, 29, 36–9, 41, 44–50, 52–5, 63, 159

Owenism 13, 38–9, 47–9, 51–3, 63, 78, 159

Patrick, J. Max 10, 20, 26–8, 32, 33

perfection 2, 3, 7, 12, 18, 19, 20, 26, 172, 176

performance principle 136–9, 143, 151

Piercy, Marge 166, 172

Pisarev, Dmitry Ivanovich 56, 94, 118

Plato 11, 15, 18, 21, 22, 23, 29, 31, 85

Plekhanov, Georgii Valentinovich 55, 63

Plutarch 14, 43

possibility 1, 3–5, 12–14, 18–20, 25–6, 28, 35–7, 57, 74, 87, 89, 92, 103–4, 114, 143, 150–5, 164, 175–7, 190–7, 199

Popper, Karl 3

post-industrialism 139–47, 161, 165–6, 173–4, 177, 196–7

progress 5, 10, 11, 13–14, 17–20, 23, 25–6, 28–9, 49, 72–4, 152, 193–5

proletariat 29–30, 37–9, 44, 47, 49, 51, 54, 57, 61–7, 80–1, 89, 93, 108, 143, 147, 150, 174, 195–7

Proudhon, Pierre-Joseph 12, 18, 46

Rabelais, François 23

rationality 19, 59, 68, 72, 79, 82, 89, 128–9, 132, 138, 141, 152, 187

Rawls, John 175, 184

reason 19, 39, 52, 72, 82, 106, 129, 144, 151

religion 1, 2, 4, 10, 18–20, 33, 37–8, 48, 69, 72, 86, 90–1, 98–100, 102–5, 121, 149, 156, 168

repression 133–9, 141, 147–8, 151, 153, 155, 181

revolution 11, 12, 25, 43, 44, 46–9, 55, 57–8, 62, 67, 80, 87, 89, 96, 107–8, 112, 114, 143, 149, 150, 154

Richter, Eugene 24, 29, 33

Ricoeur, Paul 76–7, 171, 186

Riesman, David 177, 190

Romanticism 83, 84, 105–6, 114–18, 127–30

Roshwald, Mordecai 195

Ross, Harry 10, 20–2, 32, 34

Ruge, Arnold 94

Ruskin, John 15, 107, 114, 118

Russ, Joanna 172

Saint-Simon, Claude Henri de 12, 18, 21, 36–9, 45, 46, 49, 53–5, 63

Saint-Simonism 20, 37, 39, 50, 63

Sargent, Lyman Tower 167, 168, 174, 176, 178, 198

satire 3, 4, 11, 14, 21, 23–4, 27, 29, 31–3, 175–6

Savonarola, Girolamo 18

scarcity 131, 135–6, 138–9, 141, 146, 161–4, 166, 179, 181–4, 191, 193

Scruton, Roger 123, 188

Shelley, Percy Bysshe 29, 33

sexism 15, 66, 141

sexuality 36–8, 134, 137, 162, 185, 188

Skinner, B. F. 22, 165

Sorel, Georges 6, 16, 59–68, 71, 75, 76, 78–80, 82, 98, 108, 129

Spence, Thomas 15

Stalinism 56, 168

Stravinsky, Igor 149

Suvin, Darko 175, 180

Swift, Jonathan 21, 29, 33

223

Index

224